MARIAN HOROSKO

MARTHA

GRAHAM

The Evolution of Her Dance Theory and Training

❦ **revised edition** ❦

07   06   05   04   03   02   6   5   4   3   2   1

Library of Congress Cataloging-in-Publication Data
Martha Graham: the evolution of her dance theory and training/
[compiled by] Marian Horosko.—Rev. ed.
p. cm.
Includes bibliographical references.
ISBN 0-8130-2473-0 (pbk.: alk. paper)
1. Graham, Martha. 2. Choreographers—United States—Biography.
3. Dancers—United States—Biography. I. Horosko, Marian.
GV1785.G7 M27 2002
798.8'2'092—dc21
[B]   2002016565

The University Press of Florida is the scholarly publishing
agency for the State University System of Florida, compris-
ing Florida A&M University, Florida Atlantic University,
Florida Gulf Coast University, Florida International
University, Florida State University, University of Central
Florida, University of Florida, University of North Florida,
University of South Florida, and University of West Florida.

University Press of Florida
15 Northwest 15th Street
Gainesville, FL 32611-2079
http://www.upf.com

MARTHA GRAHAM

South Sefton
6th Form College

Florida A&M University, Tallahassee

Florida Atlantic University, Boca Raton

Florida Gulf Coast University, Ft. Myers

Florida International University, Miami

Florida State University, Tallahassee

University of Central Florida, Orlando

University of Florida, Gainesville

University of North Florida, Jacksonville

University of South Florida, Tampa

University of West Florida, Pensacola

UNIVERSITY PRESS OF FLORIDA

Gainesville/Tallahassee/Tampa/Boca Raton

Pensacola/Orlando/Miami/Jacksonville/Ft. Myers

CONTENTS

FOREWORD

Martha Graham's creative genius was threefold: She was a galvanizing performer, a choreographer of astounding productivity and originality, and the creator of a systematic, coherent technique known and taught today as classical modern dance.

For the past two decades, the most requested materials at the Dance Division of the New York Public Library for the Performing Arts involve Martha Graham. Students from the world over have called, e-mailed, written, and visited the Dance Division seeking to study the books, articles, audio- and videotapes, photographs, and programs featuring Graham. The library's catalog lists more than fifteen hundred items, including films in which she appeared as early as the 1930s.

Graham was able to transmit her intensity, passion, and power to her dancers and teachers, who, to this day, maintain her aesthetic spirituality and technique. She brought a unique intellectual element to her dances, whether the subjects were a reflection of her time or of timeless dimension of mythology. Her works speak to different cultures, to peoples who have different spiritual alignments or have never before seen theatrical dance.

> Madeleine Nichols, Curator, Dance Division, New York
> Public Library for the Performing Arts at Lincoln Center

The Dance Division's catalog is available on the Internet at <http://catnyp.nypl.org> can be searched for listings on Graham and her choreography by author and subject.

PREFACE

In modern dance, one name looms over all others: Martha Graham. Her works have influenced the entire growth of dance, not only directly through her generations of dancers but also through those same dancers, who became teachers and choreographers. The impact of her life and work on dance culture has been unique and continuous. Her revolutionary dance making has been compared to the artistic innovations of Picasso and the musical genius of Stravinsky. Her contribution as a performer, choreographer, and teacher set a standard for a new movement vocabulary. Graham was the most famous, most controversial, and most prolific of all the modern dance pioneers, and her school and company the longest in operation in the modern dance world. *Martha Graham: The Evolution of Her Dance Theory and Training, 1926–1991,* was the first book to explore how Graham's dance movement developed. This second edition continues to trace that development into 2001, the restaging of her dances, and the current controversy over the performance of her works by her own company. It is tempting to believe that her dance theory sprang full and complete at her first concert in 1926. The training method, however, evolved through seventy years of teaching dancers and actors, as well as through her life-long work of making new dances for herself and her company. Her creativity made her uninterested in fixing the class work exercises in her training method into an inviolate specific rhythm or shape. Whenever asked at faculty seminars to do so, she digressed. The seminars ended in confusion, differences of opinion, and despair. All of which Graham probably enjoyed. To this day the teachers embrace what they were taught and pass it along to their students.

Graham herself kept the focus away from her contributions to dance training and somewhat disingenuously made no claim for creating a new technique of movement. "No school of movements," she insisted, should be added to her accomplishments. "I have simply rediscovered what the body can do." Of course, it is one thing to discover what the body can do and another thing to create a cumulative methodology to train dancers to move and perform expressively in a different way. The dancers who speak in this book testify to Graham's remarkable capabilities as a teacher whose system of dance training inspired their careers and later set a standard for them as teachers and choreographers.

Modern dance began as a clear and distinct alternative to ballet. While ballet sought to free the dancer from gravity in its expression, modern dance pulled the dancer back to earth to express the psychological turmoil and issues of the era—a time of change and artistic vitality. Ballet training, based on an evolving syllabus of movements, has been changed by choreographic invention, as has Graham's training by her own inventions. She encouraged her students and dancers, however, to move as individuals, while staying within the standard for the given exercises and the intention of the choreography. The testimony of the dancers, who worked with Graham from the beginning, questions her assertion that she worked without an underlying method. Graham pioneered many of the teaching methods that are now standard in modern dance pedagogy: bare feet, floor exercises (an innovation in itself) to strengthen the back and legs, standing balances, the stretch series on the floor with different arm patterns and levels, open Fourth Position, falls, side extensions, and walks, runs, skips, and leaps across the floor in diagonal. All were taught in classes as early as 1927.

The "contraction and release" principle appeared in Graham's teaching in the late 1920s as well. This ancient awareness of the physicality of movement as dependent on the breath, and the anatomical changes in the body due to the breathing process, was based on her early training in Eastern dance forms in the Denishawn Company. Although yogalike breathing was introduced into the classrooms of Western dance at the turn of the century, Graham was the first to develop breath with the contraction and release principle into an inherent basis of movement in her new dance form. The traditional ballet barre, however, was used as support in the teaching of standing falls and hip swings.

As Graham's vocabulary and training evolved through her choreography, new generations of dancers brought different abilities, body types, and challenges. As a result, her choreography developed in new directions; the new choreography was, in turn, mirrored in the training. For instance, in the thirties, when the company was composed entirely of women, her dances reflected the social climate of protest by using angular, vigorous, percussive, and purposeful movements as well as cupped hands and angular arms to confront the concept of "feminine" movements. A wide Second Position stretch (plié) in contraction with outstretched arms in a slight turnout position and parallel positions were introduced.

As new dances were created, new movements—such as leaps with the body leaning forward in contraction, arms thrust back, as in *Primitive Mysteries* (1931)—were practiced. The flying leaps in *Celebration* (1934) introduced pointed feet and the accent on the "up" movements. A variety of falls and triplets found their way into classes. A step or a combination from her dances was often lifted intact into the class work and called by the name of the piece. The names of steps in the vocabulary that were similar to ballet steps were Americanized—brushes for tendues, for instance. Graham also developed movements based on the way a dancer individualized a step and added it to the class work. Graham sought to inspire the dancers to do the movements creatively. They remember her cues as poetic, impressionistic, and sometimes amusing. "The spine is your tree," she would say, "respect it. At all times, the dancer should feel poised as if in flight—even when seated." And: "In dance, each time, it may be a mystical or religious connotation that you feel, but principally, it is the body exalting in its strength and its own power." She viewed class work not as uninspired repetition, but as a creative process, adjusted to the individual dancer, but always conforming to professional standards.

The late 1930s brought a new element to the Graham company: male dancers, most notably Erick Hawkins in 1938 and Merce Cunningham in 1939. Cunningham's naturally high jump, which he performed in *Letter to the World* (1940) as an entrance on the spoken cue "Dear March, come in . . ." entered the classroom vocabulary as "March jumps."

Graham asked Hawkins to teach rudimentary ballet as a way of expanding her movement vocabulary. The once fiercely antiballetic Graham now incorporated lifts into her dances, developed a more feminine style for her characterizations, and explored a masculine style for the new relationships in the works. Deep pliés (knee bends) in First, Fourth, and Fifth Positions entered the classroom. Hinges and a variety of falls were introduced, along with exercises designated by the number of counts required for execution. In 1948 came the infamous "knee vibrations" and the "Cave turn," from *Cave of the*

Heart (1946); the "forward split," from *Night Journey* (1947); and "spirals" that were performed at every angle. New steps, such as "bison," and acrobatics were introduced for the growing number of men in her company, whom she encouraged to find their own style.

By the 1950s, Graham and her company were at their highest level of performance. In 1952 a move from 66 Fifth Avenue to the small building at 316 East 63rd Street (later sold and now restored within a large structure on the same site) permitted the school's schedule of classes to expand. Work with actors at the Neighborhood Playhouse, begun in the 1920s, continued to employ her dancers as teachers in addition to her own classes. With the creation of the Juilliard School (1951), Graham taught along with fellow pioneers of modern dance: Doris Humphrey, José Limón, her long-time mentor and friend Louis Horst—all in the company of a celebrated faculty of musicians. Also on the Juilliard faculty was ballet teacher–choreographer Antony Tudor, whose psychological subtext in his works was not distant from her own concept in the creation of roles. Although ballet was offered at the Graham school for a short time, it was discontinued since most of the students shopped elsewhere for ballet classes. The 1950s reached a new height in the creation of her series based on Greek characters for herself, her soloists, and a dance chorus. The company and Graham were acclaimed and recognized worldwide.

In 1959 she and George Balanchine each created a section of a work called *Episodes* for the New York City Ballet's season at the City Center. Graham's role was Mary, Queen of Scots, in combat with an NYCB member as Elizabeth. Balanchine produced a section in the same ballet for his company using one of Graham's dancers, Paul Taylor, in an unforgettable solo.

The 1960s were unkind to Graham as bouts with alcoholism took over her body. But company members maintained the technique at the school with vigor and commitment. Graham gradually had lost interest in coaching her dancers in her own roles. Different body shapes and training backgrounds challenged the faculty as well. The technique continued to be disseminated throughout the country and abroad, to the point that accreditation to preserve its authenticity was necessary, and the technique became trademarked in 1976. A certification program was also inaugurated for full-time students including courses in music for dancers, repertory, composition, and Graham technique. An apprentice company was created as a preparation for entry into the main company.

In the final phase of her career in the seventies and eighties, Graham made valiant efforts to create an eclectic style in her works to reflect the changes in her dancers and their varied training. Her dancers almost universally came from a wide range of performing dance experience, as well. Although the distinctions among modern, ballet, jazz, and other dance forms are now blurred, her classic training regimen remains basic and essential in preparing the body and emotions—the instruments of dance—for the performance of almost any style of contemporary dance, because it is organic to the human body, safe and cumulative in mastery.

The dancers interviewed here present only a snapshot of the training as it existed during their tenure with the company. Today's unwritten syllabus represents the vast accumulation of movements in their basic and varied forms that now take eight to ten years to master. (According to Graham, "It takes five years to learn to run, ten to walk, and fifteen to learn to stand still.") Together, the dancer-teachers give as full a picture as possible of Graham's unique teaching style. There is also a glimpse into the future as her works are now restaged for companies other than her own.

In reading the memories of the dancers who worked with Graham, we are able to enter into the Graham mind. We can compare the class material of the thirties (as it is remembered by Gertrude Shurr and Sophie Maslow) with today's classroom material, to see how the class work was derived from the choreography that reflected the society of the time.

Her teachers, never able to pin her down to the "right" way to execute an exercise, have had to be satisfied with her aesthetic to reinterpret the past for the present, to "make it new." Graham liked to describe her training methods, her vision, and her life by paraphrasing the words of the philosopher Heraclitus: "The only constant is change."

Acknowledgments

In order to understand the development of Graham's dance theory and training, curiosity drove me to assemble a group of dancers who had studied and performed with her over the years in her company. Beate Gordon, director of the Asia Society's theater presentations, consented with enthusiasm to the public use of the society's Lila Acheson Wallace Auditorium for a day-long seminar. Madeleine Nichols, curator of the Dance Division of the New

York Public Library at Lincoln Center, offered her assistance with the video-taping and sound recording of the proceedings. Choreographer Marvin Gordon gave me the seed money for the seminar and the date was set for Thursday, May 19, 1988. With the cooperation of Ron Protas and Linda Hodes, then assistant artistic directors of the Martha Graham Dance Company, and Diane Gray, director of the Martha Graham School of Contemporary Dance, the meeting began to take shape.

Although some former dancers were on tour or out of the country on the seminar date, a representative number who had danced in her company in 1926—the date of Graham's first independent concert—and others up to 1988, were able to participate. Additional interviews with her performers up to 2001 have been added for this second edition. The result is not a textbook on Graham's methodology, but a sequential record, as told by her dancers, reflecting what was taught in the classroom and how it was altered and expanded over the years through her choreographic output. The syllabus at the end of the book is from a limited-access film of a class taught by Graham herself for her advanced and professional company members in the 1960s. Because Graham disliked documentation, it is one of the few films that exists outside visual material used by the school faculty. It has an added value because it contains imagery and comments by Graham, but it should not be regarded as contemporary or complete. Graham's class work cannot be taught from a book but must be experienced with a teacher. She valued freedom and change and the personal input of her teachers and dancers after they had mastered her basic principles.

I extend my thanks to all the participants in the original seminar as well as those who made their contribution more recently. Remarkably, the passion, dedication, and commitment to the emotional content within the methodology, as studied in the classroom and performed in her works on stage, have remained with them long after Graham's death (April 1, 1991) as an integral part of her legacy.

A special thanks also goes to Richard Carlin, editor of a cappella books (a division of Chicago Review Press), who recognized the value of documenting Graham's training methods and who published the earlier book in 1991.

My respect and admiration go to my agent, Toni Mendez, editors Meredith Morris Babb and Gillian Hillis of the University Press of Florida, Gainesville, and Harold G. Baldridge of the Neighborhood Playhouse. Personal thanks for support and advice go to friends Bill Hooks, Gloria Fokine, and Deborah Zall. Photo expert John Radovanovich deserves a special mention.

The photographs in this book are from the following sources and are used by permission and through the courtesy of the copyright owners: Soichi Sunami; Dance Collection, the New York Public Library for the Performing Arts; Astor, Lenox, and Tilden Foundations; Reiko Kopelson; Neighborhood Playhouse. All other images are from personal collections and are used by permission of the owners.

MARTHA GRAHAM

INTRODUCTION

Martha—everyone called her Martha—was born in Allegheny, Pennsylvania, in 1894, to George Graham, M.D., whose work with the mentally disturbed designated him as an "alienist," and the former Jane Beers, a direct descendant of Miles Standish. Martha had two younger sisters favored by her mother, Mary and Georgia ("Georgie"), who danced for one year, 1931, in the Graham company. Martha was her father's daughter. Martha's Irish paternal great-grandfather had come to America from Scotland to make his fortune in Pittsburgh. Although her heritage was Puritanism, her Catholic nurse, Lizzie, was full of fantasies and tales, and the Japanese gardeners who were part of her early world when the family moved to Santa Barbara in 1908 provided more than enough material for the moral, ethical, and cultural strains that would become her theater. Graham knew about witches, wee folk, and the poetic mystery of things.

Some called Martha a sorceress, in the Irish sense of having insight, intuition, and the ability to command people to do her bidding. Others said she was a witch. She was witty and scholarly, had an extremely flexible body, was mentally disciplined, and was small but powerful, approachable to the earnest but distant to the novice, quiet yet eloquent, simple yet complex. But always Martha.

She adored her father. He taught her a lesson when she was very young that she would never forget. Caught in a falsehood, her father told her that he knew she was lying because of the way she moved. He had learned from his patients that if words and movements were inconsistent, the patient was lying. "Movement doesn't lie," he said—words she would repeat emphatically throughout her life, applying that wisdom to her own performances and everyone else's thereafter. "Either a performance is honest or it is not," she would say.

In 1911, as a special event, Martha's father, after her pleading, took her to the Opera House in Los Angeles, to see her first performance of the Denishawn company. She had been transfixed by a poster announcing the performance that pictured Ruth St. Denis in one of her exotic costumes, dressed as the Hindu goddess Radha. St. Denis (1879–1968) and Ted Shawn (1891–1972) were tireless promoters of movie prologs—live package shows that featured a variety of acts before the showing of a silent film. The Denishawn company played in gigantic theaters of lavish design, with huge stages spacious enough to include choruses and a full-size orchestra.

Denishawn became the first truly popular touring company, with a dance style that was an amalgam of pseudo-Oriental, American Indian, Far Eastern, and other "exotic" styles popular on the vaudeville circuit at the time. They experimented with what St. Denis called color and music visualizations, early abstract dances that pointed the way for the modern dance that followed.

Graham's father, who died suddenly in 1914, didn't approve of Martha's interest in the theater. However, from 1913 to 1916 she was enrolled in the Comnock School of Expression, a junior college in Santa Barbara, where she studied academic and practical theater arts. The program included "interpretive" dancing three times a week.

The drama of the Denishawn productions had made an indelible impression on her, especially the dancing of Ruth St. Denis, who became her idol and was to have a great impact on her eventual path. St. Denis was originally an actress with little concern for technique or authenticity in her dances. "Miss Ruth" was tall, slim, beautiful, elegant, and had won her reputation by performing Hindu-like religious dances dressed in gorgeous costumes. She believed that she was a sacred vessel of a higher power, and those who watched her always remarked on the transcendent quality of her performances. She remained a performer onstage through her eighty-fifth year, setting a worthy example of continuity for Martha.

St. Denis was known as the First Lady of American dance and was married to Ted Shawn when Martha enrolled at the Ruth St. Denis and Ted Shawn School of Dancing and Related Arts in Los Angeles in 1916, popularly known as Denishawn. Martha, at twenty-two, was a late starter for dance training—short, plain, overweight, but serious and intent upon becoming a dancer. Her audition for St. Denis and Shawn was unimpressive and Miss Ruth, not knowing how to handle her, turned her over to Shawn to teach. The school taught ballet, ethnic dance, music, Delsarte's codified dramatic gestures, makeup, lighting, costuming, dance history, "Oriental" art, and Greek philosophy, along with sessions of yoga and meditation.

Shawn, who was impressed with Martha's diligence and her memory of everything she saw in rehearsal or performance, gave her leading roles. He created a dance for her, *Xochitl,* that was to bring her recognition. She played a Toltec Indian maiden, whose fierce dancing protected her virtue from a drunken Toltec emperor.

She was a tremendous success and also became known for her temper. During her later creative moments, she would weep, storm and dismiss the entire company, only to eventually ask for forgiveness. She was the manager of one of the Denishawn touring companies in which she danced, as well. Louis Horst, the pianist who was at her Denishawn audition, was a member of the company. When she became discontent with the Denishawn repertoire, Horst encouraged her to find her own way. He became her strong critic, an influence on her, and eventually her mentor.

There were others who were discontent with the Denishawn repertoire— Charles Weidman and Doris Humphrey broke away from the Denishawn group in 1927. They would become, along with Martha and Hanya Holm, the pioneers of what was to be called American modern dance.

One day, Alexander Pantages, owner of a chain of theaters, said to Martha, "I don't know what you have, Martha, but you have *something!*" She would rely on that something the rest of her life. She knew at that point she could stand alone.

In 1925, Charles Chaplin was judged best actor of the year for his role in the silent movie *The Gold Rush;* Will Rogers and W. C. Fields, along with Billie Burke, were stars of the extravagant Ziegfeld Follies on Broadway. These shows were the rage before and after World War I with their display of talent, elegance, and huge production numbers, a far cry from Denishawn. Irene Castle danced in the Follies and was the first to dance in the movies. Anna Pavlova danced at the Hippodrome; Marilyn Miller danced and sang her way into America's heart.

Martha, too, was ready to enter the popular entertainment world. She attracted the attention of producer-director John Murray Anderson, who hired her for his Greenwich Village Follies, arch rival of the Ziegfeld productions. The show had lavish sets and superb costumes designed by the dazzling Russian artist Erté. Martha entered that glamorous, high-paying world as a class act. But still discontent, she stayed only a short time.

It was time to gather together all she had learned and go on her own. Since she sent much of her show salary to her mother and was short on cash, she began to teach three times a week at the Eastman School of Music in Rochester, New York, 350 miles away; at John Murray Anderson's Robert Milton School of Theater Arts; and, for private students, at her own small studio in Carnegie Hall. She couldn't teach the jealously guarded Denishawn curriculum because that would have cost a franchise fee of $500, which Martha didn't have. It proved to be a blessing in disguise. She was now forced to develop her own vocabulary and technique.

In one of her cross-country Denishawn tours, she had seen an abstract painting at the Art Institute of Chicago by the Russian artist Wassily Kandinsky, of a bold slash of red across a field of blue. Just as the poster of St. Denis sparked imagination, the Kandinsky painting made her comment, "I will do that someday. I will make a dance like that."

Louis Horst, returned from a European trip, confirmed that there was a revolution occurring in the arts and that her instincts for breaking away were right. From the Eastman school she selected three young women and trained them for six months. She choreographed nine solos for herself and a total of eighteen dances for her first concert. With Horst's accompaniment at the piano, a loan to rent the Forty-Eighth Street Theater, costumes designed by Martha and sewn with help from her "girls" (Thelma Biracree, Betty Macdonald, Evelyn Sabin), the Martha Graham Concert Group presented its first performance on April 18, 1926.

PART ONE

Witnesses to the Technique

1   THE FIRST YEARS

Evelyn Sabin Mannes

Evelyn Sabin Mannes danced in Graham's first recital in 1926, and remained in the group until 1930.

I was a pupil of Martha Graham in 1925, when she came to teach at the Eastman School of Music in Rochester [New York]. When she chose not to return for a second year, I came to New York [City]—at the age of eighteen—to continue to study with her and was a member of her first small group, The Trio. After some years, I had to leave New York because of illness. Eventually I danced and taught in Rochester until my marriage in 1940.

When Martha Graham came to teach in Rochester, I think she was already committed to creating her own dance, uniquely her own. In retrospect, I think our dances in those days may have been, quite naturally, somewhat reminiscent of Denishawn, where she had her own training and was a leading member of the company. No such thought ever occurred to me at the time. I had never seen any Denishawn dancing and had studied ballet before coming to Martha.

The movement, to me, was always changing, developing, and growing. And I think now that in the most elementary, and perhaps fundamental, way, we took first steps toward the great future that has evolved so phenomenally.

I know that through the years the technique and its teaching have become more formalized. I don't even know its vocabulary so I shall have to refer to it as simply as we did sixty years ago: walking, running, jumping, leaping, contraction and release, the floor work, and the falls. These are the movements that I recognize, remember, and feel as I see the company in performance. I have never watched a class.

In the beginning, we were taught only by Martha. For the concerts, there was no orchestra. Louis Horst was always at the piano. Everything we did, insofar as we were able, was done in Martha's way. The inspiration and the vision were always there.

Ailes Gilmour

Ailes Gilmour was the sister of the late sculptor Isamu Noguchi (1904–1988). She was a member of the Graham company from 1929 to 1933. She began her study of dance at the Neighborhood Playhouse in New York City and performed with the Graham company at the opening of Radio City Music Hall. In 1929 she introduced her brother, Isamu, to the "young, new dancer and her approach to movement." She worked with the New Dance League and the Workers' Dance League, and shared recitals with Bill Matons's Experimental Unit in the 1930s.

I was born in Yokohama, Japan. My mother was the Scotch-Irish writer Leonie Gilmour—whose name I use; my father was a Japanese poet. I came to San Francisco in 1920 and moved to the East to attend the Ethical Culture School; their educational philosophy influenced my mother. I was graduated from a boarding school in Connecticut in 1929 and then applied to the Neighborhood Playhouse in New York City for a "living scholarship"—a fifteen-dollar-a-week stipend for food, lodging, and free tuition.

At that time, fifteen dollars was sufficient living money and enabled the students at the playhouse to study the arts of speech, drama, and dance. It was there that I studied under the direction of a brilliant and blazing new dancer—Martha Graham.

I had seen her dance in *Adolescence* (1929) and was now afforded the opportunity to study with her and learn her new concepts of movement based upon contraction and release. The same year, 1929, she asked me to join her professional group; that year she choreographed *Heretic,* to music based upon old Breton songs.

The public was not used to the starkness and simplicity of movement in her work. It was not "pretty" and contained none of the conventions of ballet. It was a complete break from tradition. People unused to the bare bones of dance were often repelled. I loved it! There, it seemed, was truth.

We made our own costumes. Even the leotards used in class were cut from a yard of old jersey, split like a diamond where we sewed the crotch. We wore these in class and danced to music played on the piano by Enid Dareman.

Louis Horst, Martha's musical mentor who wrote much of her music, also gave classes at the playhouse. We studied all of the arts related to theater—movement, voice, music, and stage sets. It was a new and exciting world.

When Martha won a Guggenheim Fellowship, she went to Mexico and was influenced by that country's religious fervor. She created *Primitive Mysteries* (1931). Again, we sewed our own costumes, tubular wood jerseys fashioned so tightly to our bodies that there was little room to move. Wearing it was to become a piece of sculpture as our bodies strained against the tubing. Martha was the Virgin in white organdy, like a flower blooming above the dark mass. It was simple, direct, and powerful.

My brother, Isamu Noguchi, designed the set for *Dark Meadow* in 1946, with music by Carlos Chavez. I introduced Isamu to Graham in 1929, when he was attracting the interest of people in the art world. He was interested in "the young dancer with a new concept of movement" and worked out several sets for her. Eventually, over the years, Noguchi would create sets for more than twenty works including: *Frontier* (1935, from *Perspectives*), *Chronicle* (1936), *Appalachian Spring* (1944), *Cave of the Heart* (1946), *Errand into the Maze* (1947), *Night Journey* (1947), *Clytemnestra* (1958), and *Embattled Garden* (1958).

On December 27, 1932, Radio City Music Hall opened as a place for concert artists. In addition to the Graham company, dancers Harald Kreutzberg and his partner, Yvonne Georgi, and Ray Bolger the tap dancer were on the program. The conductor was Leopold Stokowski. When we danced on the enormous stage, the *New Yorker* magazine described us as looking like mice racing across the vast expanse.

At the end of our debut in *Choric Pattern,* "Roxy" [Samuel L. Rothafeld], the founder of Radio City Music Hall, would sit in the center of the auditorium, where he could play out all manner of visual effects. He was keen to have us appear through a steam curtain, but Martha explained that our costumes were all wool and that the steam would shrink the material and immobilize us!

We had a short run, a week as I recall. Radio City was not a success until it became a movie house with the Rockettes.

I took classes with Martha at the Neighborhood Playhouse by day and again at her studio at night. We would rehearse until one or two in the morning and Martha would give us rye bread and cheese to eat at the end of rehearsal. We never got paid. It was a wonderful time to live and work. I will always remember Martha, and I'm honored to have worked with her.

Bessie Schönberg

Bessie Schönberg was a member of the Martha Graham Dance Company from 1930 to 1931, a career cut short by an injury. As an educator, she held an eminent position in teaching composition and in 1987 was awarded the New York Dance and Performance citation (a.k.a. the Bessie) for her lifetime achievement.

Schönberg studied Eurhythmics at a Jaques-Dalcroze school near Dresden, Germany, attended the University of Oregon, and received a B.A. from Bennington College. In New York City she studied with Graham at the Neighborhood Playhouse and soon joined her company. As a teacher, Schönberg was a member of the performing arts faculty at Sarah Lawrence from 1938 to 1975, as well as the director of dance and theater. In addition, she taught at Briarcliff Junior College, the New Dance group, the Juilliard School of Music, and the Bennington School of Dance, and she was director of many opera and musical-theater productions.

After her retirement, she was a guest teacher at the City College of New York, Ohio State University, Wesleyan University, and London's Contemporary Dance Center. She was artistic advisor to choreographers at the Yard at Martha's Vineyard.

Schönberg served on the dance panel of the New York State Council on the Arts and on the advisory panel of the National Endowment for the Arts, and she was chairman of the board of directors of Dance Theater Workshop.

It was a fast, amazing, heady time for me, unexpected and undeserved as well, to be taken into the Graham company. I grew up in Dresden, where my father was responsible for my seeing everything that was going on in the name of dance. I saw [Mary] Wigman in all her early years there, and Kreutzberg and the Wiesenthals. But dancing for me was completely out.

I was allowed to take some Dalcroze, not in the original institute where Dalcroze started, but in the city, in a little vegetarian restaurant, where the classes were held in the dining room.

I came to America in 1926 because my mother was a voice and opera workshop teacher at the University of Oregon in Eugene. I became a painting and sculpture student there and took dance from a disciple of Margaret H'Doubler, because we all had to have some physical education. It was hard to take for someone who had been brought up on Wigman. Fortunately, Martha Hill took the job when the other teacher retired and the classes became one of the great experiences of my life. Hill had been in New York earlier and taken a summer course with Graham. She came to Eugene in 1927; in 1929 we both left and headed for New York and the Neighborhood Playhouse.

I watched Graham's class and was breathless and tongue-tied at meeting her. Hill introduced me and I was overcome. She suggested that we, and a fellow teacher from Oregon who was with us [Mary Jo Shelley], go to the apartment of Mrs. Rita Morgenthau, the executive director of the school, in the hope that we might be given scholarships. I got a scholarship and fifteen dollars per week.

My first class was at Ruth Doing's second-floor studio, around the corner from Carnegie Hall on 56th Street [Martha's studio was on West 10th Street at that time]. After my first class, Martha asked me to come into the company. It was all too quick.

The first class that I watched was very physical. Martha seemed to be able to do anything she wanted with her body. She had the schooling, but she also had God-given strength and flexibility. She had little square feet that were elastic as well as strong, and she was small with long, black hair and had an incredible extension.

As I remember the classes at that time, we did stretches on the floor, some standing exercises, and a lot of moving in circles. I remember an amusing thing: before the class, Louis Horst would play Percy Grainger's *Country Gardens* and we would move around in a circle in a run to warm up. I loved it, cutting through the studio as fast as I could go. It was wonderful. It's still a good warm-up. We could then begin the formal class.

Later in the classes, we did triplets with a change of accent and change of direction. Twisting on the floor and spirals were important. I remember once saying, shyly, to Martha that the exercises reminded me of a snake dancing on its tail and she responded that that was exactly the image I should have. She meant that there should be no weight on the floor and the body should be almost supported in suspension. As I remember, in the 1930s the contraction was executed as a lifting up and the release as a pressing down. I don't believe they do that any more. All the percussive exercises we used to do are not done any longer. Time and Martha moved on into a more romantic and lyrical, even voluptuous, quality of movement.

Classes at the Neighborhood Playhouse lasted all day—voice, acting, Horst's composition classes, and, of course, Martha's technique classes.

As a new student, I would go back to my little room in the International House, where I was staying, and spend half the night trying to learn what I was supposed to have learned in the class. I worked at it. Then, the next day, I would find Martha saying, "Forget what we learned yesterday, it's all changed now." This was part of the freshness of being involved with her; the changes and paths she took were no mystery. She knew where she was going.

As I look back, Martha's work was a continual transition from the [François] Delsarte and Denishawn training into her own path. A deep influence, not frequently mentioned, on her path was the Japanese dancer Michio Ito (1892–1961). He was with her in the *Greenwich Village Follies* and then in *Nuages*, the first time it was performed in a Lewisohn production. [The Lewisohn Stadium performances in Manhattan were presented free of charge in the outdoor theater during the summer months. Major companies and performers were presented.]

I remember dancing in at least two of Irene Lewisohn's Orchestral Dramas. The stars were Martha Graham, Charles Weidman, Blanche Talmud, and others, as well as scholarship students from the playhouse like myself [Anna Sokolow, Sophie Maslow, Ailes Gilmour, and others]. Nikolai Sokolow and the Cleveland Symphony were engaged for the productions. These were performed, one at the YMHA at 92nd Street and Lexington Avenue, the other at City Center on 55th Street [called the Mecca Temple at that time], but were not performed at the Lewisohn Stadium.

Ruth St. Denis influenced Martha to some extent. She taught in a free-wheeling manner, totally concentrated on the subject one minute, then deciding to change, using the words: "That's boring. Let's do something else." But she was fabulous, partially exotic and partially practical. And, of course, as everyone knows, she was very beautiful and good-natured. I tell you this because I think she was a visual influence on Graham, although I feel that Ted Shawn was a greater influence on her early training. Shawn gave her many opportunities and she was a soloist in his choreography for the Denishawn Company. Although he was not as theatrical as Ruth, he was more methodical. Graham, of course, rejected a lot, as well.

I was placed immediately in the company and was quite favored. I think it was my passionate desire to dance and my eagerness that did it for me. My first dances were *Moment Rustica* (1929), which had a peasant quality, and *Danse Languide* (1926), a leftover from Graham's first concert. It was danced by Evelyn Sabin [Mannes], Betty Macdonald, and Rosina Savelli, who replaced Thelma Biracree that first summer, in 1926. *Languide* had a very sculptural quality because of its long, long scarves and full back bends on the knees. I was thrilled. Betty and Rosina were still in the company at that time, but Evelyn had left. They would come back from time to time, if they were needed, for a tour.

By the thirties, we were living a period of primitive art. It was emulated everywhere, and Martha was part of that movement in dance. Her movements were simple, strong, straight, and percussive. Those were the terms in which she created her dances. She packed movement into the instant of action. It was frustrating and exciting at the same time: a boiling point that was never really reached.

Unlike Wigman, who believed in an extraordinary, almost Oriental way of turning out the leg, Graham surprised me with her Barlach-like starkness during that period. [Ernst Barlach (1870–1938) was a German sculptor, graphic artist and playwright, whose powerful figures in bronze or wood owe much to a very personal combination of Gothic and cubist influences.] Her changes in her movements made them purer, or starker, as I saw it. More and more was stripped away. I remember seeing her in *Dance* (1929) on a little platform in a red dress, moving between the shoulders and the knees. That was it. It was powerful.

In class, we did *calls*—a twist in the torso in a percussive movement that pulled one arm up as if to call someone to follow. They were circular movements, in part. The audience was supposed to finish the circle for themselves.

Primitive Mysteries (1931) and *Heretic* (1929) were my greatest experiences with Graham. In *Primitive Mysteries* Louis Horst counted on me to set the tempo for him in each of the three sections that had a silent introduction and a silent exodus. So I was the first to come out on stage. It was with a very sharp walk that we began. Performances now don't seem to have that same bite. We worked on nothing but that bite in the movement.

Heretic was created by Graham in one night. I've never seen anyone before or since work that way, and I've seen a great deal of dance. Louis had found a very beautiful Breton song that had a verse and a chorus. It was percussive in quality and searing, as Martha put herself against a wall of resistance—the chorus of dancers. Of course, it could be interpreted as Martha, herself, against tradition or whatever you want to interpret there. It was a pleading figure against a hostile group—terse, brief, stark; I think no other dance quite represented her personal statement with such power, although all her dances were personal statements.

At this time, these were dances of the people. Although she was not of the people, her sympathies at that time were with the downtrodden.

The positions we held were you might call stuck, sustained, with changes made on three counts. They were big changes made in the whole group. We sometimes stepped on one another, but you had to keep the meaning with tremendous concentration. Graham had almost eliminated movement of the arms, and they were thrown straight up or held down. The group was almost wooden, but she was alive, and very lyrical by contrast.

I was in some of the Lewisohn performances, and those at Bennington College, but my career was cut short by a knee injury, a torn cartilage. We didn't trust operations in those days. Martha was gentle and understanding when I went to class but this was a total accident that I had had. I wasn't warmed up enough, I think. In those days, we were young and thought ourselves invincible. We have since had to learn how to prepare the body for classes and performances. But I could no longer dance. It was over.

As I look back, dance seemed simpler and deeper. There were just a few people working at that time and they—Doris Humphrey, Hanya Holm, Charles Weidman, Helen Tamiris [1905–1966; known for her dances of social criticism], and Martha Graham—were almost monastic within themselves. They were so dedicated and single-visioned in dance as they thought it should be. All these people seemed not quite of this earth, although Martha, I knew, was very much of this earth—gossiping with us as we sewed our costumes, then far, far ahead of us when she brought back her thoughts to us in the studio.

Graham dances look different to me today because the dancing technique has changed; it has been developed, opened, and widened in every aspect. Compared to the group in the thirties, the current company dances have a totally different look. It is extraordinarily beautiful. My memories are of my own excitement and deep commitment in a euphoric beginning.

2 ∾ THE THIRTIES

The 1920s were over. Martha now performed as the Chosen One in *Sacre du printemps* (1930), reconstructed by ballet's famous choreographer Léonide Massine to the music of Igor Stravinsky. (She would create her own *Rite of Spring* in 1984). The day after her performance, she told her class, "I have learned something terribly important. I have learned how to be perfectly still. And now, I will teach you."

The opening of Radio City found her group dismissed after only one week. Graham and her dance group performed *Choric Dance for an Ancient Greek Tragedy.* At one point a mother of one of the girls ran backstage and said to Martha, "You're such a nice girl, Martha. But do you have to dance like that?" Martha Hill, a staunch Graham supporter, said she called the box office each day to order a large block of tickets, although she knew that the group was no longer performing there. When she was told that the Graham company was not dancing, she said, "Well then, cancel all my tickets!"

Martha was not alone in the revolution of the arts. Arnold Schoenberg, Prokofiev, Gershwin, and Scott Joplin, among others, were blazing their own trails; Edith Wharton, Theodore Dreiser, O. Henry, Fitzgerald, Thomas Wolfe, and Hemingway were among the writers finding a new voice; Chagall, Braque, and Picasso were astounding the world. America had survived World War I and the Great Depression, knew about the Russian revolution, and saw silent movie shorts grow into a three-hour D. W. Griffith film. Isadora Duncan published her book *My Life* in 1928, but Martha, a lifelong avid reader, was not known to have read it. Anna Pavlova had visited America and was about to become the most famous dancer in the world. There were no major ballet companies in the United States until later in the decade. To this group of revolutionaries, ballet seemed antiquated and unable to express contemporary themes.

Martha continued creating concerts although the critics only found her first trio of dancers graceful. She then astounded them in 1927 with a solo,

Revolt; a moving solo in 1928, *Immigrant;* and an antiwar work, *Poems of 1917.*
Louis Horst sarcastically called this period of percussive, blunt, dynamic
dance "the revolting era of modern dance."

Martha was demanding, her temper like a tornado, and was not above
placing a sudden slap on an erring section of a student's anatomy. At the same
time, she could be charming and display a dry, sometimes naughty sense of
humor.

Adolescence and *Dance,* both solos created in 1929, returned to her sense of
joy and exploration of the human spirit. The group grew to twelve unpaid
dancers, and their performance in *Heretic,* also in 1929, moved dance critic of
the *New York Times,* John Martin, to find the work original and "glowing"
with vitality.

A key player in Graham's growth as teacher and choreographer was her
mentor and confidant, Louis Horst (1884–1964). Martha, who had left teaching at Eastman in 1927, began the part-time teaching of actors at the Neighborhood Playhouse (Graham training is taught there to this day), opened her
new dance studio in Greenwich Village, and lived just making ends meet with
loans from Horst, enough to ride the subway or buy a cup of coffee. Horst is
described by dancers of the time as having a cigar in his mouth as he played the
piano, appearing to have closed eyes, and not missing a thing. Horst studied in
Vienna and in San Francisco, where he first became a collaborator of Ruth St.
Denis from 1915 to 1925, and then of Martha, from 1928 to 1948. He composed
Primitive Mysteries (1931), *Frontier* (1935), and *El Penitente* (1940) for her. At
the playhouse he taught dance composition to generations of modern dancers. He often helped Martha demonstrate by jumping up from the piano and
moving his great bulk on little feet. Horst also founded and was editor of an
influential modern dance journal, *Dance Observer,* in 1934, a paper with a
definite pro-Graham slant. Horst would eventually introduce Martha to composers Aaron Copeland, Samuel Barber, and Gian Carlo Menotti, who would
write original compositions for her dances. Isamu Noguchi was another in-
dispensable Graham collaborator. The Japanese sculptor was introduced to
Martha by his sister, Ailes Gilmour, who danced in the company. He became
her set designer for more than twenty works from 1935 to 1958.

This period also found Graham's costumes—long woolen tubular
shapes—and makeup different from the traditional flesh-colored, mercury-
riddled greasepaint. Graham made her own five-foot three-inch frame look

larger by using white makeup with a gash of Kandinsky-red lipstick. Her dark eyes were "beaded" for full effect. A spoonful of black wax was melted over a candle and, with a brush or toothpick, painstakingly placed drop by drop on each lash, where it quickly dried. This was repeated until the lashes were long and dark. Beading, an old theatre trick that predated false eyelashes, never smeared or irritated the eyes and it was easily removed with cold cream. Notable for costuming was Graham's design for her profoundly moving *Lamentation* (1930)—a shroud of wool jersey that hooded her head and left only her face, hands, and beautiful bare feet showing. She performed it on a bench, never standing up or moving away from the bench.

The thirties proved to be a key decade in the development of Graham's work as a teacher, choreographer, and especially as a performer. It was then that her all-female dance company reached its maturity, and many legendary dancers—such as Sophie Maslow, May O'Donnell, and Anna Sokolow—performed with her. Some of her most famous dances were premiered by this ensemble, including *Primitive Mysteries*, *Celebration* (1934), and *Deep Song* (1937).

The dancers of the thirties who worked with Graham comment on the growth of a more formal class. Gertrude Shurr gives a detailed syllabus for a typical class of the era, while Sophie Maslow gives a more impressionistic description of class work. It is clear that, as Graham matured as a creative artist, she needed to develop a methodology for training her dancers to achieve her special vision. The class became the training ground. But, equally important, the class became an experimental laboratory where training could serve as a catalyst for further creativity.

Gertrude Shurr

Gertrude Shurr began her career at the Denishawn School and danced solo performances in the early Denishawn dances (1925–29), the musical acts that were interpolated into the movie prologs of that day. She danced in the first Humphrey-Weidman concerts (1927–29) and, at the same time, began to study with Martha Graham.

Shurr became a Graham teacher and a member of the Martha Graham Dance Company from 1930 to 1938. Her other professional experiences include more than forty years with the Shurr-O'Donnell Studio of Modern

Dance in New York City. (May O'Donnell was also a member of the Graham company, from 1932 to 1938 and 1944 to 1953.)

Shurr established, with O'Donnell, the San Francisco Dance Theater. Later she became a teacher and chairman of the dance department of New York's High School for the Performing Arts (1957–73), for which she earned commendation in 1973.

The first time I saw Martha Graham was during the 1926 summer session of the Denishawn School. This was a Sunday morning in Studio 61 in Carnegie Hall, just a week or two before the Denishawn Company left for their tour of the Orient. I was at the studio to see a performance of the Swedish dancer Ronnie Johansson, the first European modern dancer we had ever seen. Johansson was born in Riga, Latvia, in 1891; went to Stockholm in 1913; studied modern dance there and in Germany; toured Europe (1918–25); came to America, where she was assistant teacher at Denishawn, the Ruth St. Denis and Ted Shawn School of Dancing and Related Arts; and gave a series of recitals and demonstrations in colleges and universities. She opened her own school in Stockholm in 1932 and became a teacher at the Royal Dramatic Theater in 1942.

This particular performance was an audition for Ronnie Johansson, for the possibility of including her dances as an added attraction in the Denishawn programs. It did not work out that way. Her *Pierrot* and *Waltzes* did not fit into the programs.

The entire Denishawn Company was there, and since I was a scholarship student and worked in the office, I was permitted to be present. Louis Horst brought Martha Graham to this performance. Everyone knew Martha. She was a great dancer who had left the Denishawn Company to dance in the *Greenwich Village Follies*.

Miss Ruth [St. Denis] had no plans for Martha to join the forthcoming tour of the Orient. Martha was short, had long black hair, a long face with enormous eyes, and was very, very thin. She really looked what was thought to be Oriental. Miss Ruth was not about to take coals to Newcastle. In fact, Miss Ruth preferred the long-stemmed American beauty type of dancer, the clean-cut American look, mostly blonde and fair. Martha wanted to go to the Orient, but it was not to be with Denishawn. Years later, Graham took her own company to the Orient to great acclaim.

The next time I saw Martha Graham was at her concert performances in 1926 and 1927. All I can remember was how beautiful the concerts were. I cried. I wanted to dance like Martha; the exquisite Oriental touches that were inbred in her from Denishawn; the lyrical qualities in the Debussy series; the subtle touches of comedy in her satires. It was all quite wonderful. Did I see the future Martha Graham at that time? I do not know. All I knew was that I wanted to study with her and dance in her company.

It wasn't until 1928 that Martha's dramatic approach to dance was evident. More angular physical movement and sharper dynamics appeared in her *Revolt, Immigrant Series,* and *Poems of 1917,* showing another side of Martha— her dramatic urge to communicate, her subtle comedy, her strong satire, and her exquisite use of materials in *Tanagra.* Now, more than ever, I wanted to study with Graham.

I knew Martha had left the *Greenwich Village Follies* and was teaching in Rochester, New York, at the Eastman School of Music three days a week and three days a week at the John Murray Anderson School of Theater on East 58th Street in New York City. I also knew she was preparing for a New York concert with three of her Rochester students. I really wanted to go to Rochester and study with Martha Graham.

At this time, a friend of mine who danced in the movie prolog productions that John Murray Anderson produced and sent out on the road told me Martha Graham was teaching a children's class one afternoon a week at the school. I knew John Murray Anderson and I asked him if I could join the class. He told me to speak to his brother Hubert, who was in charge of the school. Hubert told me that Martha had a children's class of only three children at that time, but he doubted whether she would take me on as a pupil. I suppose I looked devastated. After an uncomfortable silence for both of us, he said, "Why don't you go and try it?" That was all I needed to hear. The next day, I was in class. I was not much bigger than the three girls—Ruth, Hope, and Rosina—and with my hair in a ponytail, I could easily pass for one of them. I never knew if anyone spoke to Martha about me. She never spoke to me. I just appeared and took the class each week until the end of the year.

The children's class was lovely. Martha gave direction in a sweet, quiet voice and explained what she wanted, and the class followed. Since I missed the beginning of the session, I did not know how Martha introduced her technique. The three girls seemed to know what to do and did it well. We sat on the floor and did a series of exercises to strengthen the back and develop flexibility of the hip. We did leg extensions with straight knees and flexion and extension of the feet. I don't recall Martha ever using the terms *contraction* and *release* at this time. The emphasis was placed on strengthening the back and legs. We stood up and did a series of knee bends, which later developed into the first of the lift series. We also performed this exercise with changes of arm patterns. Leg swings and torso and arm swings were performed on different levels. Then the class began with movement across the floor in walks, runs, skips, and leaps on a diagonal or in a circle. At the same time, Martha would speak of the quality of the movement she wanted the class to experience. It seemed a very short hour. I loved it and wanted more.

The next time I saw Martha outside the classroom was at the Denishawn House on West 28th Street. This three-story brownstone house with its twenty-foot ceilings was reconstructed into dance studios with one large studio, a library, and an office on the first floor; a smaller studio and dressing room was on the second floor. The third floor, or attic, was arranged for use as a dormitory for the male scholarship students. The men from the Denishawn company lived there when they were in town.

When Louis Horst came back from his trip to Vienna, he lived in the Denishawn attic until he found his own apartment. Louis played the piano for most of the classes at the Denishawn School. At this time, I was on a work scholarship at the Denishawn School, which required that I buzz into the evening classes and take attendance. I took the advanced class in the morning. After one of these classes, Louis came out of the classroom and told me he was expecting Martha Graham and would I see that she waited for him in the library. From that moment on, I was a basket case. What should I say? How should I say it? How could I tell Martha what her classes meant to me? I kept practicing my opening sentences. Martha arrived and I said, "Louis said to please wait in the library, he may be a minute or two late." Martha, without saying a word, walked over to the bookcase and stood there reading titles. Finally, class was over and Louis came out. He knew of my experience in Martha's class and how much I wanted to speak with her. He called me over and introduced me with, "Martha, this is a fan of yours!" I was so mad I couldn't say a word. I kept hearing "a fan of yours" over and over again. I could not speak and my big chance of a great thank you speech to Martha Graham was gone. Later on, I discovered that Louis was a baseball fan and often took

Martha to baseball games. I realized that being a fan was a special compliment. It was then that I forgave Louis.

While Denishawn was touring the Orient, I was busy teaching the beginning classes at the Denishawn School and learning and performing the Denishawn dances. After I left Denishawn, I stayed with Doris Humphrey and Charles Weidman until they gave their first New York concert in 1927. Louis Horst played for their rehearsals and the concert. This gave me a chance to speak to Louis every day, and I finally talked him into letting me form an adult evening class for Martha. The big studio at the John Murray Anderson School was made available for her at night. I started recruiting students for her class. Some were dancers from the Denishawn School, some from the Duncan School, and some were ballet dancers from various ballet studios. I finally recruited a sizable class.

Martha began to teach in earnest. I knew she could not teach any Denishawn technique because the rule was that no one could use any Denishawn technique or dances without a five-hundred-dollar payment to the main school. Martha never had that kind of money. She had to develop a movement series of her own so she could teach her students.

Martha knew what techniques were needed to train a dancer and that was what she began to do—train dancers. It was in these evening classes that certain teaching phrases began to appear in order to explain or enhance the movement patterns. It was the first time [1927–28] that Martha used the terms *contraction* and *release* as an awareness of a whole new approach to the physicality of movement dependent upon the breath and the anatomical changes in the body due to the breathing process.

It was this awareness of the changes of the body due to breathing in and breathing out that freed Martha Graham from her Denishawn ethnic influence as well as the ballet influence. She had found a way to create her own dances, using the contraction and release principle. She found the answer to her own need to discover and explore what the body could do. Martha would often say, "Don't say I invented a school of movement. I only rediscovered what the human body can do." This freed her to explore an infinite variety of movements for her need to communicate through dance.

It was in the evening classes that many firsts occurred. The class started on the floor—this was a first. What dance class began before this with the students seated on the floor? After a few stretching exercises for flexibility and leg extensions to the front and side, the dance technique portion of the class began. We sat upright on the hips, knees bent, soles of the feet touching, hands on the ankles, arms rounded, and the torso stretched tall. This was the first sitting position. It was in this position that Martha introduced us to the contraction and release principle. She concentrated on the body changes that took place as a result of the inhalation and exhalation of the breath. Martha wanted to know how the body responded when the breath was exhaled; what happened to the bones—the skeletal part of the body—what happened as a result of this activity. The body changes that took place upon the exhalation of air was called a contraction. The body changes that took place upon the inhalation of air was called a release. This was not a great mystery of life, but a natural phenomenon.

Martha, seated in this first sitting position, demonstrated the movements and made us aware of the body movement inherent in the contraction and release. We soon became aware of the skeletal and muscular movements involved. We found that upon the exhaling of breath, the skeleton or bones of the body moved: the pelvic bone tipped forward, the cartilage of the spine allowed the spine to stretch and curve backward, and the shoulders moved forward, always retaining the alignment of shoulder over hip, while never lowering the level of the seated position. When the breath was inhaled, the skeleton resumed its original position moving to that position in the same order: pelvis, spine, shoulders. The muscles moved with the skeleton. When the breath is out of the torso, the back muscles stretch and the front muscles shorten. The muscles return to their original position upon the release. This is the anatomical movement of the contraction and release. The anatomical count for this was: 1, pelvis; 2, spine; 3, shoulders. This count was constant.

Martha developed movement patterns in the first sitting position. These patterns usually started with a simple movement pattern as a theme that became a long dance pattern with the addition of arm and leg patterns, and changes of direction and levels. For the advanced student, Martha's emphasis was on the technical movement patterns that she was performing at the time. Martha's explanation for these movements was focused primarily on the quality of the movement she wanted. As her assistant, I approached the explanation of the contraction and release from the anatomical point of view for the beginning students.

We also began to sense the quality of movement within the contraction and release. Martha wanted to give us the feeling of the depth of movement. We were not to be two-dimensional. We had to feel the inner skeleton of the body as part of the whole movement. The deep dramatic quality came on the exhalation of the breath, or the contraction; the lyric and open quality on the inhalation of the breath, or the release.

When Martha first started teaching, her movements were quite rounded and lyrical. As she began exploring movement for her own dances, she added some of these movement patterns to her technique vocabulary. She employed "teaching cues." She would say, "Don't slump on contractions. It's a high, elevated torso in the contraction position." She added imagery to improve her student's learning process. She explored what she called the "cutoff point of sustaining movement," and "of holding a movement, not daring to move, but moving." Other phrases that added imagery were:

Move on a stationary base.

Move through space, not as just a hop, skip, and jump.

Carve a place for yourself in space.

Project through space as if space were opaque

Focus through space, not just up and down.

The hip is the motivator of movement.

Contraction is ecstasy as well as despair.

Free the head, up and back, not down and back.

Both lyric and dramatic movement must be strong.

Lengthen the sides of the neck.

The listening ear—in space and within.

The hands and feet must respond to the contraction and release.

There must be a complete articulation of the foot; all the bones of the foot must move.

The hip bone must move as a jewel in a watch movement.

There must be an inner depth of movement on the contraction.

These and other phrases were additional firsts in making us aware of the physicality and quality of movement.

Other firsts Martha gave to dance besides the use of the floor—which developed a strong back without the problem of working upright, standing balance, as well as the stretch series on the floor with four different arm patterns and levels (floor, waist, shoulder, and overhead)—were the open Fourth Position and its many patterns of movement; the beginning of the series of falls from the seated hip position; the side extensions; movement patterns with changes of levels and changes of direction seated on a stationary base; the use of the hip as the motivating factor for movement; and the challenge of encompassing space on a stationary base. All these forced a deeper use of the exploration of the workings of the human body and the use of the space around it.

Graham technique, as it is now known, came about in several ways. Some came from experimentation and some from a simplified version of movements from one of Graham's dances. Some movements were devised to aid a technical need of the class or the dance company. The technique began to be quite codified and the class quite structured. This, I believe, was about 1929 or 1930. One half hour of the class was spent seated on the floor, one half hour was standing, and one half hour moving across the floor.

Martha's use of a simple theme and variations, changes of levels, arm patterns, and directions varied the count of each technique pattern. The measures were not always in counts of four or eight. She introduced us to patterns with new counts, sometimes a slow four as a theme of movement, a three count for a lyrical quality, and a percussive or elevation quality on a two count or even an "and-one" count. This change of accent and counts, mixed rhythms, and uneven measures were additional firsts and Martha used them a great deal. Patterns of ten or five counts were not unusual.

Three events compelled Martha to further codify and structure her technique and her teaching in class. It was while she was teaching at the Neighborhood Playhouse School of the Theater in New York City that she simplified movement patterns and added imagery to help nondancers [actors] understand and learn more easily this new and exciting activity. It was at the playhouse that Martha first used the verbal consonant "ess-s-s-s-s-s" on the contraction or exhalation of the breath, in order to dramatize this physical activity.

The second event was the culminating demonstration at the end of the first summer session at Bennington College, in Vermont, in 1934. This was a technical demonstration of six weeks of student dance training presented by all the faculty and their Bennington students. Doris Humphrey and Charles Weidman, with their assistants Leticia Ide and José Limón, led their students and demonstrated Humphrey's "fall and recovery" principle, and Weidman's "kinetic movement" patterns. Hanya Holm, with Louise Kloepper as her assistant, led her students and demonstrated her "tension and relaxation" principle. Martha, with me as her assistant, demonstrated her "contraction and release" principle. This was a very special first because it was the first time the public became aware of the differences among these three schools: Humphrey/Weidman, Holm, and Graham.

A definite time limit for the demonstration was given and the technique that had been learned over a short six-week period was demonstrated by beginning students.

Martha's demonstration included the following:

I. Class seated on the floor

1. Hip warmup and bounces

2. Leg extensions, front and sides

3. Foot flexions and extension

4. First seated position

   a. Introduction of contraction and release

   b. Contraction and release with arm and head changes

   c. Changes of rhythmic pattern with resulting change in quality of movement

5. Stretches with arm patterns in four levels

6. Open Fourth Position: arm patterns, and hip-motivated direction changes, quarter turn, half turn

7. Back leg extensions with arm patterns

8. Preparation for back fall, seated on both hips, on counts of four, three, two, and a fast one count

9. Seated on both knees: exercise on six—a complete circle of the torso

10. Body upright on both knees: changes of levels with hip swing, leading to the back fall

11. A movement transition to the standing position

II. Standing position and center work in place

1. Knee bends in First and Second, side-to-side movement, arm patterns, concentric circle patterns with arms

2. Series of lifts, center front, quarter turn, half turn, whole turn on a stationary base, use of arms

3. Brushes: three different levels, front and side

4. Extension patterns of legs: front, side, and on a contraction

5. Hip thrust series

6. Cross-sit in contraction and release and half turns

7. Prancing preparation: prances center and with quarter turn

8. Back roll with change of rhythmic pattern

9. Running in place: change of directions with back roll

10. Jumps in place in First and Second; jump with one knee bent, other leg straight; jump with two knees bent, soles of feet touching; jumps with turns on eight counts; quarter, half and full turns

11. Side falls from standing position; on a contraction; on counts four, three, and two

12. Back fall on contraction and release

III. Movement across the floor

1. Walking, running, skipping, leaping; different preparations for leaps and jumps; one- or three-step preparations

2. Leaps across the floor: both knees bent; front knee bent; back leg straight; leg straight in front, bent in back; brush leaps; leaps with both legs straight; split leaps

3. Triplets, with walks, with runs, with leaps

The third event was a lecture demonstration at the New School for Social Research in New York City in 1935 or 1936. It was under the sponsorship of John Martin and presented the companies of Doris Humphrey, Charles Weidman, Martha Graham, and Hanya Holm demonstrating their respective techniques. The participants were members of these dance companies.

These three events allowed Martha to think of the class as a theater experience, and her demonstrations began to resemble a great dance. She always spoke in terms of the theater and the need for projection and awareness of self.

Today, as the added dimension of the spiral is emphasized in the training, the demands for even more awareness of the internal movements of the torso are necessary. A dramatic richness is apparent in the movement and one is conscious of the fulfillment of Martha's vision: to move fully, to explore fearlessly, and to demand the potential that is in each of us. Indeed, for Martha Graham, "dancers are the acrobats of God."

Dorothy Bird

Dorothy Bird was a member of the Graham company from 1931 to 1937. A kiss from Pavlova helped her decide to dance as a career. In the summer of 1930, Bird left her family home in western Canada to study with Martha Graham at the Cornish School in Seattle. Bird also demonstrated for Graham in classes and lectures.

After leaving the Graham company, Bird danced in Broadway shows choreographed by Agnes de Mille, Helen Tamiris, and Jack Cole. She returned to modern dance in the José Limón Trio under the direction of Doris Humphrey, then went back to show business with choreographers Eugene Loring, Jerome Robbins, Anna Sokolow, and Herbert Ross. Bird has taught at the School of American Ballet, at the Neighborhood Playhouse, for twenty-five years, and in schools throughout the New York metropolitan area. She was dance consultant for the Nassau County Office of Performing Arts and created the Nassau County Dance Ensemble.

It was in Seattle, in the summer of 1930, that I first met Martha Graham. She came for the entire summer as an artist-in-residence to choreograph and teach at the Cornish School. I'll never forget how she walked into the school's large, airy studio, brushed aside all introductions, and said, "We've no time for formalities. We have a lot of work that we are going to do together this summer. And you may call me Martha."

This was a shock because the head of the school was known as Miss Aunt Nellie. It was a different time. You can't imagine how startling this was. Then she smiled and said, "I have something very exciting that I want to share with you. I have just come from dancing the role of the Chosen One in *Le sacre du printemps,* the Léonide Massine version, on the great stage of the Metropolitan Opera in New York City. I discovered something as I stood still for a long period of time in the work, with the dancers all around me. I learned how to command the stage while standing absolutely still. And I'm going to teach you how to do that."

It was almost magical. With this promise, she distracted us from the fact that she had closed the door on the Fifth Position, port de bras, pointing the feet, and, like Isadora Duncan, had turned her back on tutus, pointe shoes, tiny jeweled crowns, and little white wings. She was prepared to go much further than Isadora. Martha warned us of the dangers of big, romantic passions. Out went all the small, delicate, sentimental themes and the last ripple of the Delsarte System that Ted Shawn had been teaching with such devotion in the Denishawn School. [François Delsarte (1811–1871), teacher of singing and declamation, founded a system of gesture and movement based on his observations of the laws of expression. Ted Shawn, a student of the movement, wrote a small book in 1963 on Delsarte, *Every Little Movement,* reprinted by Dance Horizons.] All this went into the compost pot. Along with this went the stories that can be told in words. Martha said, "Dance has nothing to do with what you can tell in words. It has to do with actions, colored by deep inarticulate feelings that can only be expressed in movement." She did not permit a single sentence, neither a subject nor an object, to be considered as a basis for movement, only verbs and adverbs. Those were the only words she had in her notebook at that time. [Graham always made a script for her movements and works in a notebook.]

We did not for one instant question the strict discipline that Martha imposed on the range of movement patterns that were gradually being introduced to us. First, she broke down the movement into its smallest particles and showed it to us. Together we examined it and learned the source of its initiation. Then she explored ways of putting the particles together again in designs and patterns infused with high levels of energy. If I were to tell you that she was an absolutely incandescent teacher at the time, it would be only words. But it was a fact that she set the students on fire; it was unbelievable.

Martha selected five dancers and was working with us to create phrases of movement for the dance interludes in the Greek play *Seven Against Thebes,* which was to be presented at the end of the summer. She used the classroom to experiment and to create exercises that fed into the choreography. She was always engaged in the process of exploring, eliminating, and simplifying in order to capture the appropriate qualities of movement for this very inexperienced group that came from various parts of the country: Alaska, California, and me from a one-room schoolhouse in Canada. She used every possible image and device to awaken our imagination, including thousands of animal images—images I never heard her use later.

I continued my studies with Graham at Bennington College from 1934 to 1938. Bennington was a marvelous experience because we had food—meals were supplied—and there was the outdoors.

Martha only allowed us music that I considered a thump! She had this idea that the body must carry the melody and the pianist would play only one note many times, then go to another note. The pianist would beg to be released from this tedious job, but the movement had such flow it needed no more support. The sound just punctuated it.

We didn't turn much at this point, but there were two turners, Marie Marchowsky and Bonnie Bird. Each of us had our own special quality. All I think I did was go up and down!

The leaps and runs were not as big as the splits you see today—that was a long time in coming. We always did the side extension leaning forward. We did barrel turns, like Russian folk dancers, and falls: done on a breath, suspended, held, and performed on the count of four up, four down; then on three. It was based upon a faint. Coming up was on a breath. There were tilting falls. Some people were really able to suspend out and fall marvelously.

Sophie Maslow

Sophie Maslow joined the Martha Graham Dance Company in 1931 and remained until 1944. Her training began at the Neighborhood Playhouse with Martha Graham, Louis Horst (in composition), Nanette Charisse (ballet), and Muriel Stuart (at the School of American Ballet). Maslow has since choreographed over a hundred works for her own company, the New York City Opera, the Israeli Batsheva and Bat-Dor Companies, the Harkness Ballet, and many other groups. She has also created works for the many colleges and universities where she has taught, as well as works for television and theater. She has been a judge on arts councils, and in 1984 received an honorary doctorate from Skidmore College. Maslow is copresident of the New Dance Group Studio in New York City, where she continues to teach and choreograph.

When Martha Graham came to the Neighborhood Playhouse, where I was a student, she had already developed her basic movements and the theory of how to train a dancer and a dancer's body to become an expressive instrument. It was a way of expanding the expressiveness of dance so that it could reflect everything in human life—or almost anything in human experience.

In the many years that I was in the company, it never occurred to me to look in a dictionary to find the meaning of contraction and release. I looked the word [contraction] up just recently, and although there are many definitions of the word, down at the bottom of the list a contraction is defined as "a basic movement in modern dance." So, we have made Webster's Dictionary!

I was in the same class as Anna [Sokolow] at the playhouse and found it as inspiring to work with Martha and Louis Horst as she did. Even though I was an adolescent, I felt that everything Martha was doing was right. We didn't turn out our legs. (That meant nothing to me since I never studied ballet.) All her movements were meaningful. Martha gave everything imagery or a meaning to guide the quality of the movement, or we found a meaning for ourselves in everything. Other kinds of dance became unimportant to me.

I remember sitting on the lawn with students at Bennington College in the thirties talking about the "dance of the future." We could feel life changing around us and new things happening in the arts, and we wanted to be part of that future.

I've chosen a few movements that we performed at the time to illustrate how deceptively simple they seem to be. They are performed in the center. The first movements are called lifts and are comparable to the opening pliés in a ballet class. The feet are parallel; there is a rise to the half-pointe and a slow descent. The torso is balanced over the feet. The contraction and release principle was included in different positions going down to a grand plié sitting on the heels. These were very broad movements done in an adagio tempo. Some of the variations alternated between parallel and turned-out legs. These movements require control and balance. It was hard to hold the movement and keep it smooth. It had to be pure and clear. Every part of the body was used so that when you finished the series, you were warmed up. Properly done, they are beautiful to see. The body was used in a spiral position as well; the hands were cupped and the arms straight, or easy, as the series progressed.

Then there was a series I secretly used to call the revolutionary étude because it gave me the image of someone standing on top of a hill and calling people to action. The tempo is as for a march and the quality of the movement should be very percussive. This is a series of bounces, or rebounds, from heel to half-pointe with an emphasis on the up movements. It involves leaning over as if you were talking down to a group of people somewhere on the floor. You turn to the side at times. The élevés, or rises, were continuous; continuous movement is what produced the strength and stamina in the dancer, and the series tightened the buttocks as well. Unfortunately, this series is no longer taught. I feel it added a quality of movement as it developed strength. It was abrupt and heroic in quality and broadened the texture of positive movements.

Turns were learned in a sequence that includes a preparation, a half rotation or turn, and a full turn. The eyes do not "spot," as in turns in ballet, and the body moving from low to high positions form the turn. The body begins in a tipped position parallel to the floor in attitude (one leg bent at the knee and raised behind to ninety degrees). The force for the turn is gained by the lift of the torso and a twist in the back—the spiral—that makes the body turn.

The head floats around with the body, as do the arms. The arm opposite the lifted leg is raised, then the arms open to the side. From the attitude position, the pivot occurs when the body is raised and the lifted foot is placed on the floor. This movement can occur without a turn, as in a preparation, or in a half- or full-turn series. The tempo is in four slow counts.

Executed across the floor on a horizontal plane, this turn was performed with a half rotation or a full rotation. As the attitude leg is placed on the floor, the supporting leg shifts the weight of the body and frees itself to do a swooping ninety-degree rond de jambe toward the direction of the horizontal series. The body, when the crest of the attitude in back is reached, pivots to face the direction of the series and the rond de jambe leg steps forward to begin the next turn in the series.

I don't remember turns included in our early classes, but I do remember turns in our early group dances performed in concerts without Martha participating in the dance. *Course* was one of the names I remember for a concert dance with turns.

Pitch turns with a straight leg usually come from a low contraction. The turn is strong and the position kept parallel in the body; often this was performed as a full turn. The first appearance of this turn, I believe, was in *Deaths and Entrances* (1943).

Walks were another deceptively simple part of the class, especially for dancers now, when they do them, because they are turned out. It's harder now to teach a simple, straight, graceful, smooth walk than it used to be. I used this walk in my early dances, one of them was *Folksay* (1942), and I found it difficult for the dancers to learn.

It is a simple walk but must carry life within it and not become boring. It was taught in a circle and was continuous. From the moment the foot is placed on the floor, the thigh and knee straighten and the other leg moves into the next forward step. It is almost like pushing into a strong wind with a straight torso, or like bravely facing a storm in a peaceful way. The movement goes into the waist, which means that the hip has to be over the foot of the forward leg. It is a beautiful stride with the torso erect and the back leg lengthened without exaggeration. The walk is performed in 4/4 time and begun slowly, each step taking four counts, then two counts, and finally taking only one count. Triplets on one count and other variations complete the series. It all has to flow.

Walking may sound like an easy and natural thing to do, but it is not easy for dancers. Then again, there are so many different kinds of walks depending upon the characterization of the role. For instance, in my ballet *Champion* (1948) it was very hard for dancers to walk like fighters who have sunken chests and protective, rounded arms. It took hours of practice!

Leaps were done with the lifted leg in back bent at the knee, the bottom of the foot facing the ceiling. Height was the objective. Usually, the leaps were performed as "run, run, leap," in a 4/4 tempo, but sometimes they were performed as a leap on every count with the accent on the crest of the movement.

Some of these things are done today with too much lightness. Dancers have spectacular technique and can do just about anything, but it seems to be less meaningful because they employ no weight in the movement. They are not interesting movements when they are just tossed off.

The differences between dancers of my generation and those of today are in their reasons for dancing. I studied at a time when we chose the way we wanted to dance. No one earned a living dancing, aside from a few dancers in Broadway shows. So we could make our own choice as to how we would dance. It was not a question of what jobs were available and what was right for us individually. It was a matter of what was right for dance. We didn't want to be embarrassed by being in poor productions. It was better not to work.

But in Martha's works, not only was the movement important to me, but her philosophy as well. She seemed to feel the pulse of the time—the anger, sharpness, aggression in life at that time—things that were part of our lives, and she seemed to be able to put those things into an art form and communicate them.

I feel today's dancers should find a place for themselves that is right for them, rather than concentrate on where dance is heading in their time and place.

Lily Mehlman

Lily Mehlman was a Graham dancer from 1931 to 1936. She began dancing at the age of seven. She came to the Graham studio when she was sixteen and shortly afterward became a member of the company. She was in the group that performed with Graham as the Chosen One in *Le sacre du printemps,* in the first presentation choreographed by ballet choreographer Léonide Massine, after the Nijinsky version.

Mehlman was also in the opening program at the Radio City Music Hall when the Graham company played the first bill. She became a choreographer for the WPA [Works Projects Administration, a Depression arts program] dance and theater division and later choreographed for ARTEF, a Jewish theatrical company.

Mehlman taught extensively at her own studio and at children's schools and performed with her own group. In 1935 she received the *Dance Magazine* award for performing the outstanding solo of the year. In 1958, Mehlman moved to Los Angeles, where she became involved in dance therapy at the University of California, Los Angeles, later working as a dance therapist at General Hospital in Los Angeles and at Mount Sinai Hospital in New York in a closed ward for disturbed children. She worked with adolescents at Gracie Square Psychiatric Hospital in New York and the Kennedy School for Retarded Children.

In remembering the performance of *Le sacre du printemps* (1930), staged by Massine with Martha as the Chosen One, I recall that Massine and Martha worked very well together. We, in the group, never saw a rehearsal between them, but somehow, in an odd way, they understood one another. The rest of us just followed what we were told to do, sometimes with difficulty because we didn't move that way. But we managed.

Martha was so extraordinary and so beautiful in that solo that I remember when she finished there was a stunned gasp from the audience.

I remember her leaping around the group as she was going into the center for the sacrifice. Her hair was flying, her legs were high in the air, she was flying. There was so much power, so much strength and beauty, you were mesmerized. We, in the group, were transfixed and wondered what she would do next. She lifted her arms, and turned her head in such a different way from the ballet movements.

Graham's *Rite of Spring* (1984) was different from Massine's folk dance quality. The men in Massine's version moved in ponderous ways. Martha's *Rite* had force but entirely lacked folk material, although there were groups of villagers that partook in the ritual in a more abstract way.

May O'Donnell

May O'Donnell was a member of the Graham company from 1932 to 1938 and rejoined the group from 1944 to 1953. Born in Sacramento, California, the young O'Donnell studied with Leila Maple, then Estelle Reed, a student of Mary Wigman in Germany.

She learned the Graham technique in New York at the Graham school and soon joined the company. Between seasons, O'Donnell spent six summers with the Graham group in Bennington, Vermont. Between 1938 and 1944, O'Donnell taught in California and created her own works. World War II and the inactivity of dance in California brought her back to New York in 1944. Following her return, O'Donnell was asked by Graham to rejoin the company and, while continuing her own dance activities, she participated in the creation and performance of major roles in Graham's new works of that period. O'Donnell received guest artist billing.

O'Donnell's active career has spanned from 1932 to 1988 as a performer, choreographer, and teacher. Her technique is taught in several colleges and schools and her works are performed by a number of companies.

I had seen Mary Wigman's work in a concert in San Francisco about 1930 or so and liked it very much. She was on a sensational tour of the United States. A student of Wigman's in San Francisco knew there was a world beyond ballet and Michio Ito. I began to study with her—Estelle Reed. Someone saw me perform and recommended that I go to New York to work with a dancer I didn't know—Martha Graham.

I studied at the Wigman School when I got to New York. The school was sponsored by Sol Hurok, the impresario. It was in Steinway Hall on 57th Street, between Sixth and Seventh Avenues, and it was crowded. The teacher was Fé Ahlff, a big, beautiful Germanic person. The class was more an experience than a lesson. Ahlff would start off with her Oriental drums. There was a big Oriental influence in Europe at that time—even Wigman wore what seemed to be an Indian Nautch costume, with its circular skirt and bare midriff bodice. Fé would do some kind of step and the rest of us, like blind mice, would follow. She never looked back at us. When she reached the end of the room, with us following, she'd return to the original place and cross the floor again, adding a little variation to the movement. It was like a theme-and-variation process. I found it interesting and fun.

One day, I was asked to be in a class that Wigman was going to watch. It was a class in improvisation; I had no idea what that meant. I was very shy and bothered by the idea and by the whole class as I observed people doing what I thought was improvising. It looked wild, with dancers doing odd movements and making funny sounds to get attention, so I just left.

I finished taking classes at Wigman because I had paid for them and went to classes by Graham. I recognized in Martha someone who had a technique, and that the technique was something I would have to hang on to.

Martha's school was on 9th Street, between University Place and Broadway on the parlor floor of a brownstone. The classes were so crowded that there was no room to move anywhere but in your own space. We did stretches and lifts, things that required that you push into your body to find the roots of the movement. It was highly concentrated and if you weren't strong enough, the work didn't look right. There was a lot of work in opposition—one part of the body working against another part. Tension, contraction, and release were taught. There were back falls—those long stretches in the thighs that took strength—brushes and prances. The attitude at that time was: "Return to the primitive—down with anything decorative; it's a tough world out there." The entire art world was searching for new ways to express itself in art, architecture, music—all to the same call. Henry Cowell had a series called New Music, and Charles Ives, Carl Ruggles, and Edgard Varèse were on the scene making new things happen in music.

Compared to the popularity of the Wigman School uptown, run by Hanya Holm, the atmosphere in the Graham school seemed more personal. We had direct contact with Martha, who taught the class.

Very soon after I began to study, Martha took me aside and asked me to study with Gertrude Shurr, one of her teachers, with the goal of my joining her group. That idea seemed made in heaven to me. It was about 1932, I believe.

When the school moved to 66 Fifth Avenue, in 1933 or 1934, the larger space permitted us to move across the floor in low walks, run in place, and take long strides in place with many variations in the counts and in direction; it was a continuous and widening series.

Prances were practiced as a lift between the raising of the knees, so that the movement was very "up." That movement was later used in *American Document* (1938), and we also did triplets in a down-up-up rhythm with the heavier accent on the first step and lighter accents on the second and third steps. We also did running steps that looked like a small leap, in two counts: down, up (heavy, light); then in a slower tempo: heavy, one, one, one. These became bigger and bigger as a logical result.

Extensions evolved in the course of her discovering what new shapes and images could be created with the body. The same extensions were done with the body held in a horizontal position, as in a standing position, with the working knee and the supporting leg parallel to each other. Falls onto the shoulder took control, opened into a release, and, with a swing of the legs, the torso came up. But the falls to the back were performed by few in the class. I did them, and I think I had more control than most because I had more strength. My knee-to-hipbone is long and that permitted me to arch and lean backwards from a standing or kneeling position and to hold my balance with the support of a strong back.

I remember one piece in which I was in the center doing this long, slow fall backwards while everyone else was running around me. It was torture! But Martha liked the contrast of one slow movement against the swift movements of the group in this dance. She gave me credit on the program for it. She was always generous in giving credit to her dancers. The only way I can describe it technically is to compare it to a craftsman working with metal to find the tension between two points. In the body, the fall took such a high release that you had to calculate the tension between the knees and upper back in order to sustain the movement for a long time. This back fall occurs in *Chronicle* (1936), which was about the Spanish civil war, in a section called "Steps in the Street."

My relationship with Martha was good but not a terribly personal one. She liked me because I worked hard. I had to. It was so difficult for me to get to New York; I just had to make it as a dancer.

During rehearsals I watched Martha search within herself. Some of the dancers became annoyed when she changed steps during the next rehearsal, but I liked to see the progress in the changes, in the molding of the work. Going with her into her search taught you a great deal about yourself. You could discover where your base was, that point within yourself where your energy is released into movement and dance.

In the early 1930s, the time of the Depression and social unrest, Martha created dances of social content that expressed the protest, anguish, frustration, and mood of the times—the angularity, the dynamic intensity, the beat of her body rhythms and movements, the search for the return to the primitive, were all part of this time. Martha could sense those things and in her dances she gave voice to those tensions and feelings that attracted an eager and responsive audience.

The first new dance that I was in was *Chorus of Youth—Companions* (1932). She spent hours trying to break away from the primitive and find more freedom and, at the same time, keep some depth.

I don't remember that she demonstrated very much. She'd do something, then get us to do it. If you made her movement look alive, made something out of it, it had value for her. We could contribute to Martha's work in that sense, not the actual steps, but in the working out of the quality she wanted.

A much more open work was *Celebration* (1934), a work with which we began concerts. It was sensational because we never stopped jumping except for a short section when we were on the floor. The audience loved it and I think it was a breakthrough. When it was reconstructed in 1977, we got Lily Mehlman, Marjorie Mazia, Anita Alvarez, Gertrude Schurr, Ethel Butler, Marie Marchowsky, Kathleen Slagle, and me together. Bonnie Bird was in England and Anna Sokolow couldn't come. Jane Dudley came from England. The reconstructed version of the work combined all our memories of how it was originally danced.

In the late 1930s, Martha's creative drive began to unfold in new ways that gave greater range to her dance technique and movement vocabulary and brought more lyricism and freedom into her work.

At Bennington, Martha had done *Panorama* (1935), which had many of the elements she was trying to capture. It culminated in *American Document* (1938) as an abstract piece but with a reference point, and led to *Letter to the World* (1940), a piece of Americana—the new phase. *Document,* for which my husband, Ray Green, wrote the music, was a full, major work. The main sections of the dance were in episodes—Indian, Puritan, Emancipation, and Declaration—all touching and creating an atmosphere that captured the spirit of a growing young nation in its struggle to find identity on the way to modern times. It was the American scene. Although other choreographers such as Lew Christensen, Agnes de Mille, and Eugene Loring were doing dance works on American themes, these works leaned toward ballet vocabulary, while Martha kept the modern dance vocabulary and used movements in a unique and innovative way.

In 1938, *American Document* was the beginning of a new phase in her life as well as in her work. It was the first time that she used a male dancer, Erick Hawkins. This led to new directions and challenges.

In 1944, I returned to New York to establish a studio with Gertrude Shurr and to carry on my own work. Following my return, Martha asked me to rejoin her company to do important major roles. It was with concern that I agreed because I did not want to disrupt my own direction. But I decided to try to work with her and carry on my activities at the same time.

Although I did not take classes in her technique and could only spend limited time in her studio, I could feel that the atmosphere had changed when men entered the company. The men weren't as docile as the ladies. For Martha, the work became full of characterizations and relationships. It was a larger palette.

You could also see that the dancers in the company in the 1940s had, in most cases, some previous dance training, especially in ballet. Pearl Lang, Ethel Winter, and Yuriko had more facility because of their ballet training, and Martha liked it very much. It gave her a greater range, and it seemed to me that the contemporary modern dancer who had—and has today—some ballet training, who has the capacity to absorb the modern dance spirit, can bring an ease to the performance in any company. Martha was able to imprint or plant her stamp on these dancers and have the quality of Graham emerge.

When I returned to the company in 1944, I took over special roles in Martha's current works but soon was involved in new dances in which I could contribute in an important and creative way. Most of my rehearsals were with her alone. She would map out the work and say, "May, this is your music," and I would know exactly what I would be doing in relationship to Martha or to the other dancers in the work. She encouraged me to use my own intuitive imagination and spirit because we had a great sense of rapport. It wasn't a question of knowing her technique, but rather being able to sense what role of compassion I was to play based upon her role.

I knew how to move accordingly. My original role in *Appalachian Spring* (1944) was stimulating and gratifying to me for that reason. It was different from the thirties, when everything was set.

I felt that my role as the Pioneer Woman in *Appalachian Spring* represented a strong, outward, visionary kind of pioneer spirit from which the American nation was founded. It was endurance over hardships and an eternal spirit. Martha never mentioned this to me but said something like, "May, do you want me to work with you or would you like to feel it out?" I said I would try something that she might like, but if not, naturally, it would come out of the piece. We had, later, when the piece was played, a kind of interplay that was wonderful. You just did what came out of the moment, although you still did the same steps.

I originated the secondary role in her *Hérodiade* (1944) in the same way. Once I knew what my character represented, I could keep it in the right relationship. Martha never explained things; you had to create from your own imagination. I developed the Handmaiden role as a simple, devoted, and compassionate figure who helped her prepare for what might be her destruction, trying to protect her from going into the unknown, which might mean death. It was a psychological relationship.

The Chorus of *Cave of the Heart* (1946) was another role created by me, so to speak. There was a story in this work, but it was again a question of relationships. I had to know where Erick, Yuriko, and Martha herself were onstage, and, like a chess game, it had to work that way. It almost dictated itself.

Dark Meadow came along in 1946. I think I sort of balanced off the tensions in her works when she created them. She could make everyone shake and shiver until she exploded. I was called She of the Ground, or the Earth. I think she thought of me that way.

Eventually, the demands of my own work made it impossible for me to give so much time to Martha. My final appearances were in *Hérodiade*. In 1953, after an interval of two years, Martha called me once again to perform this work with her. I knew that it would be our last dance together, but I also knew that it would be a beautiful way to part.

Marie Marchowsky

Marie Marchowsky, a Graham dancer from 1934 to 1940 and then again in 1944, began her study at the Graham school at the age of thirteen. In 1931 she joined Anna Sokolow's first company, the Dance Unit. After leaving the Graham company, Marchowsky created her own group in New York and taught extensively. In 1969 she moved to Los Angeles to head the dance department at the California Institute of Technology. She created a dance company and school of her own. Marchowsky then created a dance company and school in Toronto and became principal of the Toronto Dance Theatre School.

Marchowsky returned to New York to teach at the City College dance department.

My first contact with the Graham movement was in 1930 through Lily Mehlman, my dance counselor at camp and a member of the Martha Graham Dance Company. She was the catalyst for my entry into the new world of dance.

I continued to study with Lily after returning home from camp and learned that Martha was giving a concert in New York at the Craig Theater in the west Fifties. I was determined to go, and my mother arranged to take me. It was an overwhelming experience. I saw four group works: *Primitive Mysteries, Heretic, Bacchanale,* and *Moment Rustica,* and three of Martha's solos, *Two Primitive Canticles, Adolescence,* and *Harlequinade.*

After seeing the concert, my one desire was to study with this great woman. I discussed the possibilities with Lily and learned that there were no children in Martha's class, but she offered to speak with Martha about me. A few weeks later, I was told that I might take a class with Martha, with the warning that if I did not behave like an adult, I would have to leave. I was elated, and needless to say, never uttered a word in class for three years. I later learned that Martha told the women in class to refrain from mentioning sex in the dressing room when I was present!

The movement at that time was considerably different from that of today. The early thirties was a time of searching and exploration, the discarding of the old and the creating of new forms of expression. It was a time of upheaval in all the arts.

Martha's technique reflected this explosion. The movement was percussive, stripped to the bone, unadorned, dark, dramatic, and never decorative. This new path brought a new meaning to dance as it delved into the fundamentals of movement. With her vision, Martha created an art form that was unique and independent of any dance that had existed before.

Class began with floor work which was cursory compared with the floor work of today. The fundamental source was in the contraction-and-release principle, with the pelvis as the central motivating force. The exercises were primitive: legs and feet parallel, hands cupped; feet flexed as if rooted into the earth. The movement was influenced by American Indian dances—a source of inspiration to Martha.

Following this period, a development in the technique evolved from the culture and mythology of ancient Greece in which the Dionysian rites were center stage. While the movements retained their primitive quality, the body stance was locked and altered into a two-dimensional image resembling figures in a Greek frieze. Extensive exercises were created with the body in this archaic position. The classes also incorporated great body swings, or tilts, that had an abandoned and fearless quality with hard-hitting body contractions powerful enough to propel one across the floor. A great variety of falls were included: back falls in a spiral, side falls, and falls from a tilt that would send one sliding across the floor. These wonderful falls have remained in the technique to this day.

In general, the classes seemed to be built on more horizontal than vertical lines. In moving across the floor, as in walking or running, the body had to appear to be pushing through a heavy mass, much like the pressure confronted when walking through water. Forcing through a mass, using the pressure in space, made for great intensity and drama when traveling across the floor.

In the midst of all the ladies was Louis Horst, Martha's mentor. His teaching of dance composition was responsible for our development as artists. Studying with him was like going to a school of higher education. He was an integral part of the studio. There were times when Martha was too tired to conduct rehearsals and Louis would take over. What a disciplinarian he was! He'd sit at the piano, smoking his cigar, and although his hooded eyes appeared to be closed, he didn't miss a thing. His caustic comments on our performance could be formidable. We called him Eagle Eye. Louis's contribution, as the composer for Martha's early works, was unique. At that time, Martha created her dances without music, and when completed, Louis would watch the dance, record the counts, and return with a score that fit splendidly. He was a pillar of support; a man dedicated to the development and growth of modern dance.

Each year, movements were added to the classes as the experimentation and exploration continued. I believe it was in 1933 when a new set of exercises was added to the technique. Based upon the seated-Fourth-Position [with bent knee and one foot flat on the floor about twelve inches in front of the other leg, which is flat on the floor—knee to foot], the upper body moved around the spine as if in a spiral. This innovation was the root from which flowered the extensive and rich vocabulary that embraces the floor work of today. Some of these early innovations can be seen in the dance *Celebration*, particularly in the movements that were on the floor. I recall the working title as *Energio*, or energy, and the dance lived up to the title. It was the first time I was present when Martha choreographed a work. In the previous years, jumping and leaping played a minor role in the technique. But *Celebration* called for a great deal of jumping and we had to learn to use our feet from positions flexed to mostly pointed in order to jump.

This dance, choreographed for the twelve women in the company, was a departure in that its core was composed of jumping—eight to ten minutes of it. It was a tour de force that left us all breathless. We had been rehearsing the dance in sections until, one day, Martha suggested we run it straight through. It turned out to be an exercise in sheer physical endurance and we all felt slightly ill at the end. Eventually, we were able to take this physical challenge in stride.

All the costumes Martha designed were ingenious in their simplicity and were as if wedded to the dance. The wool jersey or stretch fabrics she used sculpted the body. She designed the costumes on us as she cut the fabric and pinned us into them. As the night wore on and she continued to pin, one was lucky if the pins didn't prick too often.

Much of the vocabulary introduced in the class was the result of movements created for each new work. Thus the technique was consistently growing and expanding. In the works Martha created for herself and the company, the group was antagonist to her protagonist. The group was used as a mass in an opposing force.

Including men in the company added a new dimension. The men were no longer a part of a mass but emerged as individual players in the dances. The movements became more lyrical, decorative, and formalized.

Anna Sokolow

Anna Sokolow was a member of the Graham company from 1930 to 1938. She formed her own company in 1931 and from 1939 worked extensively for the Mexican Ministry of Fine Arts, where she introduced modern dance. She was also instrumental in the formation of modern dance in Israel with her work for the Inbal Dance Theatre. In addition to choreographing for her company, the Player's Project, Sokolow created dances for the Broadway theater, the Joffrey Ballet, the Netherlands Dans Theatre, the Alvin Ailey American Dance Theater, and other companies. She taught in colleges, universities, and major acting studios and was a longtime faculty member of the Juilliard School in New York City. In 1989 she staged her work *Rooms* for the Israeli government in remembrance of the Holocaust. In 1991 she received the Samuel H. Scripps American Dance Festival Award for lifetime achievement in dance.

I will always remember how I met Martha Graham and Louis Horst. I was a student at the Neighborhood Playhouse when it was on Grand Street in New York City. It was a theater and school for dancing when I enrolled. It was a revelation for me to be introduced to Martha Graham and Louis Horst as teachers at the playhouse. At a very young age, I knew that what I wanted to do was dance and to make dance an art form that would express the way I felt about things.

This great woman then introduced me to her techniques— rather, to her way of moving the body—and it had a very great effect upon me. Another revelation occurred when Louis Horst taught me choreography. We students didn't even know how to spell the word. In his quiet, subdued, but strong way, he explained what choreography was and why it was important for dancers in our generation to learn it and become creators. The combination of Graham and Horst brought forth our creativity. Because I felt the impact of their teaching and trusted them, I learned a great deal.

At that time, it was an introduction to another world, for not even ballet was as popular as it is today. It was so important to have Graham teaching us her way of movement, it was so interesting and so deep, and it helped me find my own way of expression—but that happened at a later time.

It was all a tremendous and overwhelming experience. Being in her early works, such as *Primitive Mysteries* and *Celebration,* showed us the wide aspects of her art and what her way of moving could express. The impression on me was so profound that I will never, never forget what she taught me.

I feel that Louis Horst is not mentioned frequently enough as an influence in choreography for modern dance. Although he is honored for his teaching, it was the *way* he taught and how he encouraged us all that was so important. For instance, he taught us music by making us analyze a form such as a pavane. He would instruct us in the history of the pavane and explain its place in society, encourage us to construct a dance in that context, and then construct a dance based upon what the dance inspired in us within the structure, form, and meaning of the pavane. These classes continued once a week until we had a thorough knowledge of music and gained the ability to analyze a score— something I don't believe our choreographers today know how to do.

Not only are choreographers today insufficiently schooled in music, they lack a general cultural knowledge concerning the arts in all their forms. They have little or nothing to say, and although this may be a general condition of our society at the present time and common to all the arts, it is not a theatrical experience, not a dance experience, to present oneself on stage and indulge in acting out one's own meager ideas that have no meaning to anyone else.

Another thing I do not like to see is modern dancers insert badly performed ballet into their works, such as a poorly executed attitude, an arabesque, or a careless beat. I saw the Ballet Russe de Monte Carlo when that company first came to America in the 1930s and I loved it. It was good dancing. Although there were whisperings in the dressing room that we should not talk about or see ballet, the visiting companies were wonderful to see. That did not apply to the local groups, which were so bad, there was nothing to learn from them at all.

Primitive Mysteries, which I mentioned earlier, was the work that led me toward what I wanted to do—create religious dances. I left the Graham company to do just that, and Martha showed me the path I needed to follow. I was schooled and disciplined in her technique, but that was not my main interest, and after that, although her influence will never leave me, I found my own way. The Mexicans, with whom I have worked for so many years, call me the rebel with discipline. I could not be more pleased with any description of myself than that.

Betty Bloomer Ford

Elizabeth Ann (Betty) Bloomer was a dancer, Martha Graham student, and (as Betty Ford) first lady.

I was born in Chicago and raised in Grand Rapids, Michigan. My interest in dance began when I was eight years old and enrolled in the Calla Travis School of Dance in Grand Rapids. There we learned a little of everything from tap, ballet, Spanish, and some Mary Wigman technique. The purpose, I suppose, was to have knowledge of art, become graceful, and learn to be a young lady. But for me, dance became a twenty-four-hour focus, six days a week. Ballet, not modern dance, had a big following in the Midwest and the idea of going to New York to join a ballet company seemed a logical goal for me at the time. Of course, that was before I was introduced to Martha Graham.

As a teenager, I had seen Martha dance with her company, most likely in Chicago, where we often went to see theater. I was well aware of her and of modern dance. I had kept a large scrapbook, collecting articles from the *New York Times* about dance and all of the major modern dance choreographers.

When I first saw Martha dance, I was captivated and thought, "That's what I want to do!" Seeing her on stage, Martha seemed very tall, with a body so supple and strong that she had the ability to project every dramatic movement. I can remember her long skirts and incredible extension. She stood high on the ball of her foot and her other leg would extend behind her head. She did not appear small at all. But, in fact, she was a tiny woman.

After graduation from Central High School in 1936, my hope was to go to New York to dance with Martha. However, my mother, being concerned about the big city, wanted me to wait until I was twenty years old. Instead, I was allowed to attend the School of Dance at Bennington College in Vermont for the summer courses in 1936 and 1937.

Martha's classes at Bennington included a great deal of floor work, stretches, dramatic falls, jumps in place, and leaps, but I don't recall triplets. We also had training with Doris Humphrey, Charles Weidman, Hanya Holm, and others. Louis Horst taught and gave us choreographic assignments. I had taken a course in dance notation. I performed the stick figures but all those little vertical lines and marks never meant dance to me. I doubt that particular form of dance notation is even taught any more.

Precise is a good word to describe Martha at that time, as well as *disciplined*. You knew you had better be disciplined in her class; she had no patience or understanding for a student who was not.

Finally, in 1938 my mother kept her promise and we drove to New York. Natalie Harris, my roommate at Bennington, was with Martha's company (1937–39) in New York. We became roommates again and rented an apartment which we had hoped would be in Greenwich Village, but we were only allowed to live "on the edge" of the Village.

When I first began to model, I went to the Powers agency. From the agency I found jobs, including work at a fashion house modeling sports wear. The work gave me enough money to pay for tuition at the Graham school and to live modestly.

Those of us in Martha's auxiliary group who did not tour were in the expanded versions of her performances. I remember being in a Carnegie Hall performance of *American Document* (1938). The dancers in the Graham company that I can remember were Anna Sokolow, Gertrude Shurr, Ethel Winter, Sophie Maslow, and my roommate, Natalie Harris.

Eventually, my mother felt that I was becoming too involved in my dance career. She came to New York and suggested a break for six months at home. With the understanding, of course, I could return if I chose to. I would have liked to have stayed and perhaps join the company. Although I had only studied and danced with Martha a short time, it seemed that it was the right time to give the idea of returning home more thought. I discussed my departure with Martha, who understood and said, "Whatever you have to do, you must do."

I returned home and kept busy doing some teaching in dance, formed my own group for a while, worked as a fashion coordinator, and became interested in a young man, Gerald R. Ford, whom I had known earlier. We married in 1948, two weeks before he was elected to Congress.

After twenty-five years of our congressional lives, we planned to leave Washington. In 1973 my husband was chosen to serve as vice president of the United States, then became president in 1974.

Throughout my years in Washington, I continued to stay in touch with Martha. When I became first lady, I was able to encourage my husband to award Martha the Presidential Medal of Freedom in 1976. She received the award at a formal dinner at the White House. President Ford designated Martha as a national treasure. It was the very first time a person in dance had been so honored.

I became a board member of her company, lobbied with her for support from the National Endowment of the Arts for her company, spoke with her on a regular basis when we moved to California, and maintained my interest in the company throughout the years. Our friendship continued until her death in 1991.

Note: The Gerald R. Ford Amphitheater, in Vail, Colorado, presents an International Festival of Dance each summer with guest artists from the major companies throughout the world.

3 ⟡ THE FORTIES

The revolutionary modern-dance pioneers, Graham, Holm, Humphrey, and Weidman, were now working successfully in their new vocabularies.

On the concert stage, a wave of Americana had overcome a country proud of its culture—Doris Humphrey choreographed *The Shakers* (1930); Eugene Loring choreographed *Billy the Kid* (1938); Jerome Robbins created *Fancy Free* (1944) for Ballet Theatre; and Agnes de Mille created the dances for the Broadway musical *Oklahoma!* in 1943.

Composers Charles Ives, Virgil Thomson, and Morton Gould; artists Edward Hopper and Frederic Remington; writers John Steinbeck and William Saroyan used American themes.

Companies emerged—Mordkin Ballet, Ballet Caravan, Ballet Theatre (now American Ballet Theatre), Balanchine's Ballet Society (now New York City Ballet), and many small modern-dance companies—as government support, which began in the thirties, and foundations now added to their financial security.

America escaped the oppressiveness of the Great Depression through mass entertainment. Prohibition pushed the cabaret entertainers into the movies. The stage prologs of the past disappeared and movie production numbers with hundreds of dancers awed audiences, beginning with Busby Berkeley's precision dancing, inspired by the drills learned from his days in the army during World War I. The meteoric rise of dancing stars such as Ruby Keeler, Bill "Bojangles" Robinson, Eleanor Powell, Fred Astaire, and Ginger Rogers made movies the favorite entertainment of America and a world-wide export. Movie star dancers created a new category for dance—musical theater.

Graham's national pride was reflected early in her solo pieces: piety and judgment in *American Provincials* (1934), Indian and Puritan subjects in *Frontier* (1935) and *American Lyric* (1937). *American Document* (1938) became a full-scale major work, one in which she used spoken words for the first time. She had created fifty new dances by the end of the 1930s.

Letter to the World, based on the life of Emily Dickinson, premiered in 1940. *Salem Shore* followed in 1943. *Appalachian Spring,* created in 1944, became her signature piece.

Her fame spread. Martha and Louis Horst were invited by Eleanor Roosevelt, in 1937, to an informal dinner with President Roosevelt before she was to perform at the White House. But she was too nervous to dine with the party. Later in her career, another presidential recognition came to her by way of a former student, Betty Bloomer, who was then First Lady Ford. However, an invitation to perform at the 1936 International Dance Festival, part of the Olympic Games in Nazi Germany, she turned down in no uncertain terms.

Musicals on Broadway became an art form. Hanya Holm choreographed *Kiss Me Kate* (1948), and later, *My Fair Lady* (1956) and *Camelot* (1960). Charles Weidman worked as choreographer for the New York City Opera Company, but Graham continued to develop her concert dances. At this point, in the 1940s, however, those works were destined to take a turn.

Graham herself and her company were revolutionized by the introduction of a new element—a male dancer, Erick Hawkins. Harvard-educated, trained in ballet, and a member of two of the fledgling Balanchine ballet companies of the thirties, Hawkins introduced a new philosophical and aesthetic bent to the Graham dances. Relationships between men and women, especially those based on Greek mythology, grew from her interest in the work of Carl Jung and the mythologist Joseph Campbell. Volumes of poetry were always on her night table. She brought a shopping bag of books home each week and returned them for a new batch the next week. Her interest in Zen Buddhism, which had begun in the 1930s, also became an influence on Hawkins and Cunningham.

Hawkins had seen Graham dance at the First International Dance Festival in New York City, which featured one night of ballet and one night of modern dance. Graham was influenced by the ballet evening, as Hawkins was influenced by the modern-dance evening. He then attended the legendary Bennington summer school of dance in 1936, where he became captivated by modern dance. In 1938 he joined Graham's company, where his encounter with her led to a repudiation of his ballet training. His first job, however, as a member of the Graham company was to teach ballet to her company members. Some of the more radical dancers were shocked to see a ballet barre brought into the Graham studio; for them, ballet was the enemy, representing an outmoded form of movement that was the antithesis of everything the modernists were trying to achieve. But Graham was far too interested in the movement possibilities that ballet offered modern dance to be bound by prejudice.

Throughout the forties (1938–50), Hawkins originated a number of memorable roles in Graham's works, including *American Document* (1938), *Every Soul Is a Circus* (1939), *Letter to the World* (1940), *Deaths and Entrances* (1943), *Appalachian Spring* (1944), *Cave of the Heart* (1946), and *Diversion of Angels* (1948). *Appalachian Spring* reflected Graham's joy, doubts, hesitation, and, finally, her decision to marry Hawkins, with whom she had had a mutually abusive live-in relationship.

Other male dancers were introduced into the company, notably the talented Merce Cunningham (1939–45) and Paul Taylor (1955–62). The increased dramatic possibilities of using men in the company deepened Graham's interest in psychodrama, the eternal struggle between men and women as it is portrayed in myth.

The impact on the classes was great. While the basic class was well established in the thirties, a new emphasis on the dramatic began to show itself in the work. The introduction of ballet technique helped the dancers hone their skills while expanding their movement vocabulary.

Graham's introduction of men into the company, along with her selection of a new generation of women, led to a broader emphasis on physical speed, precise lifts, and greater overall virtuosity. The studio expanded in space by a move to 66 Fifth Avenue.

Hawkins (who died in 1994), with his matinee-idol looks and strong personality, was now her leading male dancer. Martha made him her company manager, responsible in every operation of the group, but not without resentment from some members.

Male members of the company headed off to World War II (Hawkins was exempt because of poor eyesight). Touring during the war years was difficult and even dangerous. Tensions within the company grew.

At the same time, a former student, generous patron, and loyal friend joined the cast as a nonperformer. Bethsabee de Rothschild, a member of the wealthy European banking family, toured with the company at her own expense and paid the company's yearly deficits, which amounted to tens of thousands of dollars. In 1967, Rothschild sponsored the Tel Aviv–based Graham studio and Bat-Dor Dance Company, which had an academic and contemporary dance repertory. In 1963, Rothschild founded and sponsored the Batsheva Dance Company for modern dance. It was directed by Jane Dudley and originally included dancers who had studied with Graham. The company came to be backed by Israeli state funds in the 1970s.

The forties catapulted Martha to higher fame, to personal happiness followed by despair, and to even greater challenges in her work.

Jane Dudley

Jane Dudley joined the Graham company in 1935, after studying four years with Hanya Holm at the Mary Wigman school in New York. She was with the Graham company until 1946, then returned in 1953 and 1970. From 1938 to 1952, Dudley choreographed and performed with Sophie Maslow and William Bales in their Trio Group; was Graham's teaching assistant at the Neighborhood Playhouse School of the Theater; and was a charter member with Graham, Humphrey, Limón, Maslow, and Bales of the American Dance Festival held at Connecticut College. In the 1960s, Dudley was a member of the faculty at Bennington College and, at the invitation of Graham, became artistic director of the Batsheva Dance Company in Israel. In 1970 she was appointed vice president and senior teacher at the London School of Contemporary Dance, where she continued to work. She choreographed extensively in the United States and the United Kingdom.

Martha came to the studio on 56th Street, on the top floor, where I used to study. I was sixteen and saw her coming up the stairs, with her long hair and looking very shy. I said to myself, "That's Martha Graham!" I had seen her in concerts—the ones in the late twenties when she did performances entirely as solos. There was no company—not even The Trio—when she first began. If you can imagine a concert of thirteen or fourteen solo dances, performed with the most extraordinary movement imagination and originality, and with the most beautiful and proper costumes, with lighting—all created by Martha—you can imagine what a deep experience it was to see. And it was just that for me. And an inspiring one.

I remember once dancing the *Brahms Waltzes* for Ruth St. Denis. After I danced, she came up to me and said: "You know, you're exactly Martha Graham." It must have been my long, dark hair because I can't imagine doing *Brahms Waltzes* and being like Martha Graham!

I had also seen two classes that Martha taught in the late twenties at the Neighborhood Playhouse. The studio was then on Madison Avenue. The young actors were doing a contraction, tilting back and holding the heels, turning into a high arch, and returning to the original position about three times, then rising—all holding onto their heels! There are not many dancers who can do that today with control. Martha was uncompromising and put them through a grueling but invaluable experience.

Martha had a class of about twelve women in the 56th Street studio. I watched them doing a sequence that started on the back, proceeded to a lift in a contraction (by the way, I've given up that term because it has become hard to convince a modern dancer's body to do it; I call it a rounded back). I saw Martha do this lift, raise one leg and rise to a standing position, then, still holding the raised leg, lower to the floor and back to the original position. That takes immense strength and control. Her natural facility for movement was so special and so original it made her technique exceptional.

Erick Hawkins

Erick Hawkins was born in Trinidad, Colorado, and studied with Harald Kreutzberg and at the School of American Ballet in New York City. He danced in Balanchine's opera ballets staged for the Metropolitan Opera in the early 1930s and was a charter member of Ballet Caravan, performing in works by Eugene Loring and Lew Christensen.

He attended the Bennington College summer workshop in 1936, where Martha taught until 1942, and joined the Graham company in 1938, where he remained until 1950. He married Martha Graham in 1948.

In the 1940s, Hawkins formed his own company, for which he continued to choreograph and perform until his death in 1994.

I was in Balanchine's first *Serenade* (1934) when it was performed by students of the School of American Ballet at the Felix M. Warburg estate in White Plains, New York.

Lincoln [Kirstein] later asked me to do a work, *Showpiece,* for the Ballet Caravan company he formed in 1936. The company's goal was to encourage American dancers, choreographers, composers, and designers. It toured for three years and included works by Lew Christensen, William Dollar, Eugene Loring, and me. Ballet Caravan was engaged to appear at the First International Dance Festival in New York City—one night of ballet, one night of modern dance. That is where I first met Martha Graham; she appeared on the modern dance night.

Lincoln gave me a very short time to do the second work for the company, only three weeks. The theme of the piece was the Minotaur, later used by Christensen, and even later, by Martha in *Errand into the Maze* (1947). But before that, I knew that there was a new world of dance coming. I had read about Isadora Duncan in *Theatre Arts Monthly,* a beautiful publication. I felt that, in order to do this piece as a metaphor on the theme, and because I wanted to respond to this new world of dance, I would need more time. It was not suitable to use old, standard movements for such a mysterious theme. Lincoln understood and gave me tuition to study at Bennington College, where Graham, Humphrey, Weidman, and Holm were teaching in 1936. I was convinced that I had to find my own way. The boy from Colorado did not fit into the Balanchine mold, which, at that time, was closer to St. Petersburg than the American ballet that it became. I took Martha's summer course. In a way, I think it was Balanchine's advice to me that provided some impetus for me to search for myself. When I asked him if I could be a dancer, he said, "You can't tell what you can do until you do it." I took that as a challenge that opened doors for me to do whatever I wanted.

So, Martha's course, drilled into me by Ethel Butler at that pivotal time in my development, opened doors and expanded my awareness of freedom. I don't remember any men in the class—Merce [Cunningham] came along the second year I was in the company in 1939. My new path melded with Martha's and I think I brought additional energy and expanded the use of her movement in her dances.

As an example, in *Night Journey* (1947), in the lifts, it was natural for me to participate in working them out since I was the active participant in the work. And in *Appalachian Spring* (1944), in the role of the Husbandman, and in other works, I made some participatory contribution.

But you see, since we were all trained in the same way, the source being the center of the body, any small contribution was valid to the work. From that same source, I developed my own way—from the center. I'm sorry to say that in some of the Graham students I see today that principle seems to be lost.

Losses, such as a center, I feel are the cause of so many injuries today. If your theoretical and practical use of the body is correct, you won't do a bad movement that might cause injury. The body can be driven, but it has to be within the bounds of the capacity of the student, and be accumulative, and observant of the laws of movement—the skeletal limits. I've had a long career as a performer because I developed correctly and gained stamina slowly.

The training in the classroom at that time was well established and I don't think that anything from the ballets found its way into the classroom. There may have been an excerpt from the repertoire given, but that is not basic to the principles of her training. It's true that I taught ballet at the suggestion of Martha Hill that second year at Bennington, because that is what I knew, but I don't think it had much influence on the basic training. The floor work that Martha introduced was a tremendous contribution to dance: no weight on the legs, control from the center. Weight and center are serious concepts. Wouldn't it be nice if dancers today could embody both the current concept of lightness *and* weight, using one or the other as the work demanded it? "Gravity is the root of grace" is a saying by Simone Weil that I remember as a suitable image for dance.

I think what I really contributed to Martha is what you might call an aesthetic. She was a great artist and I don't see the great artist in performance— the moving, overpowering presence—in dancers today. Perhaps that's because of a general deterioration in the arts. The motives have changed. An aesthetic vision has to be present—a desirable goal that is not based upon gaining notoriety, money, or acceptability—but is based upon reaching that aesthetic vision. That doesn't mean starving, but it does mean that a group or a dancer has to have a standard, a level, a goal that is beyond the demands of the general culture.

There is a lot of competition in dance, so many more people in dance than ever before, and not a great deal of good judgment in the people who make dance possible. Razzmatazz has found an audience. People are doing a dance for the wrong reasons. I think our generation danced for only one reason: the desire to dance to an aesthetic goal. That was satisfaction enough. I'm not talking about art for art's sake, but about being honest in the reasons for dancing and for creating dances. It is a concept I keep in mind, trusting that the result will be fresh and from innocence. It takes a clean palette every time. And it wasn't created to please anybody. There is no dance that I have done that I'm ashamed of.

In 1950, Martha created *Eye of Anguish* on the theme of [Shakespeare's] King Lear for me. It was not successful. It was performed only once in Europe and dropped for the last time. I think it failed as a piece because Martha could not enter into that character of Lear as she had in female characters. Martha thought through a work using her psyche, her emotions, but I don't think she could do it for a leading male role.

But that was an honest failure. It was dropped. That's what I mean by honest. If a work is not up to the highest standards, it should not appear on stage. We've got to stop accepting compromises.

Jean Erdman

Jean Erdman was a member of the Graham company from 1938 to 1945, in 1970, and from 1974 to 1976. Her vigorous initiation into the company required that she learn four works in ten days before a Boston performance.

Erdman made a solo world tour in 1955. She developed a "total theater" approach for *The Coach with Six Insides,* based on James Joyce's *Finnegans Wake* (1962), which won Vernon Rice and Obie Awards.

As a choreographer, Erdman has worked for the Repertory Theater of Lincoln Center, the Vivian Beaumont Theatre, and the New York Shakespeare Festival, winning the Drama Desk Acting Award and a Tony nomination. In 1972, with her late husband, the noted author-philosopher-mythologist Joseph Campbell, she founded the Theater of the Open Eye in New York City, and continued to direct numerous total theater works. In 1985 she was commissioned jointly by the government of Greece and the U.S. State Department to create an evening of theater works for the Athens festival Myth and Man Symposium at the Herod Atticus Theatre. She has created a video archive of her early repertoire. Erdman lives in Honolulu.

When I was a student at Sarah Lawrence College, I had my very first dance lesson with Martha Graham and was transported. I knew, just by the way

Martha put her feet apart and squatted into an open plié, that she had the key to dance and to life itself. Her inspiration never left me.

I grew up in Hawaii knowing only Isadora Duncan and hula dancing, so the revelation of the tremendous intensity of expression unleashed by the body as I saw it in Graham's work was totally new to me. It was an experience just to watch it.

As a student at Sarah Lawrence, we had the privilege of having Martha's dancers come to teach us once a week—either Ethel Butler, May O'Donnell, Bonnie Bird, Dorothy Bird, or Martha herself. It was wonderful to get into that beautiful world.

Martha by that time—before 1938, when I joined the company—had a company of females who loved what she did and found it sufficient. When I was invited to join the company, upon arrival at the studio, I found that I had to learn four dances in ten days prior to my first performance in Boston: *Celebration* (1934), *Heretic* (1929), the Act of Judgment section from *American Provincials* (1934), and a new piece, *American Lyric* (1937), with music by Alex North. In *American Lyric,* as the title suggests, we did some of the turns with a leg in somewhat of an attitude position.

It was a terrifying experience because Martha said to me, "Oh, you're so much taller than I thought you were!" and then placed me with Jane Dudley and Sophie Maslow, her experienced dancers. But that may have been lucky because people would watch them instead of me, I thought.

The only thing I can remember about that performance is that during those four counts toward the end of *Celebration,* when I could stop jumping and breathe, I saw stars—the only time in my life that I saw stars from sheer exhaustion! But I was forevermore involved in the meaning, the message, and the physicality of Martha's art.

The following year, she invited a young man to come into the company for a new piece called *American Document* (1938). She asked Erick Hawkins to dance in the work and another young man, an actor, to do the narration. It was the first time she included a male dancer and spoken words. She kept the style as it was, but gave Erick stronger movements to do and we performed it all over the country on tour.

Then, she said to us one day, you're going to study ballet with Erick. At that time, we wore only bathing suits, no tights, and no shoes for class. Barres came into the classroom, and shoes. It was incredibly difficult to move our legs without a torso movement. Martha began to incorporate movements that kept the body still and used the turnout, but were not balletic.

These involved a different problem of balancing and centering without impulse from the center that was so basic to Martha's technique and expressivity. They were incorporated into turns, and I remember that it was very difficult to add that new dimension to the technique. It seems so simple now, but it was innovative at the time.

Martha began to be interested in drama. Here was a man and a woman, a relationship of male and female present on stage. The arms came into greater play, and the movements had more flow. But never, never was that powerful center lost; that meaning of her vision. When she choreographed *Letter to the World* (1940), what it meant to dance as a female came into the creating and performing of the work. We found it strange to do what we had never done, but it was all part of the experience of being in her company, learning what she wanted us to do, learning who we were, learning what *life* was about, and what the art of dance can be.

Mark Ryder

Mark Ryder was a member of the Graham company from 1941 to 1949 and made his debut in the premiere of *Letter to the World* (1940). In 1950 he and Emily Frankel debuted as the Dance Drama Duo, which became, in 1954, the Dance Drama Company. In addition to their own choreography, they commissioned works by Valerie Bettis, Todd Bolender, Sophie Maslow, Zachary Solov, and Charles Weidman, and performed throughout the United States until 1958. Ryder directed the Jewish Community Center of Cleveland from 1961 to 1965; was on the faculty of Goddard College in Vermont (1966–73); and from 1974 to his retirement in 1988, was an associate professor of dance at the University of Maryland at College Park.

When I became a member of the Graham company, the tradition was already a strong movement, but my entrance into the company followed a different pattern from the other dancers.

I lived in New York City and studied in the children's classes at the Neighborhood Playhouse when it was on Madison Avenue. I was the only boy in the class for five years! Then, I studied ballet, took other modern dance classes, and studied with Marie Marchowsky before going into the senior classes at the Neighborhood Playhouse. It was in these classes that I studied with Martha and Jane Dudley. It all seemed a natural and logical development of my past study. It didn't seem exceptional—that was just how it was.

When Martha needed a man in *Letter to the World* (1940), it seemed natural to be chosen—after all, why shouldn't she choose me, I thought. That's the point I'm trying to make—that if you were a man and coming into the school or the playhouse at that time, you were spoiled rotten. Boy, was I spoiled. I expected things to come my way and they did.

I do have two small insights to offer on her technique: One deals with the "fall on four"; the second deals with the change in the makeup of the women in the Graham company, beginning in 1941, and how this change affected the technique.

When I arrived in the Graham studio, the fall on four [on four counts] was taught only to the left side. When I was trained, symmetry was an article of faith. Turns were done on both sides, extensions were done on both sides, so were the leaps and combinations. You were taught to do things on the right side and also on the left.

Martha pulled some totally unexpected rabbits out of her intuitive hat in many rehearsals. She showed me how strong a tool intuition can be—especially for geniuses. I saw her stuck, at a dead end, in a piece of choreography from which no logical development was possible. Then, blip: We'd see another miracle from her. It was always the right movement at the right moment, but seemed to come from nowhere. It made it difficult to contradict her. She might be wrong, but how can you argue with someone who always seems to be doing the right thing at the right time! How could she have been wrong about falls to the left in her choreography?

She not only used our bodies, she also used our inner lives, she co-opted our souls.

I observed a change in the bodies of the women in the company beginning in 1941. The women of the group seemed big-boned, robust. Jane Dudley, Sophie Maslow, Jean Erdman, Frieda Flier, Ethel Butler, and Pearl Lang seemed to fit in with them. I left in 1943 for the army and returned in 1945 only to find Yuriko, Helen McGehee, Ethel Winter, and Pearl Lang (who had dropped ten or fifteen pounds) and several others, along with the larger women. The basic character of the company seemed to have changed and with it, the technique. What had been slow and powerful became lightning fast, like quicksilver. If you were to compare the group in *Primitive Mysteries* to the Chorus in *Night Journey,* it would be clear to see the contrast of style in the techniques used in each.

Postwar, I took classes with Yuriko, Marjorie Mazia Guthrie [the wife of Woody Guthrie and the mother of Arlo Guthrie], and, perhaps because I was out of shape, everything seemed so much quicker. I couldn't get all the steps into the combinations any more. The smaller bodies moved more quickly. The tempos seemed changed.

I wondered if this was Martha's design, or if it was because of the new crop of dancers, who were smaller in comparison, or whether everyone was smaller, slighter, and skinnier. I think it was Martha who had changed her aesthetic at that time in an intuitive move to reflect society's swifter, sleeker, expanding world.

Helen McGehee

Helen McGehee was a member of the Martha Graham Dance Company from 1944 to 1972, and a principal dancer from 1948. She has been a choreographer, designer of theatrical costumes, director of her own company, lecturer, teacher, and author of *Helen McGehee, Dance* and *To Be a Dancer,* her most recent book. She currently lives in Virginia.

Martha Graham's creativeness is the body and soul of her technique. Her search deep within herself to objectify in terms of movement the inner life of the character to be portrayed brought discovery of movement that she then needed to teach to her dancers. Because she was so gifted with a rare, naturally talented body, she could execute and consequently demand that the dancers also execute remarkably difficult and different movements. These movements require range, skill, and incredible strength. We, as dancers, and especially as teachers, must always be aware of this source.

A technique for dancing should not solely be concerned with developing bodily skills. But dancing should be a source of commanding a deep, inner energy. The dancer has a responsibility to be vivid. In a lifetime of dancing—performing—there will be times when a dancer will feel that she cannot do what is asked of her. Illness, fatigue, and distress can make it difficult to summon up the energy needed to make a performance live again. This is why your technical training and your preparation for a role must have always been so thorough and so constant that you will know how to go about rekindling this life.

Technique is the means by which you rekindle this vitality. For this reason, the dancer must never allow herself to make a meaningless movement—one that lacks concentration.

Actually, I'm talking about how one goes about the business of taking class. Try to become totally concentrated on what you are doing; aware; without practicing carelessness; and do nothing by rote. In this way, dance technique can bridge the gap between exercising and performing on stage.

I was fortunate, during my early development, to have had many classes taught by Martha herself. I remember her saying often, "You have so little time to be born to the instant." We, from experience, knew that this was true. My generation had fewer opportunities to perform than today's dancers. Therefore, I always felt the need to take class as an act of ritual, a commitment to the theater.

The more concentration you are able to bring to bear upon your object, your role, and your images for the role, the more likely that inner energy and vividness will be released at the precise moment you perform the role. The frustration of dance as an art form is that it exists only at the moment of performance.

Martha taught me that, to make theater, every component is essential. No aspect is secondary. Theater requires the commitment of each person involved working to the utmost of his or her capacity to produce that rarity that is excitement. She made each of her dancers realize that the devotion to the performance, to the work itself, rather than to their own importance, makes the piece ring true, and also makes it work successfully for them.

This is something that must be truly believed. It cannot be faked or it comes across as false. Nothing is more destructive than competition; both to the work of art and to the competitor.

I feel lucky to have been involved in so many Graham productions that offer the rare, almost unique, opportunity to experience this kind of participation—the creation of an experience greater than the sum of its parts that makes it such a deeply joyous thing to do.

We all know about the contraction and release, the breathing of the body, but what is less frequently taught and emphasized is another element—suspension. It is the moment of hanging there between the two elements, the moment of balance before the change. Without this suspension, the breathing becomes forced, positional, and mere huffing and puffing.

Techniques for performing are discovered through experience, through doing, and, in all probability, will differ with each personality. For me, the flow of energy must be toward the performer during the act. You must be so charged that you have power to pull energy from the audience. For this reason, I find it dangerous to watch other performers immediately before performing myself because I need time for the flow to change direction. In act 1 of *Clytemnestra* (1958), after my exit as Electra, I could always enjoy Linda Hodes's Cassandra and Ethel Winter's Helen of Troy.

You must be strong enough to admit vulnerability. You are exposed on stage. The reason for being on stage is precisely this exposure. Exposure is what you are communicating, and your protection is your preparation.

Apropos of vulnerability, Martha would sometimes say, "Let the skin be like the skin of a grape." This was meant to allow ease and release of tension. After a recovery from a fall, she would say, "Let a gentle waterfall flow down the body."

I have collected during the years with Martha what you might call tips for performing. One such tip is about marking [performing a rehearsal or any activity without the use of full energy]: "Don't! If you must, then mark the physical movement, but keep intensely the dramatic meaning. Never mark that. And keep the true timing and musicality of the role. Always be involved with what you are intending."

Another tip concerns energy. Frequently, in class, when the class energy was low, she would have us do a simple sequence of movement with an added vibration, such as heel ripples or fast, soundless clapping of the hands, which, of necessity, would demand energy to be built up in the body to be released consequently into a more difficult movement. For example, on four counts, a simple circular walk using a vibration of the hand on the first two movements, released into a wide turn on the third, and recontained into the walk on the fourth step. The most demanding use of this vibration is when Medea draws the snake from her increasingly vibrating body.

Another tip is about touching. In *Appalachian Spring,* when the Followers make a picture of adoration around the Preacher, we were to look as if we were touching him, but were not literally to do so. The image would project farther without actual touching, and the energy required to hold the position would make the image more vivid. In *Night Journey,* the Daughters of Night should give the *feeling* of tearing their clothes, but not literally do so. That literalness, suddenly, would make it all too mundane.

The tremendous joy of performing lies in the opportunity to be so many different kinds of characters. The danger in the dance world is to lose variety. I feel there is so much emphasis on the extraordinary, on the splashy, and on the overextended, that there is not enough contrast through the use of restraint and composure. Consequently, the spectator becomes sated with bravura and the point is lost.

One of my favorite roles in the Graham repertoire was Artemis in *Phaedra* (1962). It was wonderful simply to stand there simply being.

I need to withdraw and become quiet before performing. I need to feel at home in the theater, and I like to be there at least two hours before curtain. Part of this quieting takes place during the ritual of makeup. The other ritual of preparation is warming up. We see changes in the technique over the decades, because dance is a living organism and therefore subject to change; without change it will die.

I feel that many changes of detail wrought, for example, in some basic technical sequences are a result of Graham's desire to get at the unteachable. She swings the pendulum in order to have the dancers experience the excitement of equilibrium at the center. The center cannot be exaggerated, as, of course, the extremes can. Her search was for the beautiful, the unteachable, but nevertheless discoverable center.

Thus, we find Martha's work still expressing continuity with the past, but with the past as the living present.

John Butler

John Butler was a member of the Graham company from 1943 to 1953. He was born in Memphis, Tennessee, and attended the University of Mississippi. As a performer, Butler appeared in the original Broadway production of *Oklahoma!* (1943) and in *On the Town*.

He had a long and notable career as a choreographer for television on *Camera Three* (CBS), the *Bell Telephone Hour* (NBC), and on WNET (now PBS). In addition, he created works for Gian Carlo Menotti, including *Amahl and the Night Visitors* and *The Unicorn, the Gorgon, and the Manticore* (later performed by the New York City Ballet) for the Spoleto Festivals.

In 1955 he founded the John Butler Dance Theater and continued to choreograph works for the Metropolitan Opera Ballet, Nederlands Dans Theater, Pennsylvania Ballet, and the Harkness Ballet. *Carmina Burana*, created in 1962 and performed at City Center, won him high praise.

History is just a series of daily things. It was not possible for us to know that we were making history by being in the Graham company. We felt that we were doing something new and exciting and we really didn't care what anyone else thought about it.

Martha had a sense of humor when she taught movement. For instance: I had a basset hound named Camille (named by Greta Garbo, to whom I gave private dance lessons at one time). I would leave Camille with Martha when I went on my various tours, because she loved Camille. He would lift his great head and stretch, as hounds will do. When he demonstrated this to a class that Martha had brought him to, she said, "This is how your throat should look when you bend backwards." Her humor was dry, and sometimes very naughty.

We had a relationship, a private friendship, outside of the professional one. I regard it now as having been almost a mystical one. Maybe it was because we were both Irish and had a sense of mystery about things. She was a sorceress, you know—in the Irish sense of having insight and being able to command people to do her bidding. She had superhuman power.

I remember something superhuman occurring after the breakup of her marriage to Erick Hawkins. I was the last one to leave a rehearsal one night and went into the studio to bid her good night. I heard her sobbing. But it wasn't the crying of someone in grief or despair—it was something deeper, almost like a wounded animal in pain. There was a torrent of tears, like something from a Gothic tale or a Greek tragedy. I sat there for about two hours until her body calmed down and I felt I could leave. It was not a human incident, but mythic. I had come straight from Mississippi to New York—green, and probably the only boy in the state at the time who ever thought about dancing. I was practically stoned out of the state. My background was ballet and ballroom dance and I taught successfully in New York, but I knew that was not what I wanted to do.

One day, in a bookshop, I saw photos of Martha by Barbara Morgan. Only in youth can you have the kind of arrogance I had to look her up in the telephone book and go to her studio.

I said to the receptionist, "I'd like to meet Miss Graham, please." Everyone within hearing distance was horrified. They buzzed around and finally Martha emerged. I said, "I would like to work for you, Miss Graham." "Come back tomorrow morning," she said in her wisdom, "before the class," knowing that if I didn't show up, I was not worth the bother.

I showed up in my prince outfit. Since I was the only boy who danced, I was everybody's prince in Mississippi high school performances. I got into my baby-blue tights and doublet—my baby-blue outfit. You can imagine what an impression I was making on her. I flew around the studio in my rotten Mississippi ballet steps until she could stand it no longer. "Sit down, young man," she commanded. I stayed for the class. It was two hours long, but I knew instantly that it was what I wanted. At that time, the movements were still percussive, strongly rhythmic, and not yet romantic. Later, when I rejoined the company several times, the movements became more lyrical.

Years later, when Martha and I had become close friends, she would sometimes look at me across a dining table and say, "Hello, prince."

The first year I went to her classes, Martha also sent me to the School of American Ballet. It was very strange. Here I was, the Graham boy, going uptown to the 59th Street and Madison Avenue SAB wearing ballet slippers in class. I think she just wanted to see my body rid of the bad ballet I had been taught in the past. It lasted for two or three years, with Muriel Stuart as my teacher—Stuart had studied briefly with Martha and had danced in the Pavlova company. Muriel put me on an egg-custard diet. Honestly, I was so innocent and trusting and so enchanted by these important and famous ladies, I would have done anything they said in order to dance.

Graham classes were not painful for me because I had ballet classes early in my life and because I was a dedicated tennis player. I had stamina.

When we became close friends, telling each other confidences, and aside from the great woman that she was, I saw her vulnerable and sensitive side. We shared feelings about our private lives, almost as if it were a secret relationship. To me, it was sacred, and whenever I was interviewed, I never gave away any of her private thoughts.

In the studio, working with her on a role, no one else existed for you or for her. She was the enchantress in this situation. Captivated by her, you were caught completely. Half of the time, I didn't know what the hell she was talking about—it was so mystical and spiritual—way out of my Southern range. But somehow, it got to me on the level of dance, and I moved as she wanted me to.

There were those in the company to whom she entrusted participation in the creation of roles. They used her language, but she guided them and respected their contribution when it was right. It may be for this reason that so many of her dancers became choreographers. They knew the process that she showed them and, as a result, but not intentionally, they became independent of her.

Something I could never understand, however, concerned her use of music. While I am so influenced and responsive to music, I find it still a mystery that she was not. She would rehearse pieces of a dance in the studio and then commission a composer to prepare the accompaniment to that section in another place. It would all fit at some point, but I never could understand how or why. As always, she wrote the libretto for the entire dance, and Samuel Barber, or Gian Carlo Menotti, or whoever, appeared to be utterly baffled when it was put together and it all seemed to work. Even if Martha decided to do her slowest passages to their liveliest sections, the contrast matched the libretto as an underlying or underscoring of the intent.

What I learned from her, and from all of this, was pure theater. I responded more to her sense of drama than to her movements. I never had a great technique. She was so articulate, and had a capacity for such diverse imagery, that I learned from her how to get to the dramatic moment with honesty, brevity, and clarity, just as she did.

When she directed you, she reached into your being to get the strength she knew you had. You always grew with her. That's the reason I kept coming back to perform in the company between my own seasons and commissions.

From some of the dancers, she called forth their physical capacities, but from me she called forth drama and theater.

Working with her was a double act of faith. She trusted you with her theater and you gave it back to her. You had to reach her plateau; she demanded nothing less. In turn, you found yourself making the same demands of others when you were entrusted to direct them. The legacy is handed down in this way. It is a sacred trust that works on sacred ground.

Martha would come to my early concerts and give me comments. It was something I valued. When I had my big success in *Carmina Burana* (1962) at the City Center, I took Martha home, as I always did, after the performance.

She kissed me long and hard when we parted and said, "Now, I tell you good-bye." I was no longer the pupil. Not her equal, but now on my own path. She never came to another performance.

Stuart Hodes

Stuart Hodes was a member of the Graham company from 1946 to 1958, and taught at the Graham school from 1950 to 1984. He has choreographed for musicals, films, his own concerts, and ballet and modern dance companies. Hodes is now director of the Martha Graham School of Contemporary Dance in New York City.

Hodes has performed in Broadway musicals, on television, including a concert with Steve Koplowitz at the Dance Theatre Workshop and has continued to perform. He was on the faculty of Manhattan Community College, where he developed a new dance major program and was director of the Dance Notation Bureau. The following is an excerpt from a proposed book by Hodes.

In 1947 Douglas Watson taught me the first piece of Graham choreography I ever learned, the party step from *Letter to the World*. It took him two hours to teach me it. That night my metatarsal arch collapsed. I wondered if I was meant to be a dancer.

In 1984, I returned to the Graham school to teach technique. I met Martha after class and mentioned that being there was stimulating.

"How, stimulating?" she asked.

"It brings back my early days with you," I said.

She fixed me with a look and said, "Write it down." It surprised me, and I must have shown it. "Stuart, write it down," she said again, commandingly.

Well, I did. Here is a portion about how it was to take Martha's class:

Martha's advanced class, 1947. The advanced class met at 4:30 P.M. By 4:15, the choice spots in the center of the studio floor and in front of the mirrors were taken, and latecomers picked their way to the places near the back and at the sides.

Before starting, I liked to rest in the squatly soles-of-the-feet-together position of the opening moves, letting the weight of my torso gently lengthen the muscles of my lower back. The maple floor, clean as a cutting board, felt good under my bare thighs.

Ethel Winter, the demonstrator, faced the class. Other demonstrators were Yuriko Kikuchi, Helen McGehee, and Pearl Lang, all members of the Graham company. One minute before 4:30, Ralph Gilbert entered, sat down at the piano, and arranged his newspaper. When Martha entered, everyone watched her alertly. She looked the class over, glanced toward Ralph, who met her eyes.

"And—!"

Ralph's clean chords cracked out as each torso dropped into opening *bounces,* sixteen with soles of the feet together, sixteen with legs outspread, sixteen extended to the front.

Breathings followed—an expansion that filled the torso and lifted the gaze. Martha taught it with images, yet the goal was a skill without mystical baggage. In particular, she never allowed breath to whistle in and out yoga-style because the need for breath varied and real breathing had to be free beneath all movement.

Then began those signature torso modulations, Graham *contractions.* From deep in my pelvis I drew my body into a concave arc from hips to head, relishing the sensation of deep muscles working and the surge of force into my bones that seemed to shoot out of my flexed hands and feet. *Release* straightened me like an uncoiling spring.

As each contraction began, my face lifted, lengthening my throat. "Open your eyes!" Martha commanded, and accused us of resistance, self-indulgence, retreat, and other contemptible things if we closed them. "Present your gaze!" she exhorted, and I presented mine to the vaulted ceiling, then through it, imagining sky, space, and beyond space. My gaze felt solid, as though it had weight. I panned it like a beam and chopped it down like a cleaver as my body gathered an accelerating sweep that articulated my spine and flowed through my torso into my mouth, where it burst into a second contraction to begin again.

"Sit to the side, Fourth Position."

Ethel Winter demonstrated and I studied her closely, trying to fathom the comfort and ease she had in this curious body posture. My tendons seemed long enough, but I was never at home in the sitting Fourth Position and believed it to be a flaw of understanding, some muscle group deep inside that hadn't learned not to resist.

The sitting Fourth generates a spiral in the body. A year earlier Martha had urged us to see the French film *Farrabique,* the story of birth and death on a French family farm. She particularly wanted us to notice the stop-motion sequences of plants growing. "Watch how they spiral upward toward the sun," she said. "Life flows along a spiral path." Soon I noticed that spirals were being emphasized in many of our technical moves and introduced into others. Decades later the scientists Crick and Watson discovered that the DNA molecule is one spiral within another. Martha's intuition was scientifically confirmed.

I extended my legs, tilted onto my right side, spread my knees, and pulled back onto the left rump, each move on a percussive chord. Ralph's music was familiar, yet his improvisation was always fresh. Once into the exercise, an elusive melody in a minor key appeared, inspired perhaps by the subtle coil of the hips.

My left hip lifted to insinuate a rotating wave through my stomach, chest, and head. My arms engaged, first left, then right, then both as head and gaze swept an arc. The room spun past my eyes yet left stillness within me. Both hips rose as my torso arched up, back, and around until my weight hung suspended over my right forearm, where I floated until a contraction caught me, sucked me up, and whirled me into a ball, until release opened me up again to end the move with a delicate flicker—like silk settling.

End of set. Suspended in the stillness that followed deep effort, I relished my quickened heartbeat and presented my gaze to the mirror, where thirty others presented their gazes to me.

Martha moved about giving corrections. She stopped over me. "Go to the count of five." I spiraled back, placing weight on my right forearm. She poked me lightly under the ribs. "Lift, *there.*" I strove into my rib cage. "At least you're wet," she said. It was approval. The floor was wet too, as sweat ran off my thighs and arms. Heavy sweating felt cleansing—a shower from the inside out. The room was hot, comforting the muscles, the air nourishing as broth.

"Over on your face." I stretched out face down, body parallel to the front wall. "Back on your knees. Exercise-on-six." Martha's almost dramatic floor sequence was named simply by the number of its counts.

I came to the starting position: body shaped like a Z, weight on knees and insteps; torso thrust out horizontally from the hips. Martha looked us over. "Lengthen your torso. Keep your back parallel to the floor, like a table."

She pushed gently on the hips of the dancer beside me to lower her torso, lifted another's shoulders, traced her finger along the spine of one who wasn't in a full release, pressed down a pair of tensely lifted heels. She took her time. Simply holding the position demanded strength so Martha kept us there. I wished she would start, not quite comfortable with my weight on my knees, or rather on the tops of my tibiae, just below the kneecaps. I felt my jaw tighten and consciously relaxed it, then tried to let go with every muscle not engaged by the position.

"One!" A powerful contraction lifted the center of my back as my head and shoulders scooped toward the floor. My torso lifted and unfolded, moving into a steep backward tilt from knees to head.

"Two!" The count caught the tilt and I held it, thighs lengthened from within. (Years later, a student from Japan, Akiko Kanda, transformed herself with the exercise-on-six. She'd arrived with muscle-heavy thighs, giving her slender torso a grounded look. But she took class three times a day and did the exercise-on-six with fierce intensity. In a year her thighs were like reeds. She became a leading dancer in the Graham company and no one could believe she'd ever been other than the steely sylph who appeared onstage.)

"Three!" I sprang into a release, the body-long contraction reversed in one count.

"Four!" The release sucked back into a second contraction and steeper tilt, buttocks inches from heels, at the limit of my strength for half a count—

"And—release, sit." Buttocks dropped onto heels, head back, gaze straight up, spine striving for length as the torso continued forward toward the floor, in hyper-release.

"Five!" The release folded into a contraction.

"And—six!" to the horizontal thrust of the opening position.

We started over. Exercise-on-six was always performed at least twice.

"Sit to the side." I settled gratefully off my knees. Martha nodded to Ethel. Ethel had done everything along with us but now she did the exercise-on-six by herself—slowly—as Martha explained the impulse beneath each move. Ethel did it effortlessly, her control almost casual in positions that had made my muscles shudder.

All dance classes had demonstrators because dance is best learned directly from one body to another. Demonstrators faced the class, danced every exercise as our mirror image, and repeated moves as many times as the teacher asked. Being Martha's demonstrator was a high honor and as tough as boot camp. Then it was our turn and we did the exercise-on-six four times more. It yielded, at last, a feeling of exultation.

"Rise from the floor." We stretched out at full length on our stomachs then pushed back onto hands and knees.

"One!" The leg reached back.

"Two!" Step onto the left leg, straighten the right, line up heel-hip-head.

"Three!" Rise on the left leg as the body turns toward the mirror and the right leg scissors in, coming to meet the left in First Position.

Mini-break—fifteen seconds. (Men tuck T-shirts into trunks and subtly adjust dance belts. Women pull leotard bottoms over exposed buttocks.)

"Brushes."

We began with the legs parallel, weight on one, the other beating like a bird's wing. "Make arrows!" said Martha, behind me.

I thought of a man who had come to class a month before, placing himself in the front row. He wasn't a bad dancer except for having unfortunate feet that were large, lumpy, and made slapping noises against the floor. It disturbed Martha but he seemed blithely unaware and bounded enthusiastically through the class with a happy smile. Martha had interrupted our last leaps across the floor and sent the whole class to the barre for a series of foot exercises. She ended the class with these words: "These are exercises you can do at home. I want you to do them every day. And one year from now you will return with feet like arrows . . . not hot-water bottles."

That was in my mind as I strove to point my feet on each brush. The brushes broke free of the floor and then pulsed higher, coming parallel to the horizon at a tempo faster than the internal pendulum rhythm so that the body had to absorb the effort, or reveal it. Martha was still behind me.

"You're gripping with your arms. Let go. Let light pass through your body." I responded with a shake of my torso as I tried to disconnect my arms from the force energizing my leg. At the same time, I used the image she gave me, trying to feel transparent, trying to float serenely above the commotion of my legs below. I tried to imagine that my pumping leg was entirely separate from me, with a job to do: I encouraged it in a friendly, yet impersonal, way.

We did deep pliés, joining every dancer who ever lived. My body neared the floor, knee angle acute as the bones lost mechanical advantage, straining thigh muscles that had to support me with sheer strength. "Lift!" exhorted Martha and I tried to imagine gravity flowing upward through my body, opposite to jumps, where the thrust is down; resolution was often sought in opposites. I believed that, with enough concentration, opposition could disappear and effort with it.

"Slow sits to the floor!"

We began in a wide Second Position, spilled weight onto the left leg, body curved like a taut sail, right foot passing behind and to the left of the left foot, sickling at the ankle—a sin in ballet but with a beauty of its own. My instep caressed the floor and accepted my weight until my right buttock touched the floor. I settled into the sit. Thirty dancers held it, dynamic, curve-powered coils of muscle from knee to shoulder.

Ralph turned the page of his newspaper while he held the pedal down. His ringing chord echoed the effort as Martha counted ". . . six, seven, eight," and Ralph slammed his forearm down on fifteen keys at once. Thirty backs snapped straight flinging weight through thighs and sickled feet into skin-polished floor. Thirty torsos cut upward to a high suspension, then settled carefully, like mountain birds landing. The music drained away.

Martha had Ethel demonstrate prances, then challenged us with a look that seemed to ask, Why don't you all dance like that? The first time I saw Ethel dance, she was as chaste as Diana the Huntress in a *Letter to the World* rehearsal. Next it was jazz improvisations at a company party, and after that steamy routines in Broadway's *Texas, L'il Darlin'.*

Daydreaming, I missed an explanation. I suddenly felt woozy and bent from the waist to drain the blood into my brain, then did the prances as a rest step, letting the spring in my calves and feet carry me through the first low set. We repeated it, knees rising high, then with jumps in the middle, ending with a double upbeat. Martha worked the prances into a turning jump combination with tricky syncopation, and I attacked it with gusto, forgetting to be tired.

A second mini-break while the class shuffled to the corner and lined up in pairs for the diagonal across the floor. Men always danced last. There were only three other men, Mark Ryder (whom we called Sasha) and Robert Cohan, both in the Graham company, and a smallish wiry newcomer in a white leotard whose horn-rimmed glasses were tied on with elastic. Cohan and the newcomer hung back, wanting to go last, so I paired up with Sasha.

We began with low walks, slowly at first, then faster, trying to keep the body centered between footfalls. After several crosses, Martha gave a ludicrous illustration, chest caved in, belly thrust out, chin poked forward. "Little babies walk like that. Selfish little babies." Her quick smile didn't fool anybody. She hated what we were doing. We started again.

"No!" She stopped us. "Watch Ethel."

Ethel moved in a seamless flow, knees flexing smoothly, toes touching the floor with the delicacy of fingers, inviting the heel that followed soundlessly with her weight—around the room, gliding like on tracks. "Do it!" We did it over and over, fast, then faster, developing into low runs that swallowed the studio in three seconds.

"Triplets." One low step, two high. Martha added a wide turn, a traveling skip, and worked up a dancy combination that reversed and cut back in a semicircle with leaps the length of the studio. Ralph hammered out the triplets on low notes, then put a four-beat under the leaps with a slashing chord accented on the second beat to give us a musical lift at the crest of the jump.

"Stop!" Martha clapped her hands together halting music and dancers. "You're missing it," she said angrily. "Push off on one, stay in the air on two. Listen to Ralph. He's trying his best to help you. Sasha and Stuart, will you please demonstrate?"

A bouquet! We leaped in unison trying to outjump each other, aware of the intermediate students watching from the doorway as they waited for their class to begin. Then everyone did leaps in a sustained crescendo until the clock said three minutes after six.

"We've run over. That's all. Thank you."

Intermediate students dashed into the studio while the advanced class applauded.

Bertram Ross

Bertram Ross performed with the Martha Graham Dance Company from 1949 to 1973 as Graham's partner and leading dancer. He was a participating creator in most of his thirty-five starring roles. In addition to performing, Ross was Graham's demonstrator from the fifties through the seventies and appeared in several films of Graham dances.

Ross pursued an active theater career after leaving the Graham company and appeared in several dramas and musical revues. He choreographed several shows as well. Most notable, Ross created *An Evening with Bertram Ross* and another cabaret act, *Wallowitch and Ross*. With this act, he has appeared in New York City, San Francisco, Washington, D.C., Los Angeles, and Palm Beach, as well as in Europe.

Martha's teaching was rich in imagery. It was a fantastic experience demonstrating for Martha. I was her demonstrator in the fifties, sixties, and seventies. I think she did her best teaching at the Neighborhood Playhouse.

At the playhouse she used all sorts of imaginative devices to get the actors to move. The technique itself is inherently dramatic and theatrical: in working with actors, Martha found ways to make the point of each exercise vivid and meaningful, and extremely clear and specific. Sometimes she was so taken with the results she was getting with actors that she would use her discoveries back in her own studio, which made the studio classes that much richer.

Demonstrating for Martha at the Neighborhood Playhouse was a revelation. Classes at the playhouse were only one hour long, as opposed to the one-and-a-half-hour classes in her studio. Martha managed to keep the class moving, say all the brilliantly wonderful things she had to say, cover all the basic Graham exercises (floor work, center, and traveling) and make corrections, all in the space of sixty minutes.

In the fifties and sixties, in order to teach at Martha's studio, the prospective teacher would be required to demonstrate for Martha for about a year. Bob Cohan, Ethel Winter, Helen McGehee, and Mary Hinkson all demonstrated for Martha. I came after them. I used to say that I was the Last of the Red-Hot Demonstrators.

It was during Martha's years at the Juilliard School that things began to change. Martha was teaching in the same building as Antony Tudor [choreographer of psychologically based works for American Ballet Theatre] and Margaret Craske [Cecchetti ballet methodology pedagogue]. It was almost as if Martha was intimidated by them, and didn't want them to observe what she was doing, as if she didn't have faith in her technique when compared to ballet. Antony Tudor said to me later, "I liked her old technique better. So people hurt their knees! But it was more inventive, it was more exciting!" Many of the exercises with parallel legs began to disappear. Certain floor exercises were also removed because Martha felt, "It's too frustrating for too many of the students. They're finding the positions too difficult."

It was during this period that I began to hear Martha say things to her Juilliard classes such as, "Do you do that in your ballet class? Do you call *that* Fifth Position? How dare you do that in my class? Those legs should be turned out, not 'sort of.'"

Most dance companies have company classes before their performances. Martha never gave such a class. She believed that all company members should assume the responsibility for doing whatever was necessary to prepare them for performance.

When, however, I began to see company members doing a strict ballet barre before a Graham performance, I questioned strongly how doing a ballet barre would prepare them for the demands of the Graham repertory. There was never a performance in all my years as Martha's leading man, as her partner, before which I did not give myself a full Graham class. And the imagery, all Martha's pieces were flooded with imagery. In order for the dances to evoke their incomparable dramatic power, these images must be there. The teacher and the artistic director should have a responsibility to keep these emotional images and subtexts alive and glowing.

It is possible, still, that a director will come along, someone who has a thorough knowledge of the works of Martha Graham, who will be uncompromising in seeking the truth of the original artistic impulse from which this marvelous oeuvre emerged. Someone who has the ability to inspire and translate and provide the imagery needed to communicate with generations farther and farther away from the creative wellspring that was Martha Graham.

The passion has to return. Graham's training is a technique for the theater. Everything has to be motivated from the inner life of the dancer-actor, that is, from the *center!* When this inner life is not involved, sterility sets in. Martha herself has said that "this lack of motivation will lead to meaningless movement, and meaningless movement leads to decadence."

Ethel Winter

Ethel Winter studied at Bennington College and with Graham in New York and joined the Graham company in 1945. She succeeded Graham in her roles in *Hérodiade* and *Frontier.* She also danced in other companies and created the title role in Sophie Maslow's *The Dybbuk* (1964). She has appeared in her own company and choreographed for the Batsheva Dance Company in Israel and the Repertory Dance Theater of Utah.

I think of Martha as a totally theatrical person. For me, her creative energies were unparalleled. Early on, when she was choreographing *Dark Meadow* (1946), I remember arriving early for a group rehearsal. She allowed me to enter the studio and watch until she finished. She was working on a section that involved yards and yards of black material. I had no idea then how it translated into words, but emotionally I was transfixed, hooked on her magical powers of theater.

I loved watching her perform in *Every Soul Is a Circus* (1939) and *Punch and Judy* (1941); Martha was a superb comedian. Few people know her as such today and no one seems to talk of it. I likened her to the comedienne Bea Lillie, although few people know of her today as well. They were great performers.

Martha, with her multifaceted personality, had quick and passionate mood changes. Several times we, the company, would be the target when she was totally frustrated and angry if the choreography wasn't working for her. She would throw us out of the studio, saying that she didn't want to see us again, ever.

We would wait outside. In twenty or thirty minutes, she would come out of her dressing room, apologize, and plead for forgiveness like a small child. In rehearsals she was always the master, but often, in those earlier years, when we were fitting or sewing costumes, she enjoyed being one of us, gossiping and joking.

The most exciting time to be with the company was when we toured the

Far East (1955). Martha was truly the great ambassador for America and for dance. She, of course, was exhilarated by all the special attention and gave speeches everywhere. She lectured and performed tirelessly, made friends freely and yet with formality. She was in peak form, and what a privilege it was to be part of the company. We would sometimes joke about her lectures because she always started them by saying, "It's a terror and a challenge." She always lived up to the challenge.

All through the Far East we had standing ovations. In Burma and Thailand our performances were outdoors and great masses of spectators would crowd around. Monks, in their saffron robes, were eager to have a look, even though they couldn't afford a ticket.

Martha enjoyed telling of an incident in Thailand with her taxi driver. He likened her mad dance in *Cave of the Heart* (1946) to an elephant that had run amok! Hers was a kind of theater all seemed to understand.

In Tokyo our last performance was greeted with the usual enthusiastic clapping. Then the audience rose to its feet and showered us with flowers and brightly colored streamers. It felt like a gala July Fourth celebration!

Martha would also bring the audience to its feet in New York City with her fabulous curtain calls. We all loved performing in New York on Sundays, when many theaters were dark and the audience was made up of other theater professionals. Their appreciation and understanding were both evident and energizing to us.

One thing I learned, after witnessing company members with psychological bruises, was that it was better to keep one's personal life separate from work. Martha, a master manipulator, could, when it suited her, really push those sensitive buttons. For the most part, she was supportive and loyal, but she enjoyed purposely upsetting the equilibrium now and again, perhaps to stimulate us.

While it's true that many things seem to have changed within the technique, for the most part I see it as having acquired more variables. Martha taught with so many images that her spirit was always in flight. When she was actively choreographing, the class vocabulary was constantly being enlarged to accommodate moves in her new dances. Because that input is gone, we now have the danger of things becoming mannered and rigid. Each generation thinks that their way is the only correct way. Martha believed in change, but I feel that if the basic principles of movement are maintained, counts and dynamics may change. We are training and tuning the instrument to take many commands. The goal is always to make knowledgeable dancers.

Pearl Lang

Pearl Lang studied with Graham, Horst, and Muriel Stuart and in 1941 joined the Graham company, where she stayed until 1954, returning from 1970 to 1978. She became one of the principal dancers and was the first to dance Graham's roles in seven ballets. She created roles in *Diversion of Angels* (1948), *Canticle for Innocent Comedians* (1952), and *Ardent Song* (1954). In 1952 she formed her own company, appeared in several musicals, and was guest choreographer in several companies, including the Batsheva Dance Company. Her works have also appeared at Het Nationale Ballet in Amsterdam, the Boston Ballet, and the American Repertory Dance Theater. She continues to teach in various colleges (thirteen years at Yale University School of the Theater) as well as at the Juilliard School and the Graham school, and to choreograph for her own company.

My mother was a great admirer of Isadora Duncan, and there were photos of her and her various companies in Russia and Germany on our walls. I come from Chicago, and she took me to see Harald Kreutzberg, as well as all the dance companies that played there. I especially remember a performance, when I must have been four years old, of *Hansel and Gretel,* the opera. In this production, when the children went to sleep at night, the angels came down a ladder from the sky two at a time. As they stepped down, each step lighted up and I thought that was the most beautiful thing I had ever seen. I went right home, got my girlfriends together and did my first choreography, walking them downstairs with lights at every step!

I had lessons with a Duncan teacher and later, ballet lessons in Chicago. And when I was about sixteen years old, I saw a Northwestern University series of American modern dancers that included Martha Graham, Doris Humphrey, Hanya Holm, and Charles Weidman. I took all their master classes and was invited by Martha and Humphrey to come to New York. I arrived when I was nineteen years old.

The traditional Graham class begins with the bounces, but in the last years, in watching the company's performances, the contraction is just not as apparent as I used to see it and the way we danced it. The contraction is Martha's great gift to dance. I begin the class with it, along with some of the things that are usually done later in the class. The contraction is the most basic use of the center of the body. There is always a stretch before a contraction, which engages the interior muscles and reacts as in a cough, a sob, or a laugh—all violent physical reactions. In order for the contraction to be visual, you have to have a smooth plane before it can happen. I try to make my students aware of the contrast in these movements. I point out that before a contraction is visible, there has to be a stretch in the other direction to make it happen. Aesthetically, too, it pleases me more to see them sit down and do contractions rather than begin with bounces. Somehow, I don't think Martha would have minded my changing the order.

Nothing in the system begins in the extremities. All the movements begin in the center of the body and move out. There is an overtone here from Duncan. In her book *My Life* [1928] she wrote that movement begins in the solar plexus, the diaphragm. When Martha devised her system, Duncan training was still around. Martha made a technique of the concept of a contraction beginning in the abdominals, while with Duncan it was a style, a quality of movement. Martha worked at a time when even painters were picturing the body in a cubist style. Picasso painted the body broken up into various planes, and choreographers of the time were emulating that kind of vision.

Martha saw Duncan dance in New York at Carnegie Hall and was enamored with her and absolutely ecstatic when she saw her dance. She wrote in her notebooks that she could hardly breathe during Duncan's performance and that her own hair, combed into two buns, had become completely undone at the end of the performance. Ruth St. Denis and Duncan were dancing at the same time—two famous and unique dancers who influenced Martha. She never talked about Mary Wigman and probably never saw her dance.

Her early background in the Denishawn company provided her technique with a strong influence in ethnic dance since their repertoire was built upon ethnic dances. St. Denis was famous for her *Nautch Dance,* which bore little resemblance to the original, but ethnic dances were all very fashionable in those days.

I find that students lose sight of a movement phrase, especially at its beginning. Just as you write a sentence with a capital letter, the beginning of a dance has to have some authority to tell us what is going to happen, and it has to have an end. If it doesn't have that finality, we don't remember it. I try to convey that when I teach. There are those students who are naturally going to dance and need some technique, and you have those who study technique, technique, technique and nothing more than that ever happens.

I have been saying for years that, in addition to classes in ballet for all the students, male dancers, especially those studying Graham's technique, should be required to study flamenco dance because Martha's posture for men was macho.

Martha listened a great deal to Joseph Campbell [company member Jean Erdman's husband and author of *Man and Myth*]. Martha was a Jungian [Swiss psychiatrist C. G. Jung (1875–1961) founded analytical psychology]. A lot of Jung's psychiatry was built upon universal archetypes. The behavior of people interested Martha, so when Campbell made parallels to something in Hopi Indians and East Indian mythology, for instance, she absorbed those similarities. She didn't want to be specific in her characterizations as much as she wanted them to resonate in other cultures.

For instance, Martha was fascinated with the beautiful Southwest, which was an artist colony in the 1930s and where Georgia O'Keeffe went to live and paint. There, the cross-culture of American Indians and Hispanic Catholics influenced her early work *Primitive Mysteries* (1931).

We are, after all, training dancers for the stage, and they have to have life in them. It can't just be steps and technique. I see so many young choreographers walk to the front of the stage, look out to the audience, and seem to say, "I'm unhappy and it's all your fault." Every company director and teacher has the responsibility to develop the possibilities of a dancer. You have to know what those possibilities are and bring them out of each one. After every class I think about what the students will need in the next class. It takes the director or teacher and the student together to make this happen.

Every class is a prayer. Some of the movements are pious; there is a spirituality in dance. Martha claimed the studio was her church, just as the Asians bless the floor on which they perform. There are so many influences in our society that the student has to ignore—the vulgarity on the screen, on television, and even on stage. If a character is vulgar, then you have to play it that way, but when it becomes pervasive in a society, it makes you wonder how you can teach the subtleties, the refinements, and the nuances and beauty within the movements. There is little or no frame of reference for them. And so little time.

Yuriko

Yuriko studied at the University of California, Los Angeles, and, although an American citizen, was wrongfully interned in 1942 in a U.S. detention camp. She joined the Martha Graham Dance Company, where she stayed from 1944 to 1967.

At the same time, Yuriko performed on the Broadway stage as Eliza in Jerome Robbins's stage and screen version of *The King and I* and restaged the same work in Israel, London, Tokyo, and throughout the United States, including the 1978 Broadway revival. Yuriko has had her own company, has taught in many countries, and has received several commissions and an honorary doctorate from France.

She has directed the Martha Graham Ensemble (the apprentice company) and taught at the Martha Graham School of Contemporary Dance. In 1989 she assisted Robbins in restaging *The King and I,* for *Jerome Robbins's Broadway.* In 2001 she staged *Appalachian Spring* for the Joffrey Ballet of Chicago, as well as other Graham works in Europe.

I arrived in New York in September of 1943 from the Gila River Relocation Center, where I was interned by the U.S. government unjustly, with one hundred dollars and a one-way ticket given to me to start anew. I was brave, in a sense, but very, very green. I didn't know New York.

I found a job as a seamstress and in the evenings took classes with Jane Dudley and Sophie Maslow. One evening, in the dressing room, Jane remarked that Martha needed a seamstress. I had a job at the Jay Thorpe department store as a seamstress, but decided to take a leave to sew for Martha as a volunteer. I sewed costumes for *Death and Entrances,* which premiered in December 1943.

My first impression of the company was a reaction to its power. I saw the work from high up in the balcony, looking down onto the stage. What I remember of Martha was her fantastic traveling falls across the length of the stage. She came through from one end of the stage to the other in about five falls as I looked on in amazement. I could not imagine how she did that.

Then I remember a dramatic, jerky, sharp movement—how did she do that?

Jane Dudley came across the stage in a swoop of a contraction—a huge wave coming "swoosh"—like that—and into a contraction. I can't take this anymore, I said to myself.

In late 1944, I became Graham's demonstrator, a position I held for over eight years. It was here that I learned the depth and logic of her teaching. I watched her teach and perform for the next twenty-three years. I learned the dynamics and approach of her basic principle—contraction and release—and witnessed her creativity.

For me, the contraction is an inner action that produces an outer position. The position depends upon how and where you start the contraction. For instance, this explanation of a hanging contraction will illustrate the point.

Hanging Contraction

Kneel on the right knee with the left leg out to the side with a straight knee, the body facing front, and the arms outstretched. Begin a contraction in the left hip, moving backwards into the bones of the lower spine in a circular motion—almost a sitting position—and continue the contraction and motion into the right hip. The circular motion then continues as a visualization from the right hip to the right elbow, which is held shoulder high, bent, and with the forearm and hand toward the floor—a right angle of the arm. This position looks as if it were hanging from that elbow.

Traveling Fall

The traveling fall that Martha performed so magnificently in *Deaths and Entrances* became part of the technique given in class. This movement begins with a contraction in the right hip, travels through the back bones to create a sitting position, continues through to the left hip, where you land in a back fall. The left leg then extends to release the body. The contraction is done as it comes around to the front, and a release raises the body to the original position. The movement is then repeated: contraction, a sit, back fall to the left side, and recovery from the kneeling position with an extension of the left leg, a contraction around with the body slightly past the right leg. The movement might be described as a back fall and may be used to travel across the stage when done continuously.

Sculptured Contraction

The sculptured contraction is my name for this movement, because when Martha first gave it to us she said that we should feel like a piece of sculpture with holes, such as in a Henry Moore sculpture. That is, we should have the feeling of air going through the holes in our bones. This movement has subsequently changed into a much more sensuous "down" feeling. But here is the original movement: standing on the right leg, knees parallel, lift the left leg into a side attitude along the same line as the right supporting leg. The left knee is only slightly bent and the right is in demi-plié. A contraction begins on the left side and travels into the back or sit bones, with the pelvis parallel to the floor, and the contraction ends on the right hip.

The position of the arm: right arm bent and in front of the body. The left arm stretches to the side; the head is turned slightly to the right. Martha said we should visualize air going through holes in our bones and ending in a reach through to the sky from the elbow.

Circle Leg Contraction

This movement begins with a high grand rond de jambe with the right leg. When the crest of the rond de jambe is reached to the side, a contraction begins in the right hip and moves to the left hip, almost to a sitting position as the leg continues around to the back and passes behind the supporting leg, which is now in a demi-plié position. The left arm is outstretched as the movement begins and remains to the side. Both arms finish to the left. The effect is somewhat like a hovering bird, with the torso almost parallel to the floor at the finish of the movement. The feeling should be *up* as the leg lifts. Martha described the pelvis as looking up at the sky as an *under* contraction, and the ending as an *over* contraction.

Because these actions come from the depth of the body as the source, I believe her technique never goes against the laws of natural movement in the body.

Upright Stance

About forty-five years ago, Martha gave a description of the stance she wanted us to assume. It is a position I still place myself into when I rehearse, or teach, for, as she said, "in this properly balanced position, your body will not become tired."

The stance is maintained in perpendicular lines. Seen from the side, the ankle bone must be perpendicular to the floor (not with a pronated arch, but held straight up); the hip bone must be in a straight line at the natural bend or crease created at the top of the leg when the leg is raised and the torso kept erect (the pelvis must not be tipped forward or backward); the shoulder at the hollow in front and below the clavicle should remain upright (should not drop forward or be held unnaturally back); the base of the neck should be held in a perpendicular line to the lobe of the ear; and the forehead between the eyebrows and hairline should make a straight line.

Images and Expressions

Martha had many images and expressions that helped us visualize the movements. For placement of the face, she would say, "point your ears upwards, straight up." In order to have us sense all parts of the body, "Get to know all your pores. Speak to them. Train them until you feel tingles from within. Do not feel flesh hanging on the bone, but a deeper tingling sensation."

Concerning contractions, she suggested we visualize circles spiraling around the outside of our ankles, continuing around and up our legs, hips, waist, chest, head, and up to the sky: "circles within circles within circles." Concerning falls: "Calculate a danger as if you just tripped and fell." Concerning contractions: "The contraction comes from the pit of the stomach."

She also illustrated a soundless sound that emanated from the innards to indicate an expression of horror, terror, revulsion, and reaction to base actions, such as the movement of the Chorus in *Night Journey.* Martha described the movement as a "pulling out of the innards from the bowels, a stretching of them to the sky followed by a contraction retracting the innards as if they were on an elastic." This dance depicts a sickness. It's awful.

I keep telling my students that they have to use their imagination if they want to take my class because I use a lot of images. When I finally get them to move a leg, for instance, from its source—at the connection to the body—it's not the end of the movement, not a period at the end of a sentence. The leg then has to go beyond itself. It starts as a physical thing at first, then it becomes a visual thing in the imagination as the body miraculously continues the movement to an even greater length. It's a very beautiful use of an extension, satisfying and even exciting to do as the body responds to the image.

The thing about any arm or leg movement is that it starts at the skeleton to which it is attached. It's not a pose or a position; it's internal. I try to get them to think in terms of their skeleton—the head, neck, spine all connected—and the ribs as a horizontal portion of the skeleton that moves in and out to allow for the breath.

The contraction, too, is internal. It is a scoop position, easier to see when the legs are in Second Position on the floor, arms lifted to the side. The contraction continues in the abdominals and goes right through to the spine and beyond. It is not to be seen as a lustful or vulgar movement, but a very beautiful and sophisticated position, so basic to the human body, so full of reverence for it. And it is one of Martha's great gifts to dance. In the contraction, for instance, there is a slight rise in the body so there is someplace for it to go. You have to train students to see this, teach them to see, not only to look; to hear, not only to listen.

But students keep trying to arrive at a position through imitation instead of initiating the position internally, which would not only get them into the position to which they are striving, but would become part of their technique instead of just a pose. This understanding of the technique also relates to expressing to an audience larger than the size of the classroom, because by using the organic source and an endless extension of a movement, the movement appears larger and projects farther in space. The movement stays alive instead of becoming static.

Students today are at a disadvantage for having seen so much of a two-dimensional, two-plane perspective on their home screens and at the movies. They see no depth or third dimension, and they are unaware of the eight directions of the studio or stage in which the body can move at angles and still be seen to have two arms and two legs from the audience viewpoint.

Moving throughout all the space of the studio or stage has to become automatic and friendly, familiar, and safe as a place to go. Going backwards is always approached by students tentatively, as if it were a black hole into which one could fall. Front, right, and left seem to be the only fixed dimensions of awareness until you teach students to devour all the space. Front is a dead end.

During the final portion of the class, when the dancer has to get across the space fast, there has to be a sense of urgency. What impels all of us to move fast is a thought, a fear, a motivation, such as one that makes us hurry to an appointment or run for a bus. The motive is what makes you move fast, the body follows.

Modern dance is not hard on the knees if the muscles around the knees have been made strong. The obvious muscles are in the thighs, inner thighs, and abdominals, but important, as well, are the anterior cruciate ligaments behind the knees. All these muscles are developed with many movements but in particular by careful pliés, with the knees over the foot, heels well grounded. Rises should go straight up through the top of the head, and the rise to the half-foot position should be steady, with the body well placed with no wobble. The knees are never bounced or slammed to the floor. Body weight is not placed directly onto the patella but lowered to it. Development and control of the surrounding muscles protect the knees from harm. And you don't just get up from your knees; you rise. And here again we use the image of rising as the body follows the image.

Another concept I always use, which is not comfortable for students to hear, is the image of hanging flesh on a leg of meat suspended from a hook in a butcher shop. The flesh hangs because it has no life in it. It's dead meat. In the same manner, flesh on the inside of the leg, the inner thigh muscles, will just hang there if you don't use those muscles. It is not a question of going on a diet, as many young people decide to do to reduce flab; it's a question of using those muscles to make them long and firm. Since most students don't understand anatomical language, and I would find it too general to use, I do place my hands on students when necessary to make sure they understand and can feel the exact spot that needs to work. The contemporary negative reaction to touching in the classroom, which is impersonal and corrective, makes no sense to me.

Doing all the things that you have to master as you go through the process of study does not dehumanize you. Quite the contrary. Students will find that there is a person emerging as each becomes aware of being one. That person can eventually become any number of characters on stage and go back to being oneself on the way home.

It is always the greatest pleasure for me to see, if only for a moment, when students do something correctly but with a quality all their own, individual, unique.

Somehow, Martha was able to reach dancers of all nationalities to become artists in her company, but strangely, I find that Asian students, although they have an affinity for being on the floor in their culture, do not realize that they *are* on the floor. As for reaching them emotionally, they pull down the shades on their faces, and it is quite a struggle to grant them permission to let go of their tradition of remaining impassive.

It's not just the student who has to be trained. The audience, as well, has to be encouraged to look beyond the obvious attractiveness or flexibility of a dancer. Responding to steps that appear difficult dulls their perception of the subtle dynamics and nuances of a performance. They have to learn to permit themselves to experience what they see, not merely to look at it. What great moments of dance we can then observe and remember.

David Zellmer

David Zellmer was a Graham student in 1940 at Bennington College, then a student at the Graham studio in Greenwich Village in New York City. He was a member of the Martha Graham Dance Company from 1940 to 1946, interrupted by service in the U.S. Air Force (1942–45). While Zellmer was in the South Pacific, Martha wrote letters to him, which he saved. He performed in Graham's *Punch and Judy* (1941) and *Letter to the World* (1940).

It is 4:30 on the afternoon of a late October day in 1941, and I am sitting on the cold linoleum studio floor, at the back of the room, screened from Martha's eyes—I hope—by the other members of the class, all more technically proficient than I. We await the arrival of Ralph, the accompanist, hoping Martha will not lose patience and begin without him. It feels more like a performance than a class with Ralph's music.

At 4:32, Ralph sidles into the hushed room, sits immediately at the battered old grand and raises his hands high on the keyboard. A few of us dare to applaud. Ralph's tentative smile instantly dissolves with Martha's flung command, "Bounces!" We poise ourselves as if preparing for a levitational flight:

back stiffened and straight to the top of the head; soles of the feet pressed together and pulled back to our crotch; heels off the floor; knees and thighs lifted; arms to the side; hands on the floor. ("The tension in the body must give the impression of a vibration.")

". . . And!" Martha warns, turning to Ralph. His hands crash down on the keys. A shattering, dissonant chord propels our first "bounce." The chord is repeated and we attempt to "bounce" our rigid torsos forward and back, forward and back. The beat is just a bit faster than we can "bounce," the chord now pianissimo and staccato. A slight melody soon becomes apparent and is repeated, slightly altered, as we extend our legs forward on Martha's cue, lean over our knees, still "bouncing," and touching our toes with the heels of our hands. The melody Ralph has devised becomes today's theme, and the variations accompany our movements for the next 90 minutes.

Without prompting, the class as one begins the next in Martha's litany of floor exercises: sit to the side; exercise on six; the pleadings. Ralph's strident, insistent music masks our groans. Martha walks among us, correcting arm positions, leg angles, hip turn-out, sometimes with a flick of her fingers or in a stage whisper everyone is meant to hear. She exhorts us to push harder, reach farther, bend deeper, turn faster.

When we finally rise from the floor, I feel I am standing erect for the first time in my life. The wall of mirrors we now face magnifies all my errors, reveals my physical inadequacies. We begin the "brushes," sliding the bare foot forward, without bending the knee, until it is just off the floor; then to the sides. The rustle and scraping of the feet is the only sound we hear until Ralph adds off-beat staccato chords to keep the tempo steady.

We assume Second Position, Martha calls it "The Battle Position of the World." She once told us that the Indian dancer Uday Shankar is a Warrior when in Second Position plié with the whole foot flat on the ground; when he lifts just his big toe, he is a hero. Ralph smooths our deep pliés with pealed glissandos. Then come the extensions and turns, followed by sits and slow falls. ("A sit or a fall does not finish on the floor. The floor is only the means by which one rises.") As we jump-in-place, Martha warns: "The beat is *UP!* Pay attention to Ralph's silences!"

An hour has passed. We are now gathered in a far corner of the studio, ready to begin the floor crossings. Ralph lights another cigarette and plays a little circus fanfare as we prance-in-place to loosen our leg muscles. The girls always lead in this procession. It begins with low walks, back leg dragging, knees bent, arms swinging. We strain to keep on the beat, which Ralph speeds up and syncopates. "Triplets" next: a *demi-plié* followed by two level steps, accent on the plié-like waltz, which Ralph simulates by plucking notes from the upper register.

The exultation of running makes everyone smile, even Martha ("The dancer must sparkle, as a spontaneous laugh.") She is now standing near the piano, calling attention to each unpointed foot, bent knee, open mouth, limp wrist. We run as fast as we dare, first high and erect, then low in a squat, next on tip-toe. Finally, we skip. Small leaps follow, then run and skip leaps. The finale is always of great leaps: UP! and UP! and UP! Ralph accents the second of each four beats with a staccato chord.

The last to cross is usually Merce [Cunningham], who does the great leaps with left arm extended, right forearm raised. He seems to briefly float in mid-air. As he lands at the far end of the studio, Ralph concludes the final variation of today's musical theme with a cascade of descending arpeggios. We face Martha and applaud. She smiles, genuflects to Ralph. He grins and drags deeply on the stub of his smoldering cigarette.

The excerpt above is from *The Spectator: A World War II Bomber Pilot's Journal of the Artist as Warrior,* by David Zellmer, copyright 1999, reproduced with permission of Greenwood Publishing Group, Inc., Westport, Conn. Zellmer, when he was in the South Pacific, bemoaned a gnawing concern at a loss of sensation, the prospect of life not as a performer but as a spectator. With distant memories of life on the stage, he found that only the threat of death could bring the same intensity of feeling.

Martha responded to his letter: "You describe the sensation of stage when you speak of yourself as a Spectator. It is the state of non-feeling that in some way is the highest condition of feeling. When people ask what I feel on the stage, I can only truthfully answer—I think I feel nothing."

Martha's last letter to Zellmer was in 1945, when he was discharged from the U.S. Air Force. He rejoined the company for one more season. Both Martha and Zellmer knew that he would never be a "real" dancer. He became a spectator.

4 ⤳ WORK WITH ACTORS AND MUSICIANS

One area of Graham's career that is not as well known is her landmark work with actors at the Neighborhood Playhouse, in New York City.

The Neighborhood Playhouse, founded by Alice and Irene Lewisohn (two philanthropic sisters), began in 1915 as a venture to enrich the lives of the underprivileged of Manhattan's Lower East Side at the Henry Street Settlement, on Grand Street. Its productions of drama, song and dance, and other cultural events became notable and acclaimed. (Anna Pavlova attended the playhouse's production of *An Arab Fantasia* in 1924.)

In 1928, with an enrollment of nine students, the Neighborhood Playhouse School of the Theater became first among professional training programs in the country. It continues as one of the most distinctive training schools of theater in the nation. Its list of former students, now prominent actors—internationally known on Broadway and in films—is legendary. Some of the first actors to benefit from working with Graham were Bette Davis, Blanche Yurka, Gertrude Lawrence, and director Rouben Mamoulian. The list of distinguished alumni includes Gregory Peck, Joanne Woodward, Tony Randall, Robert Duvall, Kirk Douglas, Lorne Greene, Eli Wallach, Amanda Plummer, Woody Allen, Mason Adams, James Caan, Suzanne Pleshette, Diane Keaton, Patrick O'Neal, Jo Van Fleet, Darren McGavin, Efrem Zimbalist Jr., Tammy Grimes, Anne Jackson, and Tyrone Power.

Martha Graham's first concert solely of her own works was in 1926. By 1928 she had joined the faculty of the Neighborhood Playhouse. The school's classes were held at several different locations until 1946. When the school moved to its present location on 54th Street in 1947, she continued to give classes in movement. To this day, her company members teach those same "movement doesn't lie" classes to young actors in training.

That same year, 1928, the playhouse, as a project of Irene Lewisohn, embarked on productions of "orchestral dance dramas," a visualized expression of orchestrated works, as if "the musical structure were being interpreted through a composite orchestra of dancers and musicians."

The first orchestral drama, *Israel* by Ernest Bloch, was performed at the Manhattan Opera House on 34th Street in collaboration with the Cleveland Orchestra under the direction of Nicolai Sokoloff. Martha Graham, Doris Humphrey, and Charles Weidman were distinctive figures as part of Bloch's mass. On the same program, Graham also danced with Japanese artist Michi Ito to Debussy's *Images*.

The following year, 1929, Graham and Weidman characterized Richard Strauss's tone poem *Ein Heldenleben (A hero's life)*, once more in collaboration with the Cleveland Orchestra. Graham's *Primitive Mysteries*, her first extended dramatic dancework, was introduced in 1931, the last year of the orchestral drama series.

Lewisohn Stadium, built in upper Manhattan, in later years provided free music and dance concerts by the foremost artists and companies of the time.

Graham choreographed and even directed plays during her early years at the playhouse. Much of this important contribution is undocumented.

Anne Jackson

Anne Jackson, like Graham, was born in Allegheny, Pennsylvania. She attended Graham's classes at the Neighborhood Playhouse from 1943 to 1944. In 1948 she attended Lee Strasberg's acting technique classes at the Actor's Studio along with James Dean, Shelley Winters, and Marlon Brando. She also studied acting with Herbert Berghof and Sanford Meisner.

As an actor, she is best known for her numerous stage performances, including Anya in *The Cherry Orchard*, Nellie in *Summer and Smoke*, Luka in *Arms and the Man*, Laura in *The Glass Menagerie*, and Daisy in *Rhinoceros*.

In the 1950s she was among the pioneering Broadway stage actors who brought theater to television viewers through major network series on NBC and CBS. She received the *Village Voice*'s Obie Award for her performance in *The Typist* and *The Tiger*.

She is married to another early Graham student, actor Eli Wallach, with whom she frequently appeared on Broadway.

I don't know how the photographs of Albert Einstein, Eleonora Duse, and Martha Graham happened to be put together on my dressing table. It was a happy accident. I keep the grouping because it seems so right and because I've grown accustomed to seeing them daily. They inspire me. I like what they stand for: simplicity, truth, beauty, and hard work.

Duse and Einstein are long gone; Graham was the youngest genius in the group and lived the longest. She was someone I could marvel at and tell her so, a living reminder that the spirit can soar long after the body is defeated by gravity.

Yet Martha was an acquired taste. In the beginning I didn't know what all the fuss was about (being green and uneducated). When I met Martha at the Neighborhood Playhouse in 1943, she was well over fifty. I was fresh out of high school. My idea of a dancer was Eleanor Powell.

I had read a quotation from a critic on seeing Graham and her modern dancing: "I expected," he said, "Miss Graham to give birth to a cube." That description certainly seemed apt. I thought she was arty and eccentric.

All those contractions and percussive movements her disciples put us through, the endless pliés and stretches on the floor—the barre work made us groan. I liked the pony trotting, the leaps, and the running; I didn't like the long black jersey tubes we wore for demonstration—but once dressed in one, the feel of the jersey sent my body into motion and I would clown around, do runs and falls in an imitation of Martha for my classmates.

We were usually drilled by one of her dancers; Martha came on rare occasions, like a general inspecting the ranks. When she entered the studio our backs grew straighter; even the walls got whiter and the mirror seemed to gleam.

I think I came under her spell after a rather silly incident. She was getting us ready for a student performance and cracking the whip. I was not on the beat, I guess, and she slapped me on my rump with force because, she said, I was not giving my all. I went wild and ran to the door. "I'm telling Mrs. Morganthau on you!" I shouted, and raced straight into the administrator's office. Mrs. Morganthau was a dear, chubby little lady with cheeks like a squirrel's. She adored Martha and, I suspect, was terrified of her. She had given me a scholarship to the school and I felt justified in coming to her with my complaint. When I blurted out my indignation at being hit, her cheeks puffed up in alarm.

"Oh dear," she said, "don't waste a moment; go back and apologize to Martha at once."

I rejoined the class. Nothing was said, but there was a silent understanding between us. My imitations after that grew less and less frequent. I tried harder to execute the leaps and falls and make them my own.

I came completely under her spell when my friend and classmate Lucille Paton said, "You'd better learn your contractions, Annie; Martha said if you don't you'll never get a man."

The man I got [Eli Wallach] was also influenced by the high priestess. Martha had locked horns with him and then won his heart several years earlier. "Eli," she ordered, "walk, walk as though you carry the seed."

What sent my heart racing was her eloquence, her passion about dance: "There is a vitality, a life force and energy, a quickening which is translated into action—and because there is only one of you in all time, this expression is unique. And if you block it, it will never exist through any other medium and will be lost. The world will not have it."

Douglas Watson

Douglas Watson performed in the Graham company in 1946, a suitable preparation for his continuous work until his death. As an actor, he was the recipient of the 1973 New York Drama Desk Acting Award, the New York Critics' *Variety* Acting Award, the Clarence Derwent Award, the Theater World Award, and a best actor Emmy Award for three years running.

Although he might be best remembered as Mac Cory in NBC TV's *Another World*, Watson played Don Parritt in O'Neill's *The Ice Man Cometh*, and later, Eben in *Desire under the Elms*. He was Romeo to Olivia de Havilland's Juliet; the clerk in T. S. Eliot's *The Confidential Clerk*, Henry VIII in *A Man for All Seasons*, and appeared with Jennifer Jones, Eva Gabor, Ruth Gordon, Katherine Cornell, Helen Hayes, Julie Harris, Judith Anderson, and Margaret Leighton in stage plays.

I am not a dancer and have never been. So I will speak from a little different viewpoint. On the other hand, I guess I was a dancer for about six months in 1946. After World War II, I came to New York to study acting—I had studied acting earlier. I had six hundred dollars—my wife had the other six hundred dollars—and with two children we lived with my parents. I had come to New York to make a fortune as an actor.

The first thing I did was enroll in a Martha Graham class. Why? I'll never know. It was the apex of my experience in theater as I think it should be. I've done about thirty-five or thirty-six plays in New York, but the high point of my career was in those few months with Martha.

When I enrolled in that class, because there weren't many men around after World War II, I was offered a place in the company for the Broadway season that year. It was the year Martha choreographed *Dark Meadow* (1946). I had never danced professionally but had had classes, since I studied with Maria Ouspenskaya, who had a Graham student teaching movement for her.

I wasn't allowed at times to come out onto the floor in the studio because the cracks on the bottom of my feet were so deep that I would bleed on the floor. The classes were very intensive, but also very rewarding.

I would just like to say what the Graham training has meant to me as an actor. Graham recommended me to Katherine Cornell, a leading actress in the 1940s. I got the role of Eros, a small part in *Antony and Cleopatra*. In the play, at one point, Antony, defeated in battle, turns his back to his sword bearer, Eros, and says, "Kill me. I don't want to be shamed by being brought before Octavius Caesar in his triumph." So, Eros draws the sword to kill Antony, but loving him so much, he can't do it. While Antony's back is toward him, Eros says, "Are you ready?" Antony answers, "Now, Eros." But Eros plunges the sword into himself. This, mind you, was my first Broadway production, and others in small parts in that production were Tony Randall, Charlton Heston, Joseph Weisman, and a few others who became famous.

I heard them say behind my back, "What is he doing! He's dancing the part, for God's sake." And indeed I was. To me, the greatest performer in the theater was Martha Graham, so I was doing Martha Graham.

So this is what I did, of course, I tamed it down, but not too much, by the time the show opened. I was into the basics. There were two basics I followed—the contraction and the extension with the fall. Don't think I still don't do these exercises every day at the gym!

I should just like to say briefly what Graham meant to me psychologically. The Method, which you probably all have heard about, was taught by Maria Ouspenskaya, who was a member of the Stanislavsky troupe and who was left here because Americans wanted to learn it. The Method, simply put, is to get the insides going so the outsides will do other things. You prepare your character's history; you think a lot; rev yourself up emotionally. What I learned when I came to Graham was that the external can create the internal, rather than the internal creating the external.

An example of how I applied this to acting can be seen in *Richard III*, the night scene. Richard says, "Guilty, guilty, guilty," because he kept killing people and needed punishment and someone who could stand up against him, which no one could do until the end, when Richmond is successful. His grandmother, in the play, describes him as a "touchy, wayward" boy of five or six years old with a humpback. I think he had a right to be a little touchy. I took it that the physical disability was an externalization of what was going on inside of him, and took place in the course of the years before the play and then to some extent afterward. (I interpose here that what Graham did for me was enable me to externalize the warmest passions I have within myself that are covered up by societal behavior. She puts this skeleton on the outside, not on the inside, whereas, in Chekhov, one never talks about what is going on inside, it's all in the subplot. You know what I mean, you are supposed to shoot the billiard ball into the second corner and it means your heart is breaking.)

In Shakespeare, everything is said, and sometimes more than needs to be said. He puts it all on the outside, into the action in front of you. And this is what Graham did so well.

Ted Dalbotten

Ted Dalbotten studied with Martha Graham at the Neighborhood Playhouse School of the Theater from 1946 to 1948. He danced in the Nina Fonaroff and Sin Cha Hong companies. Dalbotten was Graham's accompanist at the Neighborhood Playhouse from 1948 to 1953. For several years, he taught music classes at the Martha Graham School of Contemporary Dance and has been an adjunct faculty member of Columbia

Teachers' College dance education department since 1969. He recently retired as an accompanist at the Neighborhood Playhouse.

I have never taught the Graham technique. I studied with Graham at the Neighborhood Playhouse and then played for her classes there for the next five years. I have three things to share with you; one of them deals with what might be called an innovation; the others are about various aspects of her teaching.

I can't place an exact date on what I'd like to relate first. It didn't occur to me at the time to run home and write it down, but my guess is that it was about 1950.

Martha taught both first- and second-year classes at the playhouse. One day, when the first-year class had finished the floor work, but before Martha had brought them up to a standing position, she walked over to a short section of barre next to the piano, turned and faced the class, and began talking about ballet. She spoke about its long theatrical tradition, how its technique had evolved over a long period of time, and added some other things as well.

Then she put her right hand very delicately on the barre and said, "There is something the ballet has known for many years. It is called Fifth Position." She carefully brought her left foot in front of her right foot into an absolutely turned-out Fifth Position. "And," she added, "I think we can find it useful." Thereupon she lowered her eyes and proceeded to do a perfectly placed plié in Fifth. I imagine that Fifth Position had made its appearance at the studio shortly before this, but I wouldn't have known about it.

I took Martha's second-year acting class at the playhouse in the forties and fifties. Martha spent a period of time with us on speeches from Shakespeare. There was one basic approach she used—there were variations on it—but this was typical.

Martha would hold each of us across her lap, as in Michelangelo's *Pietà*, where we would go into a very deep contraction—and if it wasn't deep enough, you can be sure that Martha saw to the necessary adjustment. Then she would have us turn our heads to the side, giving the position additional dramatic tension, but also releasing the throat so that we would be able to speak more easily. And in this seemingly unlikely pose we would perform our speeches. But two rather startling things occurred if the student used his breath fully in that position: first, there was a tremendous sense of urgency and communication; second, and even more astonishing, voices that often were habitually breathy suddenly became vibrant and full with a deep sound. And, for the first time for some of the students, the girls sounded like women and the boys sounded like men.

Martha always claimed that she knew nothing about voice production, and, from a scientific point of view, she may not have. But she arrived at a startlingly effective result that neither the speech nor the singing department had been able to duplicate.

I think that many young people who had never seen Martha herself perform think of her work as being exclusively a serious and ecstatic exploration—as she herself has put it—of the deep matters of the heart. But Martha had a sense of humor second to none. And she was a marvelous comedienne.

I remember her using this aspect of her personality one day—but for a very serious purpose. One day at the beginning of an initial first-year class at the playhouse (you have to remember that most young people entering the school forty years ago had never taken a dance class in their lives—nor had heard of Martha, for that matter), she gathered the students together at the far end of the studio. She talked to them in her magical way about the formidable physical skill that theatrical performance demands, of the theater artist's responsibility to astonish and delight, and of how the work must seem effortless although it might be grueling, and must give the effect of spontaneity. As she talked, she did a développé with her right leg into a fabulous side extension (although she was now in her mid-fifties). And the leg stayed up there as she kept talking. She didn't acknowledge it, but continued to talk as if nothing out of the ordinary was happening. Of course, by now she had all the students completely mesmerized, including the male unbelievers. Then for the first and only time, she barely glanced at her foot as if to say condescendingly, "You may come down now." And down it came.

I was sitting at the piano and my impulse was to applaud this delicious bit of theatrics. But I didn't because Martha had demonstrated this piece of virtuosity for a very serious purpose. She was presenting to these neophytes a glimpse of a kind of theater that most of them didn't know existed. And she was playing for high stakes—for their allegiance to that theatrical vision she was describing.

Both she and that vision have had my allegiance for a very long time.

Tony Randall

Tony Randall has had a long and prestigious career as an actor for stage, screen, and television. He is currently artistic and executive director of the National Actors Theater.

The Neighborhood Playhouse's purpose, when it was founded by the Lewisohn sisters, Irene and Alice, was to present cultural events to the teeming masses of the Lower East Side. In 1927 the Neighborhood Playhouse Theater closed, probably as a result of the Depression. But in 1928 these two sisters founded the Neighborhood Playhouse School of the Theater. What remarkable dedication, sense of philanthropy, and ambition they had!

The school's teachers included Martha Graham, Louis Horst, Laura Elliott, and others. And later, Sanford Meisner, who developed the Meisner Technique, based on some of the theories of the Russian teacher-director Konstantin Stanislavsky, joined the faculty in 1935.

But, because there was no actual school building until 1947, Graham and the other teachers held classes at their own studios, and the students traipsed around, going to classes here and there. Before I joined the student body in 1938, the school had found two floors of an office building for classes on West 46th Street, which was a very nice location.

Rita Wallace Morganthau, who was the administrator of the school, found this big building on 54th Street, which became, and still is, the home of the school. The building cost $75,000, a fortune at that time, and she wasn't sure it was a wise move.

I remember that Martha could tell you intuitively all about a person by the way they moved. She was uncanny. What most people don't know about her is the enormous influence she had on American acting. She taught acting students for thirty years!

I went to the playhouse because of Martha. I was at Northwestern University in Evanston, Illinois, where the head of the university theater department was Garrett Leverton. He advised me to quit the school and go to the Neighborhood Playhouse. I had never heard of it. "There," he said, "you will study with Martha Graham and you'll learn how to move. You don't know how to move on stage." So I came to New York to study with this woman, Martha Graham. I didn't know about whom he was talking. What he didn't tell me was that I would also be studying with Sanford Meisner, the teacher who made me an actor.

Martha knew all about acting. She never thought of her dancers as dancers, or her movement as movement. Every move was a dramatic gesture. She was her own kind of actress, which is one reason you never see her works danced as well as she danced them. Almost no one could bring that inner life to a character as she did. There was one girl who reached her intensity. It was Yuriko. She brought an "I don't care if this is the last time I'm ever on stage, I'm going to do it if it kills me" quality to the role of St. Joan. Another Graham dancer who has never lost his intensity is Dudley Williams in Alvin Ailey's "You Got to Be Ready" solo from *Revelations*. Opening night, and every single time, live or die, he projects, "I don't care if I'm too old to do it, I'll do it," and he does it every time. It's amazing. That inner life that has to be in a character is what Martha taught us to find.

I once watched a class at American Ballet Theatre that included several of its stars. Everyone, even the most famous of them, was doing the class automatically except for Royal Ballet star Anthony Dowell. I never thought of him as a great dancer, but he gave every exercise a distinct quality. I can still see in my memory an arabesque that he did. His extended arm was pointing at something, looking at something in his mind, visualizing something in the distance. He wasn't just doing a movement, he was living the moment. The trouble is that no one dares say anything to stars about their behavior. Martha would have, no doubt about that.

The first thing we learned in the Graham training was contractions and releases. I remember them very well. But it is in the falls that you can kill yourself. One very famous actor wrecked his back doing a fall in Martha's class and it kept him out of the army during World War II, but made him a star when everyone else was recruited. Everything in her class was difficult to do well.

We had class every day and sometimes Jane Dudley was the teacher instead of Martha. There was no doubt in my mind at that time that Martha was a fanatic. My first impression of her was also that she was queenly, a priestess accustomed to acolytes. I thought her self-absorbed and I didn't understand her. Most worshipped her and that was good.

I wasn't terribly good at her work, but I loved it. I was only eighteen and refused to wear a jockstrap under my one-piece leotard. Jane Dudley, who was a wonderful teacher, asked me if I would please wear one. I hated jock-straps and wouldn't wear one.

The school did a play by Ibsen that was not to be seen by anyone except the class and teachers. Martha saw it and stopped me in the hall afterward. "You were too much in character," she said. And I, being a pompous young ass, replied, "Yes, that was what I was *trying* to do."

"No," she said, "you must always do something out of character. Human beings do things out of character. Your best friend does things that you would never dream he or she would do. It's part of the human condition and makes a character real. To develop a character fully, you must look at the other side of them and find the secrets that are there, contradictory things that are not obvious the first time you read the role. You have to do something out of character." I remembered that advice all my life.

At that time Martha was giving private lessons to Ingrid Bergman, who would come up to the studio for her class, and some of us peeked through the door at this famous movie star. One day Martha caught us and chewed us out with: "And you should see Ingrid Bergman's pliés. They are diabolically good!"

We did something rather wonderful together. For our class project at the end of the year and graduation, I wanted to do *Look Homeward Angel,* the whole book. And we did it. We worked together on it and the class did it with dance and speech, and she directed it.

Funny thing how many choreographers, before they were called choreographers and were known as dance directors, have become directors. And in every case, they're good. Herbert Ross, Jerome Robbins, Stanley Donen, Agnes de Mille, and others all knew how to talk to an actor.

On Broadway, the "gypsies" today are fabulous. Every one of them has a technique that's stunning. But they have a mentality that knows they are never going any higher in their work. They become sarcastic and bitter and invidious. I did a musical, *Oh, Captain,* in 1958. Alexandra Danilova, the Ballet Russe star, was in it. The chorus gypsies, the men especially, were all good, but within a week after we opened the show they just passively went through a performance. They would talk onstage to each other and over the actors' lines. They could not be disciplined because they didn't care. They would be late for entrances and knew nothing but their own stuff. They had stopped learning after they signed a contract.

Danilova, however, would stand in the wings transfixed, and she had been around for about fifty years! She had only one scene in the show, but her discipline and training allowed her to renew herself at each performance. She had intelligence, taste, elegance, and was present in the sense of being involved at each performance.

Martha was like that. I saw everything she ever did from 1938 to the day she stopped dancing—when she was seventy-five, in 1969. In the early days, before she was the prominent figure she became, you had to go to the YMHA or Brooklyn to see her. I saw her in everything she danced.

She also had an enormous influence on stage design in her discovery and commissioning of [Isamu] Noguchi, the sculptor and scene designer. His stark and powerful sets for her, in my opinion, were the best work he ever did (*Appalachian Spring, Alcestis, Night Journey, Errand into the Maze, Acrobats of God, Seraphic Dialogue,* and *Frontier.*)

I doubt if there will ever be another dancer like Martha. We have bigger and better stunts now, but fewer and fewer artists.

Reed Hansen

Reed Hansen has been the accompanist at the Juilliard School since 1958 and at the Martha Graham School of Contemporary Dance since 1971.

I played for Martha's classes on her tours and for her lecture demonstrations. I also played for other modern dance teachers: José Limón, Betty Jones, Pauline Koner, Lucas Hoving, and all the teachers at the Graham school.

Martha was musical. She used European and commissioned American composers for her works. I remember when she was creating *Clytemnestra* (1958) and working on *Lucifer* (1975) with composer Halim El-Dabh that it was a hand-to-hand process. The composer wrote the music in the front studio while she rehearsed the new work in another studio. He would play what he had written for her, watch the rehearsal for a short time, go away, and add more music. It was an inch-by-inch process. But it seemed to work for her. In a sense, I did the same thing when I played for Martha's classes and for the other teachers.

It is still the same. The teacher counts out about three beats as an introduction and I begin on the next beat as the count of one. I end with a few sounds to finish off the sequence musically. The combinations are sometimes in offbeats, which can include a phrase in five or seven counts, and the music is an improvisation. Sometimes I improvise on a well-known theme, such as *The Battle Hymn of the Republic,* if the sequence seems exultant! Or the Quaker hymn from *Appalachian Spring,* or a quiet theme to calm the dancers down from an energetic combination. But they usually concentrate so hard on the steps, they don't notice the improvisation except to like it.

Class consists of three sections—floor work with breathing and stretching; the contraction and release movements; center work, which includes small foot movements, rises, small jumps, arm work, and combinations that might include as many as thirty-two or more beats and are performed by two groups; and the last section, which has more vigorous crossings, when I have to play continually until the entire class has gone across the floor two or three times, repeating the combination on the right and left sides.

Martha was meticulous about the amount of time spent on each section. She paced the class to thirty minutes on the floor, thirty in the center, and thirty for the crossings. No matter where she was in a combination, she would stop and shape the class in this manner. Sometimes she would recite entire passages from Chaucer, because she was a great reader and wanted to inspire and inform the class.

She didn't like to use a drum accompaniment because she felt it had no quality, no beginning, no ending, just beats that began or ended. I use key changes to contribute tonal quality. It was hard in the beginning to understand what the class required, but now, after stating a clear theme, the dancers are free to know what I'm doing and I'm free as well. Some studio pianos, however, have only two sounds—loud and bang.

I never saw Martha warm up for a performance or class. Perhaps she did this at home or at the hotel on tour. Just her presence was a power that transfixed the students. I once saw her stop the class, slowly look at each dancer, then poke a student's abs. The class responded physically. It was scary and wonderful at the same time.

5 ∽ THE FIFTIES
AND SIXTIES

By mid-century, American ballet and modern dancers and choreographers had found a second place to work—in Europe. America too was visited by foreign companies with great stars from the Royal Ballet and the Bolshoi and Kirov companies. Later, Rudolf Nureyev and Mikhail Baryshnikov thrilled audiences with their talent and charisma. Graham too would eventually open a new world of movement to them as she gave Baryshnikov and Nureyev—as well as Liza Minelli, Margot Fonteyn, and Maya Plitsetskaya—guest-star status in her works in the 1970s.

Across the country, regional and local companies developed in peak numbers as the cost of touring large and famous groups diminished American exposure to foreign talent.

Television documented dance, and two major choreographers emerged for the musical stage, Jerome Robbins (*West Side Story,* 1957) and Bob Fosse (*The Pajama Game,* 1953). Rock 'n' roll hit the airwaves as tap dancing disappeared from musicals in favor of "musical theater dance," and the last huge dance production, which ended the Hollywood musical era, was MGM's *An American in Paris* (1950). Hollywood went on witch-hunts as Senator Joseph R. McCarthy pursued writers and performers with hearsay evidence, using an approach similar to that of the notorious House Committee on Un-American Activities. Artists were asked to sign loyalty oaths. Many left the studios in disgust.

Veterans returned from the Korean War and the hydrogen bomb was tested. Black performers gained fame in major cultural institutions; Tennessee Williams, Eugène Ionesco, Henry Moore, Marc Chagall, and Ingmar Bergman produced major works.

In the sixties, social unrest once again stirred the nation. There were desegregation demonstrations and riots. Drugs and sexual freedom entered the mainstream. Dancers, now accepted and integrated into society as members of a viable profession, became exposed to the disruptions and were not free from the eventual influence of drugs. Social dance became solo dancers gyrating without dance partners, without recognizable steps, and mainly in 4/4 rhythm. Discipline in the schools flagged and the young preferred to "let it all hang out." President John F. Kennedy, a supporter of the arts, was assassinated. Pop art took over the art galleries and the protests against the Vietnam War began. Humans alighted on the moon's surface. Abstract and multimedia dance works entered the postmodern era. Graham produced some of her most profound works in the fifties and sixties, although her personal powers began to diminish. She overcame depression and bouts with alcoholism—her father and a sister also drank—while her fame continued to grow internationally. Horst, probably jealous or dismayed by the influence of Hawkins in her life and the company, had left (he died at eighty, in 1964). Martha was devastated by Hawkins's departure from her life and her own inability to choreograph a role for him that would equal the importance of her own leading characters.

She rallied, purged herself, and made a triumphant comeback in her solo *Judith* (1951). She returned from the ashes of despair using her instinct and impeccable taste. A passage from the Bible guided her:

The Assyrian came from the mountains of the north,
He threatened to set fire to my land,
Judith disarmed him by the beauty of her face,
She put off her widow's weeds
To raise up the afflicted Israel
She anointed her face with perfume
And bound her hair with a headband
And put on a linen gown to beguile him
Her sandal entranced his eye
Her beauty took his heart captive and
the sword cut through his neck.

The pain of Hawkins was exorcised.

Martha, who was often called a genius, would say, "I'm not sure what a genius is." Edgard Varèse (1883–1965), who wrote the music for *Judith*, told her, "Every one is born with genius, Martha; the sad thing is that most people only keep it for a few minutes." She added her own definition: "There has to be about you a transparency to receive the energy around you—maybe that's what genius is; I don't really know."

Martha maintained her signature look: elegant clothes, beautifully coiffed black hair, and perfect makeup. She dressed herself and her dancers on stage with the same dramatic quality. Many of the costumes she designed herself— swirling, long dresses and floor-sweeping scarves. They made a strong statement and were wonderfully constructed. The hairpieces were symbolic and bold, as were the ornaments: a simple clasp indicated status, capes indicated mystery. She combined vivid colors—black with gold, magenta with red, pure white against dull browns. Halston, the fashion designer, also created costumes for fifteen of her dances. They included the invention of wide pants in soft materials that looked like a skirt. The dancers could raise their legs or roll on the floor without disarraying their costumes. Martha gave Halston one request: "Dress the women, and undress the men." The male dancers wore little more than bikini-type bottoms that displayed their small, tight, bare buttocks.

He dressed Martha offstage as well. She was fond of jewelry; the simple elegant stone (especially jade) in a dramatic setting; turquoise and silver pieces; and she frequently wore a long, beautiful Navaho wedding necklace from the Southwest, a place she loved. She was generous to her dancers, giving them small, precious gifts of jewelry.

Some of her masterworks produced in the fifties and sixties were *Canticle for Innocent Comedians* (1952), *Seraphic Dialogue* (1955), *Clytemnestra* (1958), *Embattled Garden* (1958), and *Cortege of Eagles* (1967), as well as twenty other dances. Martha's dances now included flashback scenes, as she held center stage while a younger member depicted the character's past.

Despite the awards and accolades that accumulated around her, it was always a struggle to find financial support. Martha was no stranger to the center of a conflict. In 1964 two American elected officials happened to attend a performance in Europe of her work *Phaedra* (1962). At that time, the work had already been running in repertory for two years in America. The officials found the work shocking, blatant, offensive. They wondered why the government, which had provided Martha with small grants, was financing an "overtly lustful" subject as American art. They made a clamor in the press. Fortunately, Martha had more supporters than critics. They suggested that the officials read the daily headlines, where they could easily find modern-day Phaedras, Medeas, and Jocastas. Far from glorifying the predicament of the women, Martha's dances offered a moral: without passing judgment, she revealed the torture, the frustration, the pain of her mythological characters, reminding us that they were all too human.

Martha, as well, was all too human as she began to face her last performances, when her body would no longer do what she wanted it to do. Arthritis wracked her body, especially her hands, and in 1969, at the age of seventy-five, she gave her last performances in *A Time of Snow* and *The Lady of the House of Sleep*. These roles dealt with age, sorrow, despair. Martha faced retirement, sank deeply into depression, and, suffering from the long-term effects of alcoholism, was hospitalized. Miraculously, she once again survived, was reborn, and returned to direct her company in 1972, bitter at no longer being able to dance but ever the creative genius and ready to produce new dances. "I'm not a choreographer," she would say, "that's too big a word. I make dances." She would create twenty new dances and thirty major revivals.

Marnie Thomas

Marnie Thomas was a member of the Martha Graham Dance Company from 1958 to 1968. She studied ballet in her home town of Charleston, West Virginia, and at summer camp at Perry-Mansfield in Steam Boat Springs, Colorado, where she first studied Graham technique. She attended Sarah Lawrence College and studied with Doris Humphrey, José Limón, Alwin Nikolais, and Merce Cunningham.

I was graduated from Sarah Lawrence College in 1958 and was at the American Dance Festival at Connecticut College during the summer. Graham technique was taught there. I was a demonstrator for David Wood, who was in the company and teaching for Martha. She saw me as his demonstrator and at the end of the summer suggested I come to the studio in Manhattan. (At Sarah Lawrence, there had been Graham dancers as teachers, but I still commuted to New York to take class at the studio on 63rd Street—a six-hour trip.) By the time I was graduated, I knew I wanted to dance.

Two weeks after arriving in New York, in 1958, I joined the company. Just before a tour to Israel, one of the dancers hurt her ankle and a replacement had to be found. Martha (already overseas), was contacted and I was "it." Two days later, I was in Israel performing as a Fury in *Clytemnestra*. Everyone was so excited to be there, no one wanted to teach me the dances! Lois Schlossberg ran up and down the halls of the hotel showing me what to do. When we finally got onstage for the one rehearsal given us, I was very confused, so Martha turned the run-through into a *Clytemnestra* teaching session. We opened that night. It was like cramming for an exam.

When I got to Israel, Humphrey wrote me a letter inviting me to join her company. But I was already committed to Martha and David. The choice to go with the Graham company was settled when, on opening night in Tel-Aviv, David asked me to marry him. Martha was excited about the fact that two of her dancers would marry on tour. We considered Israel as the place for the ceremony, but my parents wanted me to wait until we returned. Martha was attached to the couples in her company. Basically, I think, because I am physically small, that I was thought by Martha to be the Bride in *El Penitente* (1940). That was the first role of her own that she gave me. She always maintained her image of me in that role of the innocent young girl.

My choice of modern dance, instead of a career in ballet, grew out of the realization that modern dance spoke more about people. To me it had more dramatic and deeper personal expressive possibilities. In my home town, only ballet lessons were available, so it wasn't until I studied with Harriet Anne Gray at summer camp in Steam Boat Springs that I discovered modern dance. I was eleven or twelve years old and really, really excited about finding a way to continue studying it, but there was no place to do that in my world. My parents were not interested in my being serious about dance. To them on such and such a day you went to dance class, the next day you joined the Brownies, then you worked on the school newspaper, and one afternoon a week you played the piano. Their solution to my desire to study dance and drop other activities was to send me away to school so that I wouldn't be too serious about dance. Little did they know that I would be exposed to more of it and become encouraged to persevere!

David was a soloist when I joined the company as a corps member. Within two years, we started having children, so a lot of my development in the company was interrupted with five pregnancies (only three of our children lived). Martha was always involved in the lives of her dancers and encouraging to the company members who were having children. She was never negative about the fact that you might be dancing for only a few months while pregnant. (I was performing with our second child up to my third month of pregnancy.) We also took the children to Sweden, as well, where we taught each summer. Somehow we always managed to find a dance school on tour where there were students available as baby sitters.

Martha's way of preparing a member of the company to teach was by having her become her demonstrator in class. That way she would demonstrate on your body to make you more articulate in her approach and perspective. These sessions as demonstrator and her magical use of imagery were unforgettable.

There were constant changes in her approach that she would never explain, except by saying, for instance, "Today we're going to do this movement differently." She would simply give it in a different way and you would have to tune into the new concept on the spot. In the deep-plié sequence, for instance, instead of making a contraction that moved forward for all six counts, she had the demonstrator hold that contraction for three counts, then let it go forward for the next three counts. If that change occurred during the summer course at Connecticut, it was then introduced at the school and became her way of making changes in the training. She would never say that it was a change. It was simply her way of asking for a different dynamic or of inserting something that interested her. This led to many arguments in the dressing room as we compared experiences and asked each other how we taught certain movements.

Finally there would be a company gathering where we asked Martha questions about her preferences. At first, she would listen to the questions, then become irritated. She did not want to be pinned down to who was right or wrong or which way was best. She would become uncomfortable and start to give other options, change the subject, use every evasive tactic in order not to be limited to only one way of doing something that might be devoid of an awareness of new elements that she had introduced from intuition, her intellect, or from seeing it executed on a different body. Her goal was to develop choreographic nuances, not to fix or limit anything to a time or being right or wrong. She made every generation think "you're it." This is *the* way to do a contraction, *the* way to do a fall. Every dancer was convinced that he or she was the embodiment of what Martha wanted. Just think how many of us were convinced we were it! No wonder we called *Diversion of Angels* (1948) versions of angels. Each cast was right for that moment in time when they were learning or doing a ballet, but it was always different on another body at another time as Martha evolved through the years. Basic principles remained the same, but as long as Martha was moving—she was sixty-two years old when I entered the company and seventy-two when I left—she was in a constant state of physical discovery. There was no end to her inventiveness or curiosity about how different bodies did the same thing differently.

Everything was created for performance and then taken into the classroom. The school was the result of performance rather than the other way around. That's why, to her, teaching was a performance, and she looked for that in class as well as on stage.

It's true that all of us were permitted to add our own creative dimension to a role and were sometimes asked by her to come up with a movement invention. Some dancers believe that they should have been credited as choreographers. But they had contributed only the germ of an idea, which Martha refined with additions or just fiddled with until it fit into the scope of the whole piece. These were creative contributions, which some dancers bitterly felt were not acknowledged or credited. There was a pressure to contribute and she would utilize each dancer's contribution until she became interested in someone else.

When she wanted to express some emotion, she would follow her intuition and discover the way to express that emotion in movement. She was courageous enough to keep growing and to discard what was no longer valid. Her creative longevity, as in other artists of the same level of talent, who kept working and developing during an entire lifetime, was based upon never looking back or settling for what she had accomplished yesterday by compromising what she would discover today.

Linda Margoles Hodes

Linda Hodes was a member of the Graham company from 1951 to 1969. From 1977 to 1992, she was Graham's rehearsal director.

My company years were from 1951 to 1969 (Israel, 1963) and 1977 to 1992. At the age of nine I began my studies at the Graham school, when it was at 66 Fifth Avenue, at 13th Street. I lived around the corner from Martha's studio, and because I wanted to take dance classes, my parents sent me there. My idea was to be a Hollywood ice-skating star like Sonja Henie. Someone told me I should take dance classes if I wanted to be a skater, and because the difference between ballet and modern dance meant nothing to me, it was just easier for me to take modern dance.

There were Saturday morning classes for children that Martha taught. There were about eight girls in the class. She had a way of dramatizing the movements with little challenges, such as doing an exercise in a sad way, a joyous way, a more inner way, or a more outer way. She talked about alignment, but it was as an image of placing the back of the neck over the base of the spine over the heels. The class included a barre, brushes, pliés, triplets, and diagonals across the floor. Another class was added after I had been there for a year, on Wednesday afternoons, and I remember begging and begging and nagging and nagging until I was allowed to go. There were no performances for us. Martha let me take two classes on Saturdays, one with the older girls. The ice-skating goal just melted away.

After I was graduated from high school and had upset my parents by not going to college, I got into a show, *Make Mine Manhattan,* with a wonderful choreographer, Lee Sherman. I had never auditioned before. Sherman asked me if I studied with Martha Graham. When I said yes, he answered, "Well, you're probably going to be terrible in the show but I want to hire you anyway." It was a jazzy show, but I loved it, stayed for the Broadway run, and went on tour with it.

The dancers in the show took ballet classes in whatever town we played. On the Graham company tours, we sometimes gave each other classes, working together or sometimes separately.

At the end of the show's run, I joined the Graham company but it was a depressing time for the group: Martha had just gotten back from Paris (1951) after a disastrous tour, she had hurt her knee, her husband (Erick Hawkins) had left, and some of the dancers had left as well. She was to do a lecture with Walter Terry, the *Herald Tribune*'s renowned dance critic, at the 92nd Street Y, but didn't have enough dancers. So she hired Mary Hinkson and me. She decided on the sarabande section from *Dark Meadow.* That was the first dance that I performed with her company, along with Mary, Patricia Birch, Stuart Hodes, Bertram Ross, and Robert Cohan. A few months later, she choreographed *Canticle for Innocent Comedians* (1952).

Between seasons we all had office jobs or some means of support until the next rehearsal period. I danced in small performances for other choreographers. I demonstrated for Martha when she was teaching at the Juilliard School and the Neighborhood Playhouse, as we all did, because she knew that we needed those jobs. The ballet companies were better organized than we as far as compensation and unemployment benefits, but those dancers too had periods of not working while waiting for the next season.

I don't think I was a good teacher when I started, in my twenties. I was teaching elementary class and demonstrating for Martha. We had moved in 1952 to the three-story building on 63rd Street donated by Lila Wallace Acheson as a school and company site. When we first moved there the big studio had two pillars in the middle of the floor. A lot of exciting movements came from dancing around and between these pillars. This was when the turns around the back entered the technique. Martha experimented with movement during the classes she taught and certain key elements—such as the "cave turn," from *Cave of the Heart* (1946)—came from these experiments. Classes began in the morning, with a break around noon, then began again at 4:00 to 7:30 P.M. The period of the break was the time Martha rehearsed— first by herself, then with the entire company.

The Batsheva Dance Company had begun in Tel Aviv and wanted some of Martha's works. Martha asked me to go but I didn't want to do that since I had two children, was married to Stuart Hodes (who was in the company), and was performing in *The King and I*. Giving up a salary every week did not sound like a good idea. So I named what I thought was a huge amount of money and, to my surprise, got my price!

My plan was to stay three weeks, but I stayed three months. By the time I got there, the company had already studied the technique in classes taught by Robert Cohan, Donald McKayle, Ethel Winter, and Anna Sokolow, who had taught there for several years. I staged *Diversion of Angels, Embattled Garden,* and *Hérodiade* (1944). I stayed in Israel and taught at Batsheva and the Rubin Academy of Music in Jerusalem because the company at home was not doing a lot of work then and because I had fallen in love.

I stayed in Israel for fourteen years, married again, had another child, and would have remained had my husband not died. Martha, with whom I had remained close, was compassionate and offered me directorship of the school in New York, with directorship of rehearsals and some involvement in the company as associate artistic director. That position lasted from 1977 to 1992. I had originally planned to stay one year. I sat beside her for all those years, helping in any way I could and did a lot of teaching as well.

When Martha died, in 1991, the loss changed too many aspects at the center, and I no longer wanted to continue as associate director of a company in which I had no voice.

Martha wanted other companies to dance her ballets if they had the proper training in her technique. Realistically, training is an expensive and time-consuming project for any company. There was once the prospect of teaching Graham technique to members of American Ballet Theatre for six months, then permitting ABT to incorporate some of her works, providing the casting was suitable. This was a project planned shortly before she died, then abandoned until the recent performances by ABT in *Diversion of Angels* (2000).

Many changes are apparent in Martha's own company today. There are new dancers with different training, who had never done one of her works and who had to begin from scratch. I taught a course at the center, before it recently closed [in 2000], based on the chorus section of *Night Journey* (1947), and it was a very revealing experience because the choreography wasn't done at all the way I remembered it to be when I was dancing. The later generation of students were more facile, legs went higher, but placement was lacking. They were lighter in movement but too airborne, and I had to struggle to get them into the ground. But that's what I was there to do. I saw the recent ABT version of *Divert,* and it had these same qualities missing, but I thought it was beautifully, if airily, done. If you give one of Martha's works to a ballet company, it's going to look like a ballet company doing a modern work.

After leaving the center, I became director of Paul Taylor's second company. I believe that Taylor, when he danced with the company, added to Martha's technique. She was beguiled by the way he moved. She created roles for him in *Embattled Garden* and *Clytemnestra.* Working with him was a wonderful experience for me and it lasted until I no longer wanted to tour. I keep trying to retire. But I am happy to be teaching once in a while.

There was an earlier Graham experience with a ballet company. It was a work for New York City Ballet called *Episodes* (1959) to difficult music by Anton Webern. Martha composed the first half of the ballet, which was choreographed with our dancers. Martha was then to transfer the work to the

NYCB dancers. Balanchine and Lincoln Kirstein came to the studio and cringed when they saw us crawling around on our knees. We were told originally that we would not be performing that work, but were thrilled when we were told we would be performing it after all. We opened the first section of the ballet in ornate Elizabethan costumes by Karinska, dancing the story of the death of Mary, Queen of Scots. The NYCB members danced the second half with abstract movements, costumed in black leotards, pink tights, and pointe shoes, looking somewhat like modern dancers. Paul Taylor had a solo in the second-half ballet section, choreographed by Balanchine but filled with his own inventive movement.

Martha put in a lot of time alone in the studio, experimenting. She would put a red jersey strip on the studio door and we knew that we should not enter because she was working. She was a good observer of people. She would talk with taxi drivers, delivery boys, grocery boys and show an interest in life around her. She was always curious about our personal lives.

Martha, in her later years, looked for many new ways of choreographing. She became more interested in structure and pattern than she had been when she was still dancing herself. The dancers had higher extensions and bigger jumps and more facile turns and Martha liked that and she used it.

Phyllis Gutelius

I was in the company from 1962 to 1977. There are moments that stay with you through a lifetime. My first step into Martha Graham's studio on East 63rd Street was just such a moment. The vivid contrast of the hot June day, with the New York clamor behind me, as I stepped into the quiet of a cool, dark hall, still remains with me. I could hear music from a class going on upstairs. Rich with rhythm and melody, it pulsed downward, filling the entrance to the school. Mrs. Georgia Sargeant [Geordie], Martha's youngest sister, welcomed me, as she did all students, to her upstairs office with a gentle humor that gave support and comfort over the years and especially through tough transitions: from scholarship student to apprentice, company member to soloist, and ultimately, to performer of Martha's roles.

My first experiences in dance were in Wilmington, Delaware, in ballet classes taught by former Agnes de Mille dancers James Jamison and Stella

Hobson. Early performance experience in amateur productions of Broadway shows, such as *Kismet* and *Plain and Fancy,* along with seeing Hollywood's rich legacy of musicals—*American in Paris, Daddy Long Legs, Invitation to the Dance,* and the unforgettable *Red Shoes*—were the principal sources of inspiration available to aspiring dancers growing up in a small town.

At the Graham studio, the formula for the physical development of a dancer had been successful through decades. It was thorough, demanding, and effective. The first step, the ten-classes-a-week full scholarship program, molded bodies as it opened countless doors of discovery into the multidimensional world of dance. The hierarchy in the studio was clearly defined. Within the company, there were several generations represented—Bertram Ross and Helen McGehee were the principal teachers; Yuriko, Ethel Winter, Pearl Lang, and Robert Cohan were principal dancers and choreographers in their own right; and principal dancers Mary Hinkson, Linda Hodes, Matt Turney, Gene MacDonald, David Wood (who was both rehearsal director and teacher). The next group included soloists Akiko Kanda, Robert Powell, Richard Kuch, Miriam Cole, Dudley Williams, and later, Richard Gain. Because of the loyalty between Martha and her senior dancers, she would rather lose a generation of neophytes than lose one dancer from the inner circle.

The year as a scholarship student in the school was the barest preparation for the demands of the repertory. Returning to class after a rehearsal put the technical work completely into a new light. Class work, as challenging as it was, took on an entirely different character. The heart of the transformation into "a Graham dancer," lay in those first years of hard labor in those magnificent jewels—the chorus dances in *Diversion of Angels, Clytemnestra, Appalachian Spring, Primitive Mysteries, Dark Meadow, Night Journey,* and others. To perform in each of these works was an introduction to the real Martha. They provided the groundwork for soloist roles. The process of *endless* rehearsing, mostly unpaid, molded four, six, or sixteen very different chorus bodies into a single entity, demanding that they breathe as one, move as one, be one. It also provided the roots of strength and insight that were essential to the development of each artist in the Graham company. In rare instances when a dancer stepped directly into soloist roles, that dancer, in my opinion, was left an outsider and without that special quality of movement developed only through that organic experience of transformation.

When I was first invited to dance with the company, my first role was as

Saint Margaret in *Seraphic Dialogue*. There is little doubt in my mind that Geordie's knowing that a Roman Catholic saint was one of my maternal ancestors acted as a contributing factor to Martha's casting decision. It was Martha who introduced me to the works of my renowned ancestress when she gave me her own heavily notated copy of *The Interior Castle* by Saint Teresa of Avila.

When I joined the company, roles were frequently performed by the dancers who had originated them. Probably because the dancer had participated actively in the making of a role, there was a sense of signature in these parts. The role of the Warrior in *Seraphic Dialogue* was Helen McGehee's; St. Joan was Linda Hodes's. Roles could be taken over when someone left, but even in those instances, the unique quality of each dancer was important enough to Martha for her to change the choreography to better suit the newcomer. Only at the very painful and traumatic end of Martha's career as a performer were her roles left to be filled by Ethel, Helen, and Mary. As a result, their soloist roles were left for another generation to fill. Coaching was rare. If you were lucky, timing and sequences were taught in a few succinct rehearsals, after which you were left alone to succeed or fail. You knew you had gained the role *only* when Ursula Reed, the wardrobe mistress, fitted you for the costume. Competition was brutal but understandably fair since success depended upon whether the echoing ring of truth resonated in the voice of your character.

I remember Ethel Winter's first run-through in *Appalachian Spring*. The agony of Martha's bitterness almost cut the air as she watched another dancer rehearse a role in which she had been so happy. In retrospect it seems apparent that it had little to do with Ethel personally or with any of us. What it really was about was Martha's unwillingness, in her heart, to yield to the ravages of time and age.

Despite the atmosphere at that time, there were exceptions. I was very grateful to Patricia Birch, who directed me in my first solo as the Maid in *Seraphic Dialogue,* a role that she had originally performed. Her direction focused on the Maid as a tomboy, wild in her heart and fervent in her love of her inner voices. I was taken into Joan's world, moment to moment, breath by breath. My promise to Patricia, to never look in the mirror during the entire preparation, brought the stage to life for me in a way that pushed me into the direction of becoming a dramatic dancer. A very few years and many roles later, the rewards of those first steps resulted in lead roles such as the principal sister in *Deaths and Entrances, Appalachian Spring, Letter to the World, Cave of the Heart, Night Journey,* and many others.

Yuriko was very generous in teaching me her role as Iphigenia in *Clytemnestra.* Her encouragement and direction put me in touch with the instinctual and visceral nature of Martha's language, qualities clearly present in Yuriko's own dancing and choreography. Without doubt, Bertram Ross, as director, teacher, and example, was second only to Martha in his long-lasting influence. When he directed a dancer in Martha's roles, he balanced a seemingly infallible memory with a perception broad enough to encourage us when we were different from Martha's interpretation, yet true to ourselves and the role. His biting humor as a teacher was often a very welcome respite, as much for the victim as for the class. He was tireless, articulate, resourceful, patient, and very generous with his time and thoughts. His lessons brought you directly in contact with the core of the movement principles and vocabulary that are Graham's technique in a pure, unmannered simplicity.

Within the school, the shifting roster of teachers offered a multilayered, many-faceted exposure that is requisite to do justice to a language as complex and rich as the Graham idiom. Development as a teacher begins as early as the opportunity to demonstrate for the students at the lower levels. The ability to demonstrate what was *incorrect* was as important to the development of technical clarity as demonstrating the *correct* performance of a movement. Junior company members learned from questions asked by students in the coaching classes; bringing essentials into focus for someone unable as yet to master a movement inevitably made them clearer and deeper for the advanced dancer. When teachers and demonstrators were called into sessions, during which Martha dictated core elements in the teaching of her technique, I found these primary sources from which I drew for my first steps as a teacher.

Because of this process, Martha's work will always survive.

Donald McKayle

Donald McKayle studied at the Graham school and appeared with many modern dance groups and on Broadway. He formed his own group in

1951 and was artistic director of the school of dance at the California Institute of Arts.

I first met Martha Graham in 1948, at the opening session of the American Dance Festival at Connecticut College. I was a member of the New Dance Group company, directed by Jane Dudley, Sophie Maslow, and William Bales. Like the Martha Graham Dance Company, the José Limón American Dance Company, and the Valerie Bettis Dance Company, we were in residence and would perform at the Palmer Auditorium in the closing week of the festival. Jane Dudley and Sophie Maslow had been soloists with Martha Graham's earlier company and had introduced me to her technique and aesthetic. I was eager to meet her and to work directly under her instruction.

Martha was in great physical shape and her classes were not only a place for learning and absorption of her ideas but also a daily theater for her performance. She was in the process of choreographing a new work of extraordinary lyricism, a dance that celebrated the act of love. The dance, entitled *Wilderness Stair,* after a poem by Ben Belitt, was included in the program and later named *Diversion of Angels.* It remained a standard in her repertory for years to come. This dance, unlike the rest of her repertory, was choreographed for the company and did not include herself as a performer. Her own performances in the cycle of her choreographic works built on Greek themes and technical prowess. The sweeping turns that climaxed her "serpent heart" solo in *Cave of the Heart,* and that later were to become a fixture in her technique vocabulary as *cave turns,* were virtuoso movements in the fabric of those memorable performances.

At the end of the summer, I was awarded a scholarship at the Graham school at 66 Fifth Avenue in New York. The technique was constantly evolving and had yet to be strictly codified. Items from the floor work sequences that began every class were constantly reinvented. It seemed that after her yearly visits in Santa Barbara, California, she would always return with a new version of the "forward and back extensions," which gave a new attack to the sweep and carriage of the arms, the focus of the eyes, and thus the dramatic texture of the movement.

As new works entered the repertory, the vocabulary invented for the choreography would be introduced and developed in class, and sometimes would remain in the evolving unwritten syllabus. It was a time of enormous input for me as a young artist and would climax years later, when I was invited by Martha in 1955 to join the company for the State Department tour of the Far and Near East and she would create on me the central role in *Ardent Song* (1954).

Paul Taylor

Paul Taylor was a member of the company from 1955 to 1962. He is director of the Paul Taylor Dance Company.

She's come to New London for a brief visit and I first catch sight of her as she crosses the huge lawn in the center of the campus. A small dot in the distance, she's dressed in red and is carrying her own lighting equipment—a red parasol that filters the bright day, casting down a flattering shade of pink. I change direction to get a better look. Closer up, what has seemed like a smooth regal glide turns out to be a sort of lurching swagger. Her face features a crimsoned mouth artfully enlarged, and she's wearing sunglasses. Behind them the eyes—the eyes!—the eyes are dark and deep lidded and there's something very wise and undomesticated in them, like the eyes of an oracle or an orangutan. That is, they look as if they've seen everything there's to be seen in this world, maybe even more. They give the impression of being placid, yet at the same time seem to be spinning around like pinwheels. After the mouth and the eyes there's this more or less unimportant nose. And, as seen from up close, her grooming is telling me that everything possible has been done to prevent nature from taking its course. Just as our paths are about to cross, she stops, dips her chin down, and looks up at me. I've never heard Martha Graham described as cute, nevertheless that's how she looks as she waits for me to say something. I become confused. Other than throwing myself at her feet, what would be acceptable? Forgetting to disguise my Southern accent, I say that all us students sure are thrilled that she's finally come (theatrically speaking, her two-day-late entrance has been an effective buildup). Lowering her huge lashes, she whispers that being here is, for her, like atoning for all past sins. Immediately I'm dying to know exactly what all her past sins have been, but it seems best not to ask. There have been rumors that she isn't above laying out a student or two, and that she once kicked Antony Tudor in the shins for accusing her of choreographic compromise. Apocryphal or not, these kinds of incidents only add spice to her ongoing legend.

Facing a legend is a blast, but making me jittery. The mouth is uttering oracular things—something about the "little flags of celebration which fluttah all over one's bodaah" (deepest tone on the "bodaah"), and about "the miraculous little bones of the foot" and she's seeming practically gaga. Then she's telling me that she believes I can be a very great dancer if my imagination holds. (Does she mean that it would take imagination to think of myself as being great, or what?) She's also saying that I'm one of the only two people whom she's ever said this to. (Who's the other? I'll kill him.) Then she produces a slip of fortune cookie–sized paper and writes down the phone number of her school, saying that she wants me to join her company before the year is out, and that when I get to New York I should call.

Her exit is preceded by an authentic-looking Oriental bow, with flowery wrist gesture thrown in for good measure. I stand transfixed as she diminishes into a floating red dot against the wide green lawn. The lurching swagger had been pretty nice, and saying "bodaah" a big improvement over "instrument," but what I loved best were the oracular eyes.

Excerpt from Paul Taylor's book *Private Domain,* published by Knopf: distributed by Random House, copyright Taylor, 1987, and reproduced with permission.

Dudley Williams

Dudley Williams teaches Graham's technique at the Alvin Ailey School and continues to perform.

I was in the company from 1960 to 1968. It was all an accident that I dance. I had an uncle who sang, and one day, when I was youngster, he took me to the School on the Hill, at 145th Street in New York City. I heard music in a downstairs studio and peeked in. The teacher invited me to watch and I was stunned to see people dancing. I went home and told my mother that I wanted to dance. There were no objections.

Then there was another lucky accident. I wanted to audition for the High School for the Performing Arts music division because I played the piano. But I was too late to be enrolled and when they asked me if I could do anything else, I told them that I had taken dance lessons once a week on Saturdays. So I was put into the dance division and I never touched the piano again.

May O'Donnell, who was a Graham principal dancer, was a guest teacher at the high school. I was so impressed with her, I started to go to her private studio and danced in some of her concerts at the Brooklyn Academy.

Fresh out of high school, I got my first union-paying job in *Show Boat* at Jones Beach (an outdoor summer theater), where Donald McKayle had something to do with the choreography. I remember other performers in the cast—Geoffrey Holder—and others who later became well known. We performed in the Broadway shows that were reproduced there.

Ms. Graham taught a master class at Juilliard, where I eventually studied for two years. She gave me a working scholarship to her school then and there. I had to clean the mirrors in the studio and the bathrooms, collect tickets, and sew appliqués on to the costumes or do any other job that came along. I learned a lot about costuming without realizing it.

I had been at the Graham school for about a year when she asked me to teach a class. She sat very quietly in a corner on one of those Noguchi benches and stayed the entire class. At the end of the class she said, "You have my permission to teach." It was like receiving a benediction! After that, whenever a teacher was needed, I was the one who jumped in.

I think that what she saw in me was that I don't just give a class with combinations. I *teach*. And that's a different matter and something I learned by imitating all her best disciples—Ethel Winter, David Wood, Mary Hinkson, Bertram Ross. They all moved differently. I tell my students to go along with whichever teacher is giving the class. It gives a wide scope of choice to what will work best in the future for the student.

In class, I'm always calling out a loud "and" to help the class know that the next count is "one" and that the combination must begin precisely on that count. It triggers the mental and physical breath that precedes a movement—the glissade in ballet—that provides the impetus to begin a step.

It all has to flow. Students tend to worry about the steps in the sequence of a combination instead of just doing it. They don't want to make a mistake and appear foolish. But actually the mind and body compute the combination as soon as it is shown, and their concern about it is kind of an ego delay that interrupts courage and the exhilaration of risk. You can't have second thoughts on stage. So it's best to just do the step immediately.

Another thing I do is emphasize the lengthening of the neck, head, and face at the third phase of movement that begins with the lower half of the body and rises to the upper half and the arms. When the movement stops at the sternum, it is incomplete and inexpressive. Energy has to come from the center of the body and go right through the top of the head. What's frustrating is that you can't teach that. The student has to feel it. If I could teach it, I'd write a book! It takes a certain amount of daring and it won't work for everyone. Martha had that kind of projection through her entire body to the top of her head, and she was small in stature but big in movement. She used to make up her chest with white translucent powder so that it would reflect her long neck and her facial expression right up through the balcony. The red slash of her lipstick, the darkly made up eyes, the black hair, the beading on her lashes weren't a mask, but an enhancement of her stage looks. I tried to do that once and I looked like a clown. The style of her costuming on and off stage indicated that she was all theater, all the time, even when she spoke. She was bigger than life. Powerful. She called upon the fantasy of her role. The cupped hand with the energy in the wrist that you see in her photos and that is used in class work is an ancient pose that is somewhat defiant but so expressive.

Every body is different and everybody will interpret a step differently. No matter how accurate or precise that step will be executed, it will look different on a different body and not be incorrect or violate the technique. Alvin [Ailey] and I used to talk about our dislike for cookie-cutter dancers. They all think a dancer has to have a certain look when all they have to have is talent.

It takes courage to bring your deep-down dancer self and your imagination to a movement. Everything has to be alive, including your innards. You can't blink, you can't lose your focus. Your whole being has to work. The student has to pledge that hour-and-a-half class to the teacher, to the movements, to themselves.

I pledge myself to each performance. I concentrate on the spot I'm supposed to hit onstage and let nothing interfere. Then I let the role take over.

I am small in stature and because I stood next to tall men in the company, I had to learn from Ms. Graham how to project. She wasn't going to be upstaged by the tall dancers; neither was I.

A Greek god I'm not, and at one point, when Graham was doing a lot of myths in her dances, I decided to leave and join the Alvin Ailey American Dance Theater. I had danced a lot of roles for Graham, but it was time for me to move on. Alvin dealt with the here and now in concept, and that's where I wanted to be. And that's where I still am.

6 ⟳ THE SEVENTIES
AND EIGHTIES

The Beatles continued to dominate the music world, along with rock 'n' roll, punk rock, and New Wave music. Disco dancing became popular with the "me" generation. The *New York Times* published the Pentagon Papers, concerning U.S. involvement in Vietnam; musicals turned to religious subjects in *Jesus Christ Superstar* and *Godspell*. *Cabaret* won Liza Minnelli and Bob Fosse Academy Awards. The Moog synthesizer, an electronic apparatus that duplicates the sounds of various musical instruments, was invented.

Robert Cohan (in the Graham company from 1946 to 1957 and 1962 to 1969) became director of the London Contemporary Dance School and its affiliated London Contemporary Dance Theatre. The repertory consisted of works by Graham, Sokolow, Taylor, and Ailey.

Riots and unrest found college students and radicals in protest marches. Inflation and recession sent businesses crashing, but recovery was quick. More public recognition was bestowed upon Martha, with a crowning Medal of Freedom from President Ford in 1976, who called her a national treasure.

At the Martha Graham Center for Contemporary Dance, Martha remained at the helm of her school, teaching, coaching, and supervising rehearsals and reconstructing some of her older masterworks. In 1974 she embarked on a trip to East Asia with the company and lectured and taught.

In 1975, Rudolf Nureyev and Margot Fonteyn performed in Graham's *Lucifer;* Mikhail Baryshnikov appeared with Nureyev in *Appalachian Spring;* and Liza Minnelli, in 1978, narrated *The Owl and the Pussycat.*

In 1980, a Picasso retrospective of a thousand items was shown for the first time at the Museum of Modern Art in New York, and his self-portrait brought $5.3 million at auction in Paris. Baryshnikov became director of American Ballet Theatre; Ronald Reagan became president; computers reached $1 billion in annual sales. Michael Jackson gyrated on the MTV network (whose programming features video versions of popular songs) and he broke all sales records, topping 37 million copies with his *Thriller* album; there were now 350,000 homeless Americans; a Picasso now fetched $48 million at auction in New York City (1989).

The 1980s became the golden age of dance, with more performances and support than ever in American history. Martha's dances and classes on videotape, her works on television, and taped interviews, books, and photographs made her the most documented dance artist in history. She continued to tour, and in 1984 Pope John Paul II gave her an audience following the company's performance in Rimini, where three thousand people had to be turned away.

Peter Sparling

Peter Sparling danced in the Graham company from 1973 to 1987. Sparling is a native of Michigan, where he attended Interlochen Arts Academy. At the Juilliard School he was awarded the Louis Horst Memorial Scholarship and became a member of the José Limón Company.

Sparling presented his own dance company in 1983 for five successive seasons. He taught and choreographed at Juilliard, Australia's Victoria College of the Arts, Portugal's Ballet Gulbenkian, American Ballet Theatre II, Taiwan's Cloudgate Contemporary Dance Theatre, the London Contemporary Dance Theatre, and the Laban/Bartenieff Institute of Movement Studies. He became assistant professor of dance at the University of Michigan in Ann Arbor.

Those of us who came into the company in the 1970s followed in the footsteps of so many wonderful dancers. We had the Rosetta Stone—the technique—a presence unto itself. We had role models, the dancers we had seen on stage. Although we were coming into a company quite green—the apprentice company became the main company in 1973—we held onto the technique. But times had changed.

We learned the roles in the apprenticeship company under the direction of Bertram Ross and Mary Hinkson, or in Juilliard, but we were children of the media and, with the proliferation of dance at that time, it was important for us to fill a Broadway house during a season.

The pressure was on. We had spent many weeks learning the roles and handling the props, learning from films, and although the choreography was learned, it was up to us to bring the roles to life, as they had been done in the previous decades. We were not involved in the creation of the dances, although Martha was always creating, but we knew we would be compared to members of the original casts.

Many times, the critics and the public labeled us lightweight, without the maturity or the gravity of dancers in past Graham companies. That taught us all a lesson. We had to go back continually to Martha's original ideas, as they were embedded in the technique, to get deeper into the roles that we saw in videocassettes or film versions. The actual strength of a live performance was not there for us to see. And the mechanics of running the video machine were intrusive and disruptive: rewind, press, pause.

We are now taking the dance works into an era of long touring, annual seasons, and five performances a week. The technique was what we depended upon, not only to maintain our stamina and to keep our roots, but to give us the source and motivation for the emotional content.

I think we can see today how Martha's idiosyncratic gift influenced the technique and how the artistic goals contributed to the technique as well. The progression is marvelous to observe over the years—how it all developed into a streamlined and expanded form.

For me, it is proof of the strength of that technique that I can go on my way and be as idiosyncratic as I want to be and still depend upon the basic structure and principles of the Graham technique.

Martha was the first to say that she stole from the best and that she expected us to do the same. I've taken her at her word. We have not only learned from her physical way to move, but we've learned an attitude toward life, toward theater, and a moral obligation to an audience to find and project something significant.

Joyce Herring

Joyce Herring performed in the Graham company from 1981 to 1994 and was guest artist to 1999.

In 1971, I had never seen a modern dance, nor even heard of it. I came from an upstate New York ballet school and by some miracle got accepted by the

Juilliard School, where, through the guidance of Martha Hill, I was retrained. Alfredo Corvino became my main ballet teacher and I saw modern dance for the first time in the classes of Ethel Winter and Helen McGehee. I thought it strange and didn't understand it at all. But when I saw a performance of *Diversion of Angels*, I became entranced, mesmerized, and couldn't think of anything else. For me, modern dance had a voice, a purpose. I began to take my modern dance classes with a purpose.

After four years at Juilliard, I thought about going to the Graham school but everybody warned me against it: "They never take anybody into the company who goes to the school," rumor had it. "When they see you there day after day, they have contempt for you. And when they need someone in the company, they choose a fresh face!" I listened and decided to work for a small dance company instead of going to the school.

Three years passed before I got up enough nerve to go to the Graham school. It was then or never. I was twenty-seven years old. I took some classes there that were different from the Juilliard classes. Juilliard taught more of an overview of the technique, while the center trained in a difficult, detailed, focused, and intense way. Martha, who was in her eighties at that time and involved in everything, attended the scholarship auditions. She asked me, "Do you want to be a dancer?" "Yeeessss. Is there a chance that I could ever work for you?" I dared ask. "That's why I'm talking to you," she responded. She gave me a scholarship. But what a shock. I thought I was already a dancer. Martha always made it clear that dance was a never-ending mission, a life's work. I spent the full time from 1981 to 1994 in the company and thereafter as a guest.

Martha at that time was involved in the seminars on technique, and although there was a lot of disagreement, I could see why things changed from year to year depending upon what new works she had created, who her dancers were at a particular time, and how the changes kept the technique a living thing. When I later became director of the school, the seminars helped and I thought a lot about the changes. I had a good idea about what Martha liked to see in the studio every day. I had been trained carefully by teachers from later and earlier generations. It was only with the many changes in the technique that you could perform the works of the seventies and eighties because the requirements had been extended. The later generation of dancers had had more ballet training and were able to do different things and get into different shapes. Martha, seeing the different attributes and being the great artist that she was, used those traits as material for new works. The demands on the company dancer today are broad because the older works, such as *Heretic* (1929) and "Steps in the Street" from *Chronicle* (1936) are still in the repertory, as are the newer, which require jumps and twirls that were not in the earlier works.

I spent a lot of time with Martha and the teachers of her generation—especially with Anna Sokolow—and they each had the courage to get to a basic principle, whether it was understood by the class right away or if it took the entire class time to get one thing right. They didn't care if there were twenty-five people in the class or two students. For them, it wasn't a question of filling a class or making it popular. They did what they had to do in the spirit of rebellion—the motto that had guided them in their early days—and their attitude continued to be: "I don't give a damn if you like this movement or not."

Martha and Anna both would place hands and poke fingers on a student's body without gentleness and would go so far as to yank you around. It was frightening, yet wonderful, wonderful training. We were scolded, felt belittled, and given corrections and attention that would mold us the rest of our lives as artists and teachers. What they were doing sometimes would be a complete mystery, until we finally got it. We hesitate to teach that way now because we're attempting to make it all more accessible. We struggle for words, while they struggled with repetition, repetition, repetition, until the mysteries were unfolded to us. I try to do the same thing in my classes but with a little less angst for the student. The simple things are so profound, such as a demi-plié, the lift of an arm, the turn of the head, the reach of a gaze. They are dedications. The student must be made aware of the inner and outer beauty of even a simple movement, as well as their importance and the sanctity of all movements. The world is different now, and we must find ways to reach the students of today without losing the strength and integrity of the work.

I feel that one of the things that gets lost in the Graham technique, in our efforts to be accurate, is a sense of abandonment. There's a dynamic that involves the weight of the body that was described to us again and again by the earlier teachers as "fall and catch." It meant that you had to let the weight of the body fall and catch it instantaneously. There is an excitement in the moment when the student takes a precarious position and recovers safely. It can be breathtaking as the performer risks falling off balance, but doesn't.

I was taught and I teach dancers to find the extreme distinctions between different movements. When you jump, it should look like a jump; a reach should look like a reach, which means that each movement must have a quality that is suited to its inherent shape, energy, purpose, and singularity.

Just as not falling after a number of attempts becomes an act of faith, so must the student have the courage to commit to going forward into the unknown discovery and mastery of the technique.

Martha would talk about "quickening," and "vibrations," as energy takes hold of the body in response to something that moves you. Even when she was sitting in her chair at the age of ninety-seven you could see her vibrate with every fiber of her body when she watched a rehearsal or had something to say. It was electrifying. She was *there*, living the moment, and if you weren't, she wasn't interested in you. It was ruthless.

Older dancers would visit the studio and remark about the changes in the technique and attribute it to Martha's failing eyesight. Ironically, she could sit in Studio One along the mirrors and gesture to someone in the doorway far across the studio to come in. Although no artistic director can control everything, many of the changes were purposefully made by Martha.

Especially during her later years, she had little patience. The technique got sharper, bigger, harder, less subtle, almost brash. She had little time left and must have sensed it. She came to the studio every day and demanded full energy from each dancer. She needed their energy to keep herself moving. If she didn't get it from a dancer, that dancer was ignored.

There was a considerable turnover of artistic directors beginning in 1992, and my term as director of the school came during the sale of the 63rd Street building that we all revered. The school made a temporary move downtown, which the students accepted with dignity, dedication, and grace, but a serious illness, which I overcame, made it necessary for me to leave my position a year later.

At this moment [2000], there is a crisis in deciding where to continue and in the survival of the company. But Martha's work will always live, not only in her dances, but in the work of the artists her work has fostered.

The thing that helped me most in my understanding of the technique was Martha's coaching. She coached me personally in many roles, including *Primitive Mysteries, Lamentation* (which I performed at the White House),

Appalachian Spring, Deep Song, Serenata Morisca, Mary in *El Penitente* and others. She was encouraging and supportive.

She was especially forthcoming when she set a new work on me, a new version of *American Document,* which I performed with Mikhail Baryshnikov. These unforgettable experiences with Martha gave me a deeper insight into the technique and what it was intended to accomplish.

Jacqulyn Buglisi

༉

Donlin Foreman

Jacqulyn Buglisi was in the Graham company from 1977 to 1989; Donlin Foreman, from 1977 to 1994.

JB: It was at the Boston Conservatory of Music that my mother found a teacher, Jan Veen, who had studied with Mary Wigman. On a very special day, I got to give Wigman a bouquet of flowers after she had taught a master class. I was probably the youngest permitted to take that class. Wigman encouraged me to study with Martha Graham, so when my family moved back to New York in 1964, I took an audition to study at the High School for the Performing Arts. There, my teachers were former Graham dancers Gertrude Shurr, David Wood, and May O'Donnell. At the same time, I went to the Graham school and had my first classes with Martha.

Technically at that time, we did a lot of work in parallel position, in contractions, in balances, with a flexed foot, shifting our weight forward over the front thigh and turning our torso against that. It was very difficult but it strengthened the back muscles in an incredible way. We don't do much of that aspect of the technique at this point and lean more heavily on turned-out legs. When Martha was working on something in her choreography, it always became part of the class and part of her technique.

In 1973 I returned from Rome, where I had started (with five others) the first modern dance company based upon Graham technique, the first school of contemporary dance technique in Spoleto, and a contemporary-dance school in Rome. We started with small classes, then demonstrations sponsored by Francesca Astaldi, who had a school for ballet but was interested in modern dance. That same year, Martha had an audition, which I took and got an offer to join the company. But because I was committed to the Rome company, I returned to do some performances there. Pearl Lang saw our performances in Rome and offered me a job if I would come back to New York. Pearl had done the choreography for a play, *Hard to Be a Jew,* which turned out to be a perfect job for me and Christine Dakin, with whom I shared a dressing room for three months. At the same time, I was able to rehearse with Joyce Trisler (who eventually had a company), take class, and have an income. It was a time in New York when there were many small companies—the early Alvin Ailey company, Pearl's group, Mary Anthony's, and many others. At one point, when we were rehearsing at the New Dance Group studio with Joyce and getting ready to perform at Jacob's Pillow, we needed another male dancer. I was told to have a look at Donlin Foreman, who was also rehearsing in the New Dance Group building. I thought he had gorgeous bones! I invited him out to dinner, and we became inseparable before we went to Jacob's Pillow. After the Pillow engagement, I learned that he had signed a contract with the Royal Winnipeg Ballet. "Why do you want to go there?" I asked him and convinced him that his future was in modern dance.

Five weeks later, we married and performed together in Joyce Trisler's company (where I was a founding member) for her New York Roundabout Theater engagement of Denishawn pieces. There was a great deal of research involved in reproducing those early dances and we had classes in the Denishawn technique for weeks in preparation. It was a unique experience.

Donlin and I joined the Graham company in 1977. I had been at the school since 1964 and Martha chose me to be in the company after seeing me at a rehearsal of *Primitive Mysteries.* In preparation for the tours, we took class, rehearsed until the dinner break, and resumed until 10:00 P.M. We had contracts and were always working. It was a golden time for the company. One of our first tours was cross-country for nine weeks, booked by Columbia Artists Management. Martha taught company class, choreographed *Frescoes* in 1978, and spoke to the audience before each performance. At that point in her life, that was the extent of her being able to perform. It was a brilliant piece of theater to introduce the company, and a loss when she didn't appear in the smaller towns. In Europe she used a translator and it was just as effective. The

European tours were sponsored by the U.S. State Department. Some audiences were still shocked by the Greek mythological content of her dances.

We had visited Norway and Denmark, where their dark nights and legends inspired Martha to create *Tangled Night* (1986) and *Acts of Light* (1981). Halston designed the costumes for both works. The *Acts of Light* costumes were controversial tight-fitting gold unitards that everyone wears now. Martha always collaborated on the costumes with Halston. In the Lament section, he designed black dance belt–like costumes for the men. Some people in mid-America found that offensive, although there was nothing suggestive about the costume or the ballet. Actually, it was quite reverential. This exciting period of touring exposed the work to people in countries such as Egypt and Saudi Arabia who had never seen the company.

By the late 1980s the company had lost its manager through internal differences. It was a turbulent period. The manager who left had been a caring person, always there for the dancers, for Martha, for the image of the company, but it was over. Martha gave the rights to her ballets and a great deal of power to just one person. I believe she realized her mistake and tried to make repairs, but it was too late. She was dying.

We had to make a courageous choice: if Martha wasn't going to be there, we didn't want to continue with the company. It was wrenching for me because I had spent so many years involved with her, the company, the technique, and so much of my life. I was moved by Martha's compassion during the time of the death of my parents, and was delighted when she held Donlin's and my newborn son, Bradley, in her arms in 1988. But it was time to move away physically, although that is never really possible in your mind and heart.

I remember one night. It was very late; Donlin and I were alone in Studio One with Martha. We were rehearsing *Cave of the Heart* (1946), a work about a terrible love out of which grows revenge and jealousy. Martha began to speak about Miss Ruth [St. Denis] and, with her uncanny intuition, mentioned many things. But mostly I will always remember her words: "Miss Ruth's tongue was on me and my tongue is on you." It was a great challenge that I still embrace.

I had performed in Europe until I was four months pregnant, danced the New York season, and then left to teach at the High School for the Performing

Arts, the Alvin Ailey Dance Center, and the Graham studio. My choreography, which is now included in our Buglisi/Foreman Dance Company, had begun as early as school in Massachusetts, where I wrote a play, directed the action, and did the choreography. Since then, I have created many dances for workshops and ballets for our company, using my roots in Graham technique. Martha was always encouraging; the company had presented my ballet *Sospiri* in their 1989 New York City Center season. She had pioneered for herself; now we had to pioneer for ourselves.

ᏊᎧ

DF: Martha's movements didn't spring spontaneously from some sudden inspiration. They came from her blood, her bones, and her psyche, from other great arts, written and visual, and from the Denishawn work she had done. She said that she had rediscovered what was already there. She never spoke about creating a work—it was the process of discovering it. That's why I feel that her movement voice speaks directly from and to the core of instinct.

Many brilliant dancers with special gifts contributed to Martha's work and technique through the roles she "discovered" for them. I felt more like a throwback to Bertram Ross and Erick Hawkins, from that earlier period. I learned my roles from the films at the Martha Graham Center, watching Bertram (he had been "excommunicated," but not by Martha, before I arrived) and I felt connected to his way of moving. In his class one day, not at the Graham studio, when we were doing turns around the back in Fourth Position, Bertram stopped the musician, pointed to a person on the other side of the studio and said, "You don't love this. You have to love this to do it the way it should be done!" And I understood immediately that I did love it, though I had never thought of it that way. Martha never spoke of love except twice that I remember. Once, she threw me into a run-through for Halston, in *Acts of Light,* which she was choreographing simultaneously on Tim Wengerd and me. Tim had walked out of the room for a moment and she told Peggy Lyman and me, in Tim's absence, to dance the duet, Conversation of Lovers. I threw myself into it as if I owned it. When we finished I went to get some water in a room next to the studio. As I turned around, Martha was standing behind me. She grabbed me in an embrace, then pushed me back, looking into my face, and exclaimed, "I see you know how to love," then turned and walked away.

The second time she mentioned love was before a run-through of *Cave of the Heart*. We were working on a few of the more ferocious sections. Before starting—I don't remember how she began speaking—she said to us in a pensive voice, with her brow furrowed in a question, "People think this is only about jealousy, that it is about hating someone and revenge. It's not. It's about love. A love so terribly deep that you go mad if it is denied. She [Medea] killed her brother for Jason. She left her home for him, and he denied her. She became like a wounded animal tearing and killing the things closest to her."

Originally I came from a town in Alabama of three thousand people where I did typical things such as play football and perform in a rock band. I went to the University of Montevallo [Alabama]—a small school—where I changed subjects from marine biology to courses in drama and movement, and eventually went to Aspen, Colorado, through Milorad Miskovitch, who had introduced me to ballet. Willem Christensen in Salt Lake City gave me free classes in his school and I became an unsatisfied apprentice of the Ballet West company. So I went off to New York, where I asked Leon Danielian at the Ballet Theatre school for advice. He offered me free classes. After about a year, I joined Joyce Trisler's company. She was doing a work called *Four against the Gods* and Jacqulyn was the figure of Graham. I saw her dance using Graham technique, which was new to me, and I was awestruck.

Shortly after we were married and had joined the Graham company together, I worked through severe physical back pain that lasted most of the sixteen years I worked with Martha and for three years after her death. My point of view was that I didn't work for the Graham company, I worked with Martha. I always felt an apprentice to a master. I was consumed by the symbolism of the work and by working with her. I was permitted to look at the life of "man" as I demanded the strength to master the roles that I danced. It was, to me, about cultivating a physical voice with which to speak these amazing plays that had been written for us—this voice cultivated by and through her technique.

One night on tour, I was limping to my dressing room after a performance and didn't realize that Martha was standing near. I paused before attempting the stairs and she spoke suddenly and loudly in an accusatory tone, "You're limping." I replied, "No." She demanded, "Yes, you are." In order to take another step I would have to confirm her statement, so I acknowledged that she was right—I had had surgery on my back at that point and she knew about the chronic pain I was fighting. To that confirmation, with her head held high as if she had discovered something I had tried to hide, she said, "I know." Then she lowered her head and spoke into the deepest part of my chest and said, "I know. I know you would die if you couldn't do this." And she walked away and I walked away. Although it all seemed a little extreme, we both knew she was right for both of us.

The technique, as we start sitting on the floor on the earth, pressing down to rise up, becomes potentially symbolic of all real things, and, as do several great philosophies and sayings, it affirms that the most important things of this world are the *symbols* of the real and tangible, not the real itself. Oedipus and Jocasta become archetypes, symbols of fate. It is not the people but the archetypes that speak to us. This technique that we practice becomes a saying, a story, and an affirmation of what has always been a part of man, our terrors and our beauties. Martha was a great discoverer, so we continue her legacy by continuing to discover, through our own dances now, with a voice that was forged in the fire of her works and her technique.

Terese Capucilli

Terese Capucilli has been a member of the Graham company since 1979.

Many students develop bad habits in their hometown schools and when they reach the intensity of study required at a school such as the Juilliard, or at a university dance program, they always have to expect some tearing apart and relearning. Often they feel that the work is slower than they would like it to be, but by embracing the process of working slowly there is a redefining, a letting go, and the acquiring of a different focus of even the most simple movements. Old physical injuries, which usually show themselves in such intense programs, hopefully, if corrected early, will not become chronic through the dancer's career.

I have been there. In my first year at SUNY [State University of New York] at Purchase, I had come from a background that was strongly defined by many years in musical theater in my hometown in Syracuse. I had studied voice along with tap, ballet, and jazz and had had a lot of experience performing, mostly in musical theater. But I had only about a year of what was called modern technique. Earlier, I had experienced a problem with a knee, and in the intense program at Purchase I had to learn how to work in a new way. My first year I had to sit out of most of the *Night Journey* repertory class because of my knee problem! No one can help you listen to your body or teach you how to work by yourself. Those helpful therapies that are available can provide a basis for this understanding. However, it is through constant discovery of one's own strengths and weaknesses that you are able to set a work standard for your entire career.

At Purchase, modern dance studies included the techniques of Cunningham, Limón, and Graham. It was all so new and very exciting for me; I embraced all the techniques at once since I had never before known any of them. Carol Fried staged excerpts from the Graham repertoire, including *Diversion of Angels,* where we could apply the Graham technique. Martha had actually come to a performance one year. Mel Wong taught the Cunningham technique, and there were others who exposed us to different forms of techniques and very interestingly, different viewpoints of the same technique. From Kazuko Hirabayashi I learned a much more lyrical approach to the Graham technique than the viewpoint that Carol Fried held. To see how much dimension is possible within the same technique was particularly enlightening.

At Purchase it was a great honor for me to be chosen by Anna Sokolow to perform in her Charles Ives piece *Central Park in the Dark.* I was told years later that I was chosen because I sat bolt upright when she spoke and stared her directly in the face in anticipation at the prospect of performing in her piece. She couldn't ignore me! The experience of working with her was actually the first time that I was exposed to a certain sense of dramatic theater and the power of the individual in the stage space. This initial awareness left quite an impression on me.

The Graham company came to Westchester in 1975, where I saw them for the first time. It was my first contemporary dance concert. *Cave of the Heart* and *Diversion of Angels* were on the program, and it was unlike anything I had ever experienced. Again, it was a time of revelation for me to be moved in this way by a performance. I had not known that feeling before.

I made the choice to go to Graham through a door that opened for me. In my senior year, Carol Fried told me that she had spoken to Linda Hodes [then associate artistic director of the company] about giving me a scholarship at the center. It was the summer of 1978, and with my B.F.A. in hand I headed for the Graham Center. As a scholarship student, I was required to demonstrate for the classes and this was an incredible learning process. Martha taught many of the classes along with members of the company.

By March of 1979 I was asked to join the company and have spent the last twenty-one years living the Graham technique and developing a voice within the technique that is inherently my own.

My relationship with Martha was always constructive. That was not always the case with dancers who found her driving a way that was not always healthy for them. She despised mediocrity and individuals who did not work beyond their capacity. She demanded more and more from each of us, and since I was always kicking myself in the head about everything and never satisfied, that created a good relationship between us. She gave me the lead role, as the Chosen One, in her *Rite of Spring* (1984). It was a role that Martha had done in ballet choreographer Léonide Massine's version of the Stravinsky work in 1930. We spent a lot of time alone in the studio rehearsing the solo. There was her driving voice, as she sat on the edge of her chair, enticing me to go beyond what I could ever do physically in the contorting, twisting, and immense emotional intensity of fear of someone about to be sacrificed. Basically, it was not so much about the emotional content of the work, but about the depth of physicality to which she responded. It was again a turning point for me in an understanding of Martha's theater, as well as an awareness of the enormity of physicality it demanded.

As a teacher, I find that it's difficult for students to come to the realization that the body doesn't end at the top of the head or the bottom of the feet; that you can move through space beyond the limits that you think possible. The body can be voluminous and carry its weight in either a grand or subtle way if one teaches it to breathe from every pore. It takes a tremendous amount of energy to sustain, and many students are unaware of just how much energy it takes to even be still. I like to envision the spine as having the strength of a tree trunk with its roots clearly into the ground, but with the ability to bend with the wind and to extend its limbs from that strong center. For every lengthening of the spine or limb, there is a pull deeper into the earth.

As Pearl Lang often did when I was studying with her, I include the yoga "blessing," which begins with the hands, fingers touching, elbows up, lightly touching the body at four chakras, or centers of spiritual energy and consciousness. The first touch is to the inner fire of the navel chakra; then the heart, or air principle; the speech, or sound principle; and at the space between the eyebrows, or mind principle—the "third eye." This blessing also gives the student the opportunity to visualize space between the vertebrae as they sit with the weight on the sit [ischium] bones, with a straight spine, energy emanating up and through the body. With the touch of each chakra there is the perception of a breath between each vertebra as the spine lengthens. This helps students understand that when they do a contraction, it is a continuation of the spine lengthening, as the front of the body softens and lifts, rather than dropping into the pelvis.

I also emphasize the correct use of the inner thigh muscles when I teach, especially in parallel position, while sitting on the floor or standing. There is often a misconception that *parallel* translates into "turn-in." In fact, the inside muscles of the legs work just as strongly in parallel as they should in a turn-out position. When the legs are standing in a parallel position in relevé [heels up with the metatarsals-though-toes still on the floor], the image is one leg, not two legs, not two hips, but one leg moving from a strong connection to the floor and rising through the strength inside and behind the legs. It is important that both sides of the legs work evenly. This lengthening continues with a suspension from behind the ears.

When the new student stands up from the floor exercises, and the weight is now on the legs, the tendency is for the body to sag and droop. Students have no idea of the possibilities that are there for them in learning how to sustain energy that is vibrating throughout their bodies when they work through a class. Martha taught me the undeniable vibrancy that can and should be present in a still movement. An awareness through every pore that brings a sense of the back of the body, as you observe the image of the front of the body in the mirror. Every part of your being is alive and breathing.

Imagery helps students from becoming bogged down by technical directions. After a few months of study, they become more comfortable with themselves and begin to learn how much the body will respond to their creative mind. It's a matter of self-discovery and teaching the body to see inside as well as see each movement from the outside.

My class also includes the "pleadings." That position begins with lying on the back in a contraction that slightly raises the upper part of the body, with the head falling backward, arms to the side, heels of the hands moving away from the softening in the heart area. It is similar to the position seen in Michelangelo's famous sculpture *Pietà*. I try to have the students gather that image before the exercise, as it brings this very difficult movement into something quite human for them. Through an image, the technique for this movement eventually finds its way more easily into the body. There is a subtlety and a vulnerability there that can be quite beautiful.

Every movement has a life force in it and students tend to lose an awareness of the blood flowing through their veins—of their own life force. They become lethargic and insecure and need prompting, and this is where the voice of the teacher is very important in pointing out the dynamics inherent in the technique.

Many students have never seen a Graham work. I ask myself how I can bring the essence of her work and her technique to them so that class work doesn't settle into just a series of exercises. How to keep it alive! A great deal of my discovery of the technique came through actually doing her work, by performing her dances over and over again, and by learning the technique through the repetition of rehearsals in the studio and performances on stage. Because so much of the technique came out of the dances Martha choreographed, it is important for them to experience an aspect of that in their classes. That is a challenge for all of us teaching the technique. The first-year students' eagerness is encouraging and I tell them that they have to approach learning in a childlike manner, with curiosity. It is a repetition, like a child who hears a new word and repeats it endlessly, over and over again, until they understand what it actually means and realize that it can be linked with other words to make sentences that express what they want to say. This technique has to be approached as if learning a new language.

When I had first been given some of Martha's roles, my worst fear was being compared to her and other dancers in earlier interpretations. It was frightening that first time when I showed Martha my interpretation of one of her roles. It was from *Errand into the Maze.* However, I quickly discovered that Martha never made comparisons with one dancer to another. She cared only about the individual she was working with at the time and tried to enlarge their perception of that role, which translated into a larger-than-life physicality. She never wanted a carbon copy of anyone, especially of herself. That is not something she would ever just give away. She expected you, and dared you, to challenge yourself, to question yourself and to work to find your own voice. That was part of her genius and ultimately a way of finding one's own freedom. In teaching I hope to put the students at the edge of the path that will ultimately lead them to find their own freedom. It is up to them to accept the challenge and make the journey.

Christine Dakin

Christine Dakin joined the Graham company in 1976 and is still a member.

I began dancing at the University of Michigan when Elizabeth Bergmann was creating a dance department. She introduced us to Limón and Graham techniques. From the very first the Graham work felt right to my untrained body and gave me a way into technique. When I came to New York, I came to the Graham studio, worked in the apprentice company in 1971 and '72 and felt transformed through learning Martha's choreography. I studied and performed with Pearl Lang and Kazuko Hirabayashi, who were powerful and inspired influences on my performing and teaching. Later I began studying with Vladimir Dokoudovsky, who introduced me to a ballet technique and style that connected in a fascinating way to the Graham work. It was his urging that pushed me to choreography. He was insistent that it was a duty to take the knowledge of stage and choreography that I had been privileged to receive and pass it on in my own voice. This ran parallel with my work with Graham, where the tradition of passing the choreography from artist to artist was the life's blood of each generation, as was passing on the technique.

Q: What do you think about the fact that so many former Graham dancers have said that the entire movement system is no longer taught?

D: I'm not sure why that is true, but I don't think it's a question of right or wrong, or if it's bad or good. Change in dance and in a technique is natural. Martha herself was constantly in the process of change and growth, and that is reflected in which parts of the technique are taught and how the movement develops. It may be that teachers who have not experienced the older parts of the technique feel uncomfortable in teaching it, and that today's students are not comfortable with the physical demands of the older technique.

Some of Martha's works throughout the years were dropped from the repertory, perhaps because, for her, they didn't have "necessity." Her instinct for the deeply visceral made her critical of what she called the frankly decorative in her work. The purpose of choreography for her, I think, was the creative process itself. It was never an exercise to make a product or to arrive at some finite point, but to create a physical and emotional world. However, in following that process, decade to decade, she could indulge in and use elements that were "frankly, decorative" and others that in the end did not give the dances the power she required. She had no problem dropping weaker works from the repertory. And she was rarely interested in revisiting any of her old works.

For the most part, all the movements that form the historical parts of the technique are in Martha's choreography. In reality, however, not many of the students are going to be involved in learning the choreography by performing in the company, so there is some validity in concentrating the teaching on a more general body of exercises, supplemented with repertory workshops and special courses.

There is no doubt that having performed the Graham works brings a level of understanding of the technique that is much deeper. Being a demonstrator for a teacher is a great asset in learning to teach as it gives you first hand experience with the point of view and direction of a more experienced teacher. But, as with a performer, it is from the technique itself, its repetition and re-creation every day, that we learn the most.

Q: Which movements in the syllabus system seem to be missing?

D: It's hard to say, because the technique is not a finite or static entity. Dancers are always remembering and forgetting exercises as they teach, and drawing from the new choreography for new material. You have to keep in mind that Martha created choreography, not exercises, so the shape that classroom exercises take is somewhat up to the teacher.

Dancers today want an exact description of exercises, when in reality they are phrases from dances that may have no specific answer; is it turned in or turned out? It can't always be broken down.

From my experience with old films, and working with the previous generation of teachers, I can say that the basic floor work exercises are missing. These were part of the germinating process of Martha's work, worked out on her own and her dancers' bodies at that time, and they reflect a very different kind of body and physicality. It is quite beautiful to see and it would be good to try and retrieve some of it, but the basic principles are still embodied in the core of the exercises today.

Q: Is there actually a syllabus?

D: Yes, the faculty has a syllabus from which it works. Obviously it is different from earlier syllabi as it contains some of the more recent additions to the technique and leaves out some others. The choreography has given us a vocabulary of movement that is vast and can be taught as a series that progresses from exercises that work for beginners to their more complex developments for advanced students.

We approach the syllabus with our own individual styles. It is a guide for students through the levels of class and makes consistency possible from teacher to teacher. It is important to use the syllabus only as a guideline since each class is as unique in its level and ability, as is each individual. The work of a class is a creative process and its structure must take into account the physical and emotional development of the students. This is determined by each teacher's experience and personal exploration of the technique. It cannot be regulated strictly by a syllabus. Martha's own presence was incredibly dynamic in the class as a unifying force. Although she is no longer physically present, that force exists inside the technique and the choreography. The power of that continuity remains alive in us as teachers and performers.

Q: If the entire technique is not taught, how do people who are taken into the company learn these movements in order to perform the dances as created by the choreographer?

D: You learn these things as they come. The basics are taught to everyone and you learn to apply those basics to new situations. The rehearsal directors and the other dancers help, and you learn the movements as Martha created them, within a dramatic context of the individual dancer, which helps tremendously.

Q: What is the requirement for a student who wants to study dance?

D: As with any kind of movement, dance requires first a desire to move, to explore oneself moving. For Martha's technique in particular, there must be a willingness to push the limits we believe we have, to enter into each class as a new challenge, a ritual which leads us to deepen our awareness, concentrate our energies, expand our ability.

As a student of the technique, you can start at any age. The drive and physical energy of the student determines how far and fast one can go. In a certain way, the more mature person, though sometimes of limited physicality, can bring more to the study of the work and can get more out of it. There is, of course, a different window of opportunity in terms of a dancer performing with the company. Of necessity that involves an advanced physical talent as well as a unique performing presence.

Martha's creative process always demanded the full mental and physical engagement of the dancer. The power of that collaboration enriched Martha's work and could move the dancer to become an artist. By being so involved in that process, it seems inevitable that many were drawn to make their own choreography.

Q: Is ballet a larger influence now than it was earlier?

D: I think dancers of necessity have had to become more versatile to meet today's expectations. Martha was much more interested in using movement that came directly from ballet in her later works than she previously was, and it both changed and broadened her movement vocabulary. Naturally, as always, we dancers had to keep up with her.

Q: How long does it take to master today's syllabus?

D: As you know, on the deepest level, it is a life's work. On a more practical level, we have developed four levels of classes and a certification program that takes about three years to complete. It consists of as much technique as possible, music, composition, repertory classes, teaching seminars, and performances.

Inevitably, dancers want to teach what they have been taught. But good dancers don't necessarily make good teachers.

Q: Is there a procedure or a mechanism in place that assures correct teaching of the movements?

D: This is the reason for the certification course. It does assure that the minimum understanding of the technique has been achieved. The rest is a matter of individual ability, of course. I think, as a general rule, someone who has been with the company is a better choice of teacher because in performing the choreography you can discover *why* you are doing what you do in the classroom. Your goal as a teacher is clearer as you see the breadth of Martha's dramatic world and the physical means it requires to express it.

Q: What is the goal?

D: The goal is to pass on the technique Martha created, but not as so many steps or exercises. Nothing could be further from her concept of dance. She drew movement out of herself to portray characters and emotions. It is pieces of her dances that we call exercises. In re-creating that movement for ourselves, we must turn it back into dance and hope to find a glimpse of the core from which it came.

Q: Are the students chosen on a scholarship basis?

D: Our school is open to anyone. Few non-government-sponsored schools can choose only the most talented students. I have seen Martha, however, come into a class and threaten to kick all of them out of her school. The class shapes up very quickly after that. It was her way of demanding the concentration and work required to master her technique.

Q: How do you see modern dance changing during your career?

D: I see all of dance moving in the direction of athleticism and tricks. Audiences are easily entertained by this, but it dulls them, I think, to more subtle parts of choreography. Especially for Martha's work, the technique shouldn't be noticed for itself, since it is the means to show the soul of a character. On the other hand, Martha's technique has always been a bravura technique, starting with her own incredible body and the extraordinary things she did to create larger-than-life characters and universal ideas. As audiences get fewer opportunities to see subtlety—the excitement of stillness, the control of raw energy, and, above all, theatricality—Martha's work is increasingly unique. She didn't want to entertain or have you like it, just be touched and aroused by what she did. We, as Graham dancers, are also very fortunate to have so many dancers who came before us to pass down the choreography and the teaching. It gives us a continuity that is powerful and increases our responsibility to maintain the integrity of the work. It is deeply satisfying to learn Martha's dances from those who did them before us, then to enjoy them as your own.

Q: When does all this commitment begin?

D: It can begin with a child or a teenager. Many people studied with Martha for a good part of their lives. She always enjoyed the energy and creativity of children, though the more visceral aspects of the technique are hard to pass on at that stage. Teenagers are self-conscious and just becoming aware of their own physicality. It is an interesting time to see them make discoveries through the technique.

Q: How would you sum up what has been said about Graham movement by the performers of the past and present?

D: A great part of the difficulty in being a dancer today might be part of a societal problem. Both the cost of living and the speed of living have increased tremendously. When I first came to New York, you could make it as a dancer working with a few small companies and taking a little extra work on the side to make expenses. Now it is nearly impossible to study without financial help or to earn a living as a dancer. It is a sobering thought, creating a fearful state of mind where getting any dance job becomes the overriding goal. Along with this, the pace of life has made it difficult to dedicate oneself to a particular choreographer or to a teacher for the time it takes to know something about one's work on a deep level. Everyone seems to share a joy in the physical experience of the technique and in having found such a profound way to express oneself through movement. Martha's theater, her dance, is really a ritual on many levels, one we all share in some way and which we carry within us always.

Wherever I go throughout the world, I find students and dancers hungry for what Martha offers. They are transformed by the depth and physical demands of her technique in class and drawn into her theatrical world on stage. When, as a teacher and director, I put what I know about Martha's work in front of these dancers, they take it in their teeth and go with it very far and deep. In that there is no doubt about the future.

Susan Kikuchi

Susan Kikuchi was a member of the Graham company from 1978 to 1984.

My studies began at birth! Martha Graham came to look at me when I was two days old to check me out as the first child born to one of her people, Yuriko, my mother. Yuriko danced with Martha during three decades—the 1940s, '50s, and '60s. My father was a psychiatric social worker at the Brooklyn

Veterans' Hospital and was the steady person in the family. He was a great supporter of my mother's career and her company. Both my parents were evacuated to the Gila River Relocation Camp in Arizona during World War II but did not know each other there; they later met on a blind date in New York City.

Whenever there was no baby-sitter available, I was taken to class or backstage, but in response to people asking if I wanted to be a dancer, I said a definite no. As a child I watched Martha rehearse and teach classes. I went on the first European tour of the Graham company, in 1954, which lasted for several months and toured several countries. I was a small part of a sparse audience for the first performances of the company in London. I remember the technical rehearsal as I watched *Night Journey* and *Appalachian Spring.* I got lost in the balcony!

Martha had incredible presence in her dancing. It was as if she were speaking her inner dialogue through space, directly to you, even if you were in the last row of the theater. The last gesture in *Spring,* with her arm raising downstage of the proscenium, her gaze out to the future, her internal questioning resolved—the decision of such importance in the human experience, the decision of marriage—stands out in my memory.

During my grade school years, I visited Martha at her studio on 63rd Street. We were in her room, adjacent to a small studio [Studio Two] and next to the outdoor garden, which she loved. She had given me a bracelet from Tiffany's and she asked me to come look at a class with her. She then threw open the door to Studio Two and revealed to us the class in progress. I was nervous standing there next to her and I suppose the class was startled too. The class proceeded and she whispered to me, "See all the students in this room? Very few will become professional dancers, if any." She interrupted the class to say a few words, and we then retreated back to her small room and shut the door behind us.

Yuriko often taught abroad or in colleges and universities, and my brother Lawrence and I would go with her. I remember summers at Connecticut College, Salt Lake City, the Place in London, Paris, Mexico, and Cologne. If I was bored, I would often take classes but I was not serious about it. When I went off to college, my grandmother died and Martha went to her funeral. In a way, for many years after that, I suppose I felt an attachment to Martha as a grandmother. I went to college during the radical sixties and subsequently grew apart from Martha as she became more and more a part of the establishment, the formalized art world, and a dance icon, and less revolutionary than in her early days as a choreographer, in the 1930s. When I was graduated from the University of Rochester, without having a career game plan, I returned to New York and took classes at the Alvin Ailey school, as well as some jazz classes, and since my mother had a small dance company at that time, I joined it and danced there a couple of years. In the year that Ailey II (the apprentice company) was established, the school held an audition and gave scholarships and I was lucky to get one for a year of study at the Alvin Ailey School of American Dance, which led to a broad-based dance education. I eventually auditioned and was cast in a Broadway show, *Pacific Overtures*.

In 1978, I was performing at the Uris Theater in a Broadway revival of *The King and I*, starring Yul Brynner. The production was directed by Yuriko. I was dance captain and danced the role of Eliza, which my mother originally created in the Jerome Robbins ballet "The Little House of Uncle Thomas" within that show. That year I also had the opportunity to dance in the Martha Graham Dance Company in their performances at the Metropolitan Opera House. I was in *Appalachian Spring* and *Diversion of Angels*. It was the year Liza Minelli acted as narrator in Martha's *Owl and the Pussycat*. Halston designed many costumes and there were galas and glitzy parties. Martha was designated a National Treasure by then. She was adamant that I should not try to follow in my mother's footsteps, as I would always be in her shadow. That was the same thought I had for many years about Martha and her own roles. Only Martha knew her roles and could dance her work with such feeling, depth, and passion. Only she had that power as a dancer-actor to move an audience with great dramatic presence. Those who followed had their own interpretations of her roles, often coached and changed by her, but those performers could never be Martha in my eyes. Not imitation, but re-creation and reinvention; an individual reinterpretation was key for any artist to follow in the footsteps of those who preceded them in roles.

The roles in which I could potentially be cast in the Graham repertory were my mother's, and Martha did not think I should be doing them! I did not want to do any of Martha's roles because I had seen her dance them. But I got the experience of dancing in group works as an ensemble dancer in her company. There was not much else left for me to do. Because of backstage politics and company intrigue, I decided to continue on with my career on Broadway whenever possible, get married, and raise a family. My love for Martha, the Graham technique, and the repertory continued in my career as a teacher, artistic director of the Martha Graham ensemble, and director of the Martha Graham School. I also began to be assigned dances to stage or rehearse for the company and the Graham Trust in the late 1990s—*Panorama, Celebration, Primitive Mysteries,* and *Appalachian Spring.* Much of my knowledge comes from many years as assistant to Yuriko, who, as in the Kabuki tradition in Japan, was trying to pass down to every dancer her understanding of Martha, her choreography, and her art. In Japan, if you do not have an heir for your lineage, you must adopt one to carry on the tradition. In this case, it came from mother to daughter. But I was not the only one; she continues to pass on her knowledge to any dancer who is sincerely interested in learning.

In the early 1980s, I performed in, and got to watch Martha create, *Rite of Spring.* She had many images to conjure up to evoke the feeling of the piece and its sense of place. She would say, "Be the beat," as she would hammer on her chest to make us feel a sense of immediacy and to dance in the present more aggressively and passionately. I got to watch the whole choreographic process, which stretched on for weeks, and saw her emerge with two different dances for the soloist in the ballet. She was no longer Martha, the dancer; she was the choreographer and she had a different viewpoint. Even though she was in pain from a bad case of shingles, she fussed over how a piece of material should be draped, the design of the costumes, the total creative product, and I observed the degree and the level of perfection she would pursue for her art.

Yuriko's contribution to Martha's company, besides her dedication to Martha as a dancer, was in her reconstructions, revivals, and reproduction of Martha's earlier works, many from the 1930s, and I assisted her on many of those projects. Yuriko was the founder of the Martha Graham Ensemble, in 1983. An early project was *Heretic* and I danced Martha's role. It was an easy one to reproduce as there was a film, with music and a score. It was later taken into the main company, after the workshop was completed, and performed in their repertory.

Celebration involved a process of collecting original dancers into Studio One to have a session of remembering dance sequences, etching out sections of the dance from memory, and using photos to evoke memory. Yuriko put together the final interpretation. "Steps in the Street" and *Panorama* had to be reinvented from a few minutes of film clips and old photos.

During the reconstruction of *Steps,* Martha said to Yuriko, "Did I choreograph that?" The music for the work could not be found, so Stanley Sussman, the musical director of the company, found a piece of music by the same composer, Wallingford Riegger, that had been used by Doris Humphrey in one of her dance works. They used that piece for the 1988 reconstruction. Subsequently the original score was found.

Janet Eilber

Janet Eilber joined the company from 1972 to 1980 and returned for several seasons: 1981, 1985, 1993, 1994, and 1998.

In the past few years, my work for Martha has expanded to include not only performing and teaching but reconstructing, directing, and documenting, as well as new areas of interest that I did not pursue or even acknowledge when I single-mindedly performed as a Graham artist.

These new pursuits, as well as my work with the American Repertory Dance Company as an actress, have given me fresh perspectives on Martha's theater. So much so that when I returned to roles in the 1990s that I had not performed in ten or fifteen years—*Lamentation* (1930), St. Joan in *Seraphic Dialogue* (1955), and the Pioneering Woman in *Appalachian Spring* (1944)—I better understood how to fulfill the needs of the Graham ballets. In the years that I was away from the company, I encountered her influence in everything else I did and could more clearly define the breadth of her contribution.

My first dance classes were in Detroit from Rose Marie Floyd, who gave me excellent basic ballet training in Cecchetti technique. My introduction to Martha came when I was a high school student at the Interlochen Arts Academy, where my parents, Charles and Carol Eilber, were on the founding faculty. During my senior year Carlos Surinach, who composed the scores for Martha's *Acrobats of God* (1960) and *Embattled Garden* (1958), saw me dance and arranged for a private audition with Martha. Bertram Ross later told me that everyone was surprised that she showed up, but Martha was sweet and charming and very generous. Sensing that my parents wanted me to go to college, she suggested that we visit Juilliard: that was "where my best teachers teach."

Attending the Juilliard School introduced me to the Graham technique and to the unending controversy about the right way to do her exercises. For years I avoided being drawn into the argument. At Juilliard I did indeed have Martha's best teachers—the drama and wit of Bertram Ross, the exacting attack of Helen McGehee, the breadth and lyricism of Ethel Winter. And I somehow knew that, though one might teach the Fourth Position spiral on the diagonal and the other might teach it parallel to the wall, these interchangeable details were only the means to an end. The style, presence, and commitment of those master artists taught me that it was the visceral power and emotional intent of the movement that was all important. Now that the technique has grown since my training, I must admit that I too take exception to some of the "improvements."

The technique has a living, evolving quality that some ignore and others do not. Because Martha incorporated movements from her choreography into the classroom, there were constantly new exercises and new approaches to old exercises. Pearl Lang says that the technique changed considerably when Martha choreographed *Diversion of Angels* (1948), but that she remained true to the version done prior to that time. Other elements affected the evolution—for example, when men joined the company for the first time. Many of the women of my generation were taller than the previous groups. Several of us were five-foot eight, nine, or ten and Martha loved to take advantage of our long legs. She invented the Lake Placid Combination while teaching company class at our residency there. It began with a long striding run, arms flung off of a spiraling back, spinning into a handstand pitch to the floor, bringing the heels together overhead, landing stretched horizontal to the floor, contracting into a recovery, and off again. "And go, and go and go!" she would urge us, clearly invigorated by the rush of movement.

In the 1970s, between contracts with the Graham company, I danced with the American Dance Machine, directed by Lee Theodore. It was a repertory company of excerpts by great Broadway choreographers—dances from *Cabaret* by Ron Field, Bob Fosse's *Little Me,* Agnes de Mille's *Brigadoon* and *Carousel,* and works by Peter Gennaro, Donald Saddler, Danny Daniels, and others. When I first took the job, I figured that I would be "the tall one in the back" since I had had no experience in the dance styles of musical theater.

But, with her choreography for *Oklahoma!* (1943), Agnes de Mille had revolutionized musical theater dance using Martha's concepts. All that I had learned from Martha about the use of emotional image and development of character was now also essential to theater dance. I was able to acquire a new physical technique fairly quickly because of my training in delivering the emotional life in a work. And, because of Martha's influence on them and on me, I had the opportunity to work with the giants of Broadway, dancing the leads in some of their finest works.

This idea of thorough specific emotional support was continually reinforced as I began to study singing and acting. In these disciplines, the technique of providing subtext for lyrics or text is widely accepted and taught, as it should be, but almost never is, in dance.

What is the best way to teach a student how to constantly draw upon personal experience and make emotional choices before moving? The methods are elusive and demanding. We should encourage a different individual response from each student. Most dance teachers shy away from intense emotional work, or were never trained in it themselves, and emphasize only the physical. I think the current trend in dance for frenetic physicality reveals this lack of internal awareness. It's much easier to demand perfection of the physical shapes—to place an arm where it belongs—rather than to understand a reason for moving it. That becomes imitation instead of an experience.

The dancer on stage who fills each move and transition with vital specifics commands undivided attention. The dancer whose intentions are general and sporadic fades in and out of focus. I was fortunate to have been trained by Martha, who never shied from emotional work, and by her greatest generation of dancers, who were steeped in the dramatic images and theatrical experimentation of her most creative period. The good news is that there are others of my generation who continue this essential style of teaching.

This emotional training has been invaluable in many areas but particularly as I stage Martha's ballet for dancers not familiar with the Graham technique. Whether I am directing student dancers at universities or the stars of international ballet companies, the dancers invariably assimilate Martha's physicality more quickly as they begin to understand the use of emotional images. The student dancer, whose technique is still in formative stages, is more open to the new physicality but has difficulty understanding how to infuse dancing with emotion. For the professional dancers, it is the reverse.

Many of them are well practiced at filling their dancing with feeling but find it difficult to relinquish the ballet technique they have spent so many years perfecting.

In these teaching experiences, I have kept in mind Martha's style of directing new dancers in her classic roles. She would never try to freeze an earlier interpretation or have a dancer repeat another's choices. As long as she knew the central theme of the ballet was served, Martha would encourage an artist to choose an interpretation that would mine their own unique strengths.

When I was very new to the company, Martha flew into a rage about something I had done. I can't remember exactly what it was, but it was probably about doing something too prettily, with sentimentality, which was Martha's bane. I remember being so astonished and fascinated by her theatricality, the finesse of her frenzy, that I forgot to be upset. Later, she delighted in telling the story of how she had tried and failed to make me cry. She thought my seeming courage showed that I "had something." I never tried to convince her otherwise.

When I returned to the company in 1985, after doing films and commercial theater, Martha asked me to step into the role of Jocasta from *Night Journey* (1947). We were in the studio with Linda Hodes, the rehearsal director at the time, rehearsing the solo in which Jocasta frantically runs from place to place in her bedroom, running, stopping, turning, and running again. Martha said, "You know, you have to talk to yourself the whole time, telling yourself what happened in this spot or that, remembering where you weaned him as a babe or where he took you as a lover, trying to escape one memory only to encounter another. Talk to yourself. I think I used to do that automatically." She had never before spoken so directly about subtext and its specificity.

The physical moves are rehearsed until they become subservient to the inner scenario, which drives the role and literally moves you. Neither Martha's technique or her theater can be complete without this total physical and emotional dedication to the moment.

Regardless of the current turmoil over who owns Martha's technique and whether her legacy will be allowed to flourish, Martha's innovations are permanently ingrained in our culture and in the work of all subsequent artists. It is impossible to hoard her pervasive influence. Her seminal teachings and concepts will thrive, to be discovered again and again by future generations.

Peggy Lyman

Peggy Lyman was a member of the company from 1973 to 1988.

I kept growing and growing and growing until, at the ripe old age of nineteen, Robert Joffrey told me that I was too tall for his company. At the same time, Balanchine told me I was too old for his company. I outgrew my ballet training, begun in Cincinnati, and returned home, where I began modern dance training. Unable to resist the lure of New York, I returned to sing and dance in the Gower Champion/David Merrick production of *Sugar*. There, I was released from my rigid classical training and encouraged to use my inherent dramatic and theatrical instincts.

At the same time, I started my training at the Graham school with Martha, Jane Dudley, Diane Gray, Mary Hinkson, Pearl Lang, Bertram Ross, Ethel Winter, and Yuriko. I was immediately excited by and drawn to the work, almost as if I had been waiting for it my whole life. My eyes were opened to a new and dynamic way of moving combining the formal training of muscle groups, as in ballet, with imagery that nourished my interest in acting. I found an entirely new world of energy motivation, shapes, dynamics, and feelings. And, very important, here size didn't matter.

My first three years of training in the school and dancing in the company were filled with discoveries about Martha's technique and about being an interpretive artist. So much was new to me—the more natural alignment of the pelvis, the power of the pelvic-initiated contraction and release, the strong use of the back in spiral, the corkscrew image of a spiraling ascent from pelvis to the top of the head—it all created a new awareness in me of the inner activity that resulted in the outer form.

Once I had absorbed and assimilated the technique into my classically trained body, I was inspired anew with the richness of Martha's choreography. There seemed nothing one couldn't communicate through her movement vocabulary, with a tremendous amount of freedom for personal interpretation. In fact, she demanded that solo and principal dancers bring some of their own personal movement style to her choreography. The steps themselves weren't as important to her as what the steps communicated. She frequently changed movements to suit my long, tall body. Then again she also put me in a tight, nonstretch costume to force me to find ways of moving without relying on my very flexible leg extensions.

I had plenty of opportunities to grow dramatically in the company because we traveled the world between 1973 and 1988, when I retired from the stage. I especially enjoyed going to the Far East because the people there were so excited to see a new dance vocabulary that related to their ancient stance and movements. The floor was as familiar a place to them as it was to us. The deep plié was a daily sitting position for everyone. But we had to be careful not to offend. Martha was very sensitive to Asian sensibilities. For instance, the sole of the foot to the Asian was an affront, an insult when seen from the front of the stage. So we demonstrated everything in our lecture-demonstrations on the diagonal.

Martha had her own sense of discourtesy. We were not allowed to drink water three hours before a performance because she didn't want us to sweat during the performance. She considered it self-indulgent. Of course, we did sweat. We also found ways, unbeknownst to Martha, of replacing lost body fluids and minerals. We considered it part of her Puritan background and her sense of elegant behavior to require us to wear only dresses, never to be seen publicly in jeans or pants. She often charged us to "make fashion, not follow it" and expected us to be as glamorous offstage as we were onstage. I once horrified her and got reprimanded by her for wearing jeans in the hotel elevator going from my room to visit another dancer. She, of course, was always perfectly groomed and dressed in simple but elegant clothes.

Although I always taught in the Graham school while I was performing with the company, I now relish my role as mentor of the Graham technique, even more now that I chair the dance division of the Hartt School of the University of Hartford in Connecticut. I feel that it is important, from a student's first day in class, to infuse the mechanics of the technique with Martha's dramatic and behavioral imagery. And because it is such a muscularly defined technique, I spend a lot of time correcting students with my hands. In today's world of lawsuits and legal liability, this can be a dangerous practice. I always make an announcement to new students that I will be placing my hands on them to create isometric resistance—a flat, clinical, impersonal hand—so that they can feel through my hand how and where a specific area should be in use. Some students, although very few, do have trouble with this, which seems to be a contemporary objection. We Graham students of past generations accepted it as a simple correction and a sign of concerned teaching.

I speak often of Martha's belief, taught to her by her father, that movement never lies. And since her movement vocabulary was built out of choreo-graphic necessity, the classroom work is far more than just technique. For me and my students it becomes a theatrical building block for learning to dance, motivated by exploration of primitive and natural forces. It is the only way I know to teach Graham, and it provides students a unique experience in the art, not just the craft, of being a dancer.

If the technique is to live and flourish, those of us in mentoring positions of the Graham tradition must unite in carefully training teachers with equal knowledge of both the physical and the theatrical elements of the technique, supported by an in-depth knowledge of the repertory. This is a tall order, but essential.

PART TWO

The Later Years

INTERVIEWS WITH
MARTHA GRAHAM

The Martha Graham School of Contemporary Dance, a red-brick, three-story building, had been the home of Graham's school since 1952, when it was donated by Lila Acheson Wallace, a patron of the arts. It dated from the turn of the century and was the home of several organizations, including a dance school and a training school for show dogs, before it was purchased for Graham. The school's apprentice group and the administration of the company were also housed in it.

Here, Graham taught her "acrobats of God," rehearsed her company, and created her dances. At one time, more than four hundred students were enrolled in the school and practiced in the small studio to the left of the hallway or took classes in the large studio past the narrow admissions desk. Off the hallway was a tiny room—supposedly Graham's private office—although it was always filled with dancers viewing videotapes of Graham's works, overflowing with music scores, practice props, bits of costume, and visitors who came to have a "private" chat about the workings of the school or the company. Upstairs, the administration offices squeezed into cubicles that resembled rooms in an attic, although a more modern office was also maintained in another building.

Graham made the following comments about her training regimen to me in an interview conducted for a radio program in 1963 at WRVR, the Rockefeller station, at Riverside Church. Martha arrived swathed in a pale blue turban and elegant matching blue dress and coat. She sensed that it was my first broadcast and that I was so in awe of her that I didn't know what to ask. She took over the interview with my gratitude.

I'm fortunate to have a building for a school. It's a darling little building. The dancers are not supposed to run around the garden or the school in bare feet. I scold them for it. They must dance in bare feet in the studio because that's part of their costume, and they must come to class with beautifully clean feet and organized bodies, ready for work.

The school is a disciplined place because there is only one freedom. And that freedom is discipline. I think the only freedom we have in life is what we choose and select to discipline ourselves about. When people are not willing to do that, they have no freedom. Freedom is discipline. It is a philosophy for all of life, whether your discipline is law or language. If you have not disciplined yourself in what you choose, then you do not have the courage to break its laws. It is the people who have broken the old laws that have become great figures.

I prefer to have my students begin to study dance at the age of nine, and I don't object to previous training. I would prefer that it be in ballet for the simple reason that Western dance stems out of more than three hundred years of study. There are certain things that one has to learn: the five positions, for instance. These positions are in every dance in the world, even in Indonesian and Cambodian dance, where the Fifth Position has been in Asia for hundreds and hundreds of years. The use of the plié and the use of the body is different, but any discipline that is not imposed emotionally or by fantasy on the body, and is not rigid in the sense that it is against the body, is wonderful to begin with. My only fear is always with people who decide they want to begin with what I would call creativity—and use that word in the sense of just letting oneself go—instead of permitting themselves to go away from tradition after having a thorough knowledge of what one is going away from.

A musician, for instance, learns certain marvelous rules and abides by them. But when a *great* composer decides to break those rules, it is not because he does not know them, but because he does know.

The demands of our century require that another dimension to movement, another accepted use of the language of the body, be made. An artist is not ahead of his time; an artist is his time. Movement is very different from what it used to be in our society and in other places as well. I received a clipping from an Indonesian paper just this last week from a dancer who studied with me. Her audience was deeply disturbed, in a way, by a performance of her dancers, but they still thought it was absolutely marvelous as well. The girls were dressed in tights and leotards and were extending the legs higher than the hips, where in their dance, a leg is never extended very much higher than the floor. You see, it all has to do with freedom of the spirit. What moves the spirit in its time makes the outer changes that we see in dance.

The following interview was conducted on Graham's ninety-fifth birthday, in 1989. Although I was a one of those "ballet people," she was always gracious when I wanted an interview. I remember one instance when I came to her studio sometime in the eighties after a hateful day at *Dance Magazine,* where I was education editor, to seek relief and be renewed by dance. She saw me standing in the doorway and beckoned me in to sit by her. I was reminded of the rehearsals with Balanchine, when I was a member of the New York City Ballet—the quiet, the intensity of concentration by the dancers, the beauty of the movements. Tears came to my eyes. I felt like a fool. Martha, without apparently noticing, looking straight ahead, reached over to hand me some tissues and said, "Here, dear, I think you need this." It was a demonstration of her intuition. She saw that I admired and respected her work.

At this point in her life, Martha had danced the longest (she ended her performing career at seventy-five, in 1969); had composed more than two hundred works; had remained the sole artistic director of her company, founded in 1926 (the oldest continuously performing company in America); had created the most extensive methodology and vocabulary, now taught throughout the world as classic training for modern dance; and had influenced some of the foremost actors of our time through her classes for actors at the Neighborhood Playhouse.

Martha Graham lived a short distance from her school, in an apartment full of small figures and statuettes, symbols of her dances, displayed on several levels of a bookcase. White orchids in clay pots swayed before billowing, transparent curtains. A red, hand-carved wooden Indonesian-type canopy bed was enthroned on a slightly raised platform, as if a piece of scenery for her theatrical atmosphere. Spotlights dramatized a black coromandel screen, inlaid with an Oriental scene, giving her living room a center for the eye.

She wore a purple long-sleeved tunic with matching trousers. A white fur rug covered her legs and hid her arthritic hands. She wore her ornate Navaho wedding necklace and she wanted me to admire it.

When I cast a role, I look for avidity, an eagerness for life, a blood memory in the sense that the dancer remembers and can call upon more of his or her life than has yet been lived. There has to be a hunger and a need in the dancer. Of course, the formal training must be there, but there also has to be courage, a willingness to explore unknown feelings and daring to feel them and let them become part of your being. It's scary. Terrifying. But you do it because you have no choice.

Sometimes a dancer I have chosen is not brave enough to meet the challenge. There is no training for this. The dancer has to be able to respond to the imagery that shapes a movement, to the logic of why a move is from here to there, and must understand the underlying motives and feelings of a character at a given moment.

Some do, some don't. It has always been so. Some respond to a quote or saying on a deeper level and are stimulated to search within themselves. Some listen, but do not hear; some look, but do not see; some understand a character, but never become that character.

There are three things I won't talk about: politics, religion, and sex. I'm interested in human rights, not politics. That's why I did not accept an invitation from Joseph Goebbels [Hitler's propaganda chief] to appear in Germany and why I would not permit my group to perform in South Africa today, if we were asked. As for religion, it's a personal choice. My thoughts are not confined to any one belief system. As for sex, to me it is holy and sacred. I don't discuss it. For these reasons, I have cast and trained dancers from all parts of the world, from all religions, and both sexes equally. It was never a matter of politics, religion, or sex in my doing so.

I still make dances. I don't call myself a choreographer because that's a big, wonderful word that can cover up a lot of sins. I work. That's what I call what I do when I make dances.

Dance has changed and I have changed. We live in a different time, but that is no reason for not reconstructing dances of the past and performing them now. The past is not dead; it is not even past. People live on inner time—the moment in which a decisive thought or feeling takes place and can be at any time. Timeless feelings are common to all of us. A work is dated if it does not speak to us about those timeless feelings. It doesn't matter when the work was done, or when those feelings are experienced. The past can be as fresh as now.

I'm reminded of all the times Miss Ruth [St. Denis] had an idea for a dance, made the costumes, posed for photographs, and then never did the dance. I save all my energy for rehearsing and I don't want to dissipate those ideas by talking about them [new works]. I use my energy for that. The energy of the world is available to all of us. It moves the planets and makes everything work. We can all use it. Only we become frightened or frustrated or too tired to use it. I use it.

I'd like to clear up two points that have troubled me over the years. It disturbs me deeply that some dancers date my technique from the time they learned it and know only one aspect of it. They limit themselves and their own knowledge by not having an overview from the time they studied to the present.

The other point concerns claims that I have or have had codirectors. A long time ago, I decided that my place was front and center. That's where I chose to be, and that's where I remain.

7 ∾ THE NINETIES AND BEYOND

The decade was characterized by noise. Cell phones invaded public places—theaters, restaurants, buses, cars, and planes. People talked loudly into them while walking on the streets. Equipment beeped, rang, banged, or clanged everywhere. Almost every block in New York had a construction site for yet another high-rise building. Martha's 63rd Street home gave way to a high-rise to pay the company's debts. Gloom descended, but eventually a grant provided funds for renovation, placing the school in the basement of the building.

Immigration grew throughout the country, along with an increasing number of tourists in the major cities. Computers provided information, games, entertainment, and isolation.

Step dancing and Irish clogging, along with tap dancing, returned to the stage. Revivals continued to appear on Broadway. In street and theater performances, ethnic groups beat drums, sticks, or gourds.

The Russians, released from travel and immigration restrictions, initiated a second coming to follow their exodus after the Russian Revolution. They settled in Western, Midwestern, and Southern cities—not the usual cultural centers—to teach ballet with or without accreditation from their St. Petersburg or Bolshoi schools.

Van Gogh's *Portrait du Dr. Gachet* fetched $82.5 million at auction. The Contemporary Arts Center in Cincinnati and its director were tried on obscenity charges for exhibiting Robert Mapplethorpe's photography, but a jury acquitted them.

A Chorus Line closed after fifteen years, the longest run in the history of Broadway. The next big hit was the British import *Miss Saigon*.

Rap talk invaded the airwaves with patter, without musical accompaniment, and included subjects such as sex discrimination, abuse, drugs, and violence, all sprinkled with obscenities. First Amendment rights protected its existence.

As the economy heated up, government support for the arts cooled down. Dance became sport; sport became dance; ballet became acrobatic; ice dancing became balletic.

Disney characters in films and videos and theme parks provided new opportunities for dancers to work. The large ballet companies received strong private financial support, and their number of guest artists from foreign companies increased. The number of small American dance companies also increased, crowding May and October calendars—the most popular months for reviews—to an unprecedented level. Competitions at home and abroad encouraged young dancers with offers of scholarships, cash, and apprentice jobs in the major companies.

Martha Graham created her last works: *Maple Leaf Rag* (1990) and *Eyes of the Goddess* (1991). In 1991 she died of pneumonia. Since then, ownership of her works has been a subject of legal debate.

Robert Fitzgerald

Robert Fitzgerald has been a dance therapist to members of the Martha Graham Contemporary Dance Company, American Ballet Theatre, Broadway musical performers, and Martha Graham.

I had taken modern dance at Kansas State College with Jacqueline Van Gaasbeek for a phys ed credit. She was a frustrated dancer who came to New York regularly to take the intensive course in teacher training at the Graham center. The dance club at the college gave me a scholarship to go to the American Dance Festival in New London, Connecticut. There I had my first encounter with Martha, who taught for the first two weeks at the festival. Everyone was terrified of her and I stayed in the back row in the class. As we left the studio and passed her at the door, most of us left quickly. But one day she stopped me and asked, "Who are you? I like the way you use your feet." The next day she put me in the front row. When she left, Robert Cohan taught us for the rest of the summer. And because he said nothing to me, I couldn't decide if I was good, bad, awful, or hopeless. Martha came back for the last week and offered me a scholarship if I would come to New York.

In New York, for some reason, Martha and I would end up after class sitting on that nasty little bench outside Studio One. She talked and I listened. She would start sitting very straight and as she became involved in what she was saying, her back would start to round. Suddenly I would see this flash or spark in those black eyes and she would pull herself up ramrod straight. It was astounding to see how she would fight to keep her body awake, alive, alert, and functioning.

Our talks were basically her explaining to me that one had to take all the steps in her dance ladder sequentially, without jumping from the first to the sixth step. I had started to perform in works by her former dancers who were choreographing, and I didn't have the time to be her acolyte for eight to ten years, doing the sequence up the ladder, hoping that I would be taken into the company. Touring interrupted my study so that I couldn't maintain the discipline. The loss foreshortened my career. Martha was right about following the sequence of training, but for me it was not possible.

After performing for a while, I was offered a choice of a three-month tour in South America or an audition for the leading dance role in the City Center revival of the Broadway show *Can Can*. I was broke and the South American tour looked like a better move, although the City Center role would have been better for my career. As luck would have it, the South American tour fell through and the dance career was lost. So I became an assistant to a Pilates-based therapist and eventually went on my own. Since the Pilates technique is based upon the pelvis as the controlling factor—as is the Graham technique, pelvis and breath—it was a natural choice for me.

There was a gap of contact with Martha until about 1968, when Bertram Ross called me. Bertram said that Martha was in bad shape and needed to get back on stage. She could hardly stand up, had no strength, and had to perform. She came to my studio and I worked with her privately. She said, "Just treat me like anybody else," which was, of course, impossible.

We did a mat work warm-up, développés lying flat, used ankle weights, worked on the apparatus doing pliés, and I found that she could do a great deal. She could do a battement [high kick] that would hit her shoulder. She had that capacity to the day she died. She had a naturally flexible body. She could use her feet like an inchworm, they were so flexible and beautiful in the instep, although arthritic in the toes. There is no doubt that she was physically gifted and used her technique carefully—she had once hurt her knee as a result of being dropped—but it was her spirit that amazed everyone. I had the feeling that she had discovered, at an early point, that she had an incredible and unlimited range of movement and that she had to find something to do with it.

Then there was the day when I had to explain to her that she had to contract to do an exercise. The words stuck in my throat. Was I going to explain to the creator of a methodology based upon the contraction how to do a contraction?! She laughed with me.

She came for sessions with me three times a week, beginning with thirty minutes of work because she was weak, but eventually stayed a full ninety minutes. For me, it was such a treat to give back to someone who had given me so much.

Her last season, there were really only three steps she could do: throw her leg up past her shoulder, bourées [tiny moving steps], and a split fall forward, with help getting up. But you couldn't take your eyes off her! At seventy-five, she still had such power. Her last performance was in *The Lady of the House of Sleep,* in 1968.

When she was in her nineties, I always saw her, in my mind's eye, as she was when I first met her. But she was, near the end, an old woman struggling to make her body do things it could no longer do. I could see the visible frustration of her mind. She knew what to do and how to do it but was no longer being able to command her body to do what she loved best in the world, to dance. There would be tears in her eyes, and I found it heartbreaking. She kept making valiant efforts, but the machinery wasn't there any longer.

Her sessions were sporadic after a while and limited to the beginning of a season, when she would phone me and say, "I have to be able to stand up and take a bow. My legs are weak." Then she would work during her sessions with me and appear at the last bow with two strong male dancers at her side, who had just lifted her from her wheelchair when the curtain was down and who stood beside her as she bowed on stage. Her spot to watch the performances was on stage right in her wheelchair. The dancers said she would frequently fly out of that chair during rehearsals and do phenomenal things, as if she were not confined to it. Then she would sit down again.

Martha was a performer first and an amoral person. She did exactly what she wanted to do, when she wanted to do it, without any thought about rules or cultural conventions, in order to produce what she produced. It gave her freedom from guilt. There were no victims. People came to get something from her, and they took what they could or wanted. It was not her responsibility.

Susan Kikuchi
(as restager)

Panorama was re-created after Martha died and was very well received. It had been performed at Bennington College in 1935. Those who followed and believed in Martha used their own creative ability to piece together, recompose, and reconstruct from those film clips and photos a spirit of the piece. It was not the original to the step or a replication. There was no record. Those works bear the creative signature of the artists who were dedicated to and who worked with Martha. Until her death, Martha Graham gave her seal of approval to those pieces. After death, they were done for Martha with love.

In 1998 the longtime site of the school, on East 63rd Street in Manhattan, was sold to pay off a deficit. Plans to move the headquarters to a new building erected on the same site were canceled because the company was unable to raise the money necessary to convert the raw space into studios and offices. Nor was there enough money to pay rent elsewhere. Legal complications of every kind seemed to descend upon the entire organization. Students, teachers, accompanists, and office personnel were in tears, angered, and disheartened.

On May 25, 2000, the Martha Graham Dance Company pulled out of two major festivals, the American Dance Festival in Durham, North Carolina, and the Kennedy Center in Washington, D.C., and suspended operations because of financial problems. The board of the Martha Graham Center of Contemporary Dance, the umbrella organization for the company, school, and junior group, announced that operations would be suspended for the foreseeable future.

However, Graham's legacy had a tiny stronghold at the Peridance studio in lower Manhattan, where Yuriko was giving classes independent of the school. There I organized a Graham-based program for foreign students on visas, summer students, and certificate students abandoned by the Graham school's closure. I enlisted teachers from the school and former company members of the Graham family: Marnie Thomas, Ethel Winter, Dudley Williams, Jeanne Ruddy, Armgard von Bardeleben, Donlin Foreman, Joyce Herring, Steve Rooks, Susan McGuire, Linda Hodes, Jacqulyn Buglisi, Pearl Lang, Yuriko, and myself, as well as current members of the Martha Graham Dance Company.

By some quirk of fate, I was videotaping Yuriko's class at Peridance when we heard the announcement that the school, company, and ensemble operations were closed as of May 25, 2000. After class, Igal Perry, the director of the Peridance Studio, who had studied Graham technique and had been in the Bat-Dor Dance Company in Israel, asked my mother and me to come to his office. For several years, my mother had been declining his offer to create a modern Graham-based department at Peridance because of her teaching schedule and freelance work for other companies out of town. But here was an opportunity to help the dance community with classes, first offered as a summer workshop, on three levels of technique.

So, in June, we started the program to give the students of the dance world another place to study the technique. Company members were allowed to take class free of tuition. They were also able to earn some money by teaching classes at Peridance. We called it a Graham-based program since we are not the official school. My calls were answered with enthusiasm, and the roster of teachers, dancers, and accompanists represented a wide spectrum of generations from early days to the present. The program continued through the summer, fall, and winter with an eye to the future.

Yuriko and I then set off to stage *Appalachian Spring* for the Joffrey Ballet of Chicago.

Note: A state grant was made to renovate the basement of the new building on the old site at 63rd Street to make the school operational in 2001.

Takako Asakawa

(as restager)

Takako Asakawa was in the Graham company from 1962 to 1990. She was asked to restage *Diversion of Angels* for American Ballet Theatre in the spring of 2000.

I was born in Japan and came to the United States in 1962. I had studied dance in Tokyo from childhood. Then as a teenager, I started teaching younger students. When the Graham company came to Japan, I was overwhelmed with the performance. I knew then that I wanted to dance like that someday. So, in spite of my parents' objection, I came to New York. My father said to me, "If you go to New York, you are no longer my daughter." But I was determined. I convinced them to let me go by promising that I would return within one year.

Soon after starting to study at the Martha Graham school, I became aware that her style was very similar to my Oriental background—the use of the ground, the pull of gravity, and use of the upper back, as well as the yogalike breathing—and the connection of all these things made her technique easy for me to understand.

I had been studying for one month when an announcement was made that there would be an audition held for scholarships. When I went to the audition, I was first because the lineup was alphabetical. So I had no one to go before me that I could watch. I had to do the steps as described in English, which I couldn't understand. It was a disaster! But somehow, I received a scholarship. Two months after that, I was asked to join the company. I was so determined to do well, I took three classes a day and watched as many rehearsals as I could. Martha commented, "You work too hard. You are going to hurt yourself." But I didn't feel, at that time, that it was too much work. I was so eager and had so much energy.

It was a very difficult time for me. I had very little money and I could feel strong resistance from the other dancers, who were not doing as well. I called my mother. She said, "Why are you there?" I answered, "I want to dance." The answer seemed to be so simple. I would put up with anything in order to dance and learn that technique.

On one of the early tours, I asked Ethel Winters if I could room with her. She accepted. This lifted my spirits and things became a bit easier. Three months later, we were touring Japan and my parents came to see me dance. They were very proud of me but did not know what to say. My mother just held my hand and I knew everything was forgiven. My return to Japan was not discussed again.

When we assumed one of Martha's roles, she would give us total freedom to discover our own values within the character. She seemed to be so secure emotionally that she was not threatened by someone else. If she liked what we did, we could keep it within the role. If not, it would be removed without explanation. There were times when I would question my work and would ask for her help. Then she would say, "Just do it," and this somehow would help me find what I was looking for and prove it acceptable for both of us.

My favorite roles were Medea in *Cave of the Heart,* St. Joan in *Seraphic Dialogue,* the Red Girl in *Diversion of Angels,* and just the sheer joy of dancing in *Every Soul Is a Circus.* Once after a performance as Medea, I couldn't get out of the character and return to myself. The role is so demanding. I felt consumed after the performance and couldn't shake it off.

For American Ballet Theatre, I mounted *Diversion of Angels* for their spring 2000 season at City Center. The dancers were so eager to learn something new, they wore me out with their enthusiasm.

When I was asked to mount *Diversion of Angels,* I hesitated because of an unpleasant memory I had experienced with the Paris Opéra Ballet when I staged *Temptations of the Moon* for them. Martha's choreography is based more on phrases than on strict musical measures. And even more on a free form, especially in that work. They screamed and cried. We went around and around. And finally I went to the director and explained the problem and declared the situation insane. "We are fighting history and strong tradition here," I said. The performance was not that good, even though it received a warm response from the audience.

After accepting ABT's request, I found their dancers to be exactly the opposite. Their attitude was very open and accepting and they seemed more mature. Not all of them, of course, but the majority wanted to expand their knowledge by learning something new.

Young dancers today seem to have very little patience and time. Unfortunately, artistry does not arrive quickly. Martha's work and her technique cannot be performed without a long-term emotional commitment.

ABT's artistic director, Kevin McKenzie, helped me with the first step, which was casting the roles. Some of the dancers had prior experience in modern dance. But the first rehearsals for the work were during their performance season and they came to my sessions quite tired. My first request was for them to remove their shoes. That is not instantly accepted by ballet dancers. But soon after we started, they became very enthusiastic and would constantly ask me to show them this step and that exercise to the point that I was very soon as exhausted as they were.

They also found it uncomfortable to work on their knees, to fall backward, and to sit on the side of the hip, or anything that required working on the ground. After one week, however, they began to understand and were encouraged. Martha's advice to me—"Just do it!"—seemed to be helpful to them also. I felt that what I was giving them was an entirely new vocabulary. So I began by showing them a film of *Diversion of Angels* and patiently explained each movement over and over again. I didn't have enough rehearsal time to ground them—one of my challenges when I teach floor work. More rehearsal time would have helped.

The classes started from the basics: how to sit, how to fall, how to get up. It all sounds so simple. But it must be done within the technique, using all the muscles and with concentration and an understanding of the mechanics involved. The technique is important, but without the ability to project feelings the performance is empty.

While Martha had physical gifts and a well-developed technique, she had also developed her soul. To excel as a dancer requires sacrifice and dedication. So many dancers today make only meaningless movement without communicating anything.

If I were starting again, I would follow the same path as in the past and would continue to follow the learning-discovering-growing-living-and-loving pattern that I have followed all my life. Then, ultimately pass on what I know best.

The American Ballet Studio Performance Company, ABT II, has begun classes in Martha's technique. I am pleased to be teaching that.

Yuriko

(as restager)

Yuriko Kikuchi staged *Appalachian Spring* for the Boston Conservatory and the Joffrey Ballet of Chicago in September 2000.

Staging a modern dance work with the Joffrey ballet dancers had some advantages: they have trained bodies (which must be rehearsed to move a different way, although some may have had some modern dance training); there are members of a company who have performed some modern dance works;

the dancers are young adults who are eager to attempt a new kind of movement to add to their repertoire.

I was anxious that they do well and gave them daily and minute by minute all the information they needed to perform a solid and good interpretation of the work. I had seen one of their performances and found them youthful-minded, uncontaminated, and eager. By watching a performance and their class work, I was able to cast the eight roles and understudies. The artistic director of the company, Gerald Arpino, approved of the casting.

There was no time to teach classes. I had only twenty-five hours to teach the choreography, another five days (twenty-five hours) to polish the steps, with no more time available, except for one run-through with notes for the dancers. Here and there we had special rehearsals for the principals and the group of Followers, a total, at most, of ten hours for two more weeks. The work is thirty minutes long.

The company had notes from me in advance describing each entrance, the dances, and other points of importance. The cast saw a video of a performance of the work that I had staged earlier for the Boston Conservatory and a video of the Graham company performing the same work. The roles are single characters, with solos and interaction with other characters, which takes individual time to teach. This may seem like a good deal of time for staging, but it was actually a very tight schedule. My daughter, Susan, assisted me.

The group had their daily class before rehearsals and were ready to go. First, they were taught the steps and observed the music for exactness. Clues to the characters are in the steps and the quality of each dance. They must see that.

I emphasized that they must learn, learn, learn every minute movement, rhythm, and pattern on the stage and know their relationship to each other. At the same time as I rehearsed one group, another group was in another studio learning from the video. So it was a constant matter of moving the two casts around to use every moment of time, with at least two rehearsals going on at all times. The solos for the Preacher, the Husband, Bride, Pioneer Woman, and the four Followers were rehearsed and their interaction with each other. In about three days, the piece was put together, but it was by no means ready.

The advantage that I have in having been in Martha's company and knowing what she wanted brought an immediacy to her works. I could explain what happens, not only in the work, but what was happening in Martha's life when she created the dance. Thus the work was no longer in the past; it became the present.

I described the locale, a strict Quaker community in Pennsylvania, where the action takes place. I described the landscape, so that when the characters looked out to the distance, they could imagine the beauty of nature, their dreams for the future, and renew their resolve and strong commitment to them. An event is about to take place and they must all bring expectation and hope to the stage. The Pioneer Woman is an older, experienced woman who has courage, is stoic, steadfast, strong, and has the ability to cope with any emergency. She has hopes for the couple, but knows that there might be hardships ahead, but that they can be overcome, as she has overcome them. May O'Donnell was the first Pioneer Woman in Martha's work and was perfectly cast. Martha told me the role was patterned after a relative, who was beautiful and silent.

The Bride is full of happiness as well as concern. This ballet was choreographed when Martha was getting ready to marry Erick Hawkins. There are questions in her mind, as there were in Martha's at that time. She was concerned about her career, her independence, but at the same time she wanted this marriage. There are moments in her solo that indicate her questioning the wisdom of what she is doing, of conflict, and of joy. But she loves him. It's a role that goes from youthful anticipation, to questioning herself and the marriage, to a maturing and calm acceptance. The role is rich with movements and subtext. I remember sitting on the bench as one of the Followers, watching Martha do this role. She was never on a beat, but on a phrase, and she would change every performance as the unraveling of the role required in that particular performance. In a kick, for instance, it would have been a positive movement to be on the beat, but she was a character who was not positive but questioning. Her facial expression asked herself, What am I doing? Is this the right move to make in my life? In the short dance with the Husband, I told the Joffrey Bride, "I don't care what your understanding is, you must follow him in that duet. That indicates your commitment to him." Finally, the Bride settles into a private moment by going into the house.

The Husband is a manly, strong, confident character, who looks out over the land as he stands by a railing, ready to accept responsibility and to build his future. He is the he-man in the group. This was Erick's offstage personality as well.

The Preacher is often played as an amusing character, but he is not. He warns all of the consequence of fire and brimstone for those who stray from the path. He is not without ego, and his four young Followers obviously worship him without question. The strictness of the Quaker teaching permits their fascination with him to be expressed only in religious fervor. He's the boss, and sometimes playful without being playful. He gives approval and manipulates everyone. Merce Cunningham, who danced the role originally, was a deep person who played the Preacher as a cool, almost cruel, and powerful authority figure. He walked with a stride. The role is often misinterpreted.

I enjoyed being one of the Followers when I first joined the company and was sorry to give up the role. The four girls must work in perfect unison, as they bring a light touch to the scene and surround the Preacher with lively, quick movements. They are like a bunch of chicks, with twittering movements, absolute devotion, and in awe of the Preacher.

Every dancer has to make a journey from the beginning to the end as the work plays out. I give them the original intention of each role, because that is the way Martha choreographed. But each dancer will have to create a personal story, individual but interacting with the other characters. Imitation is not acceptable; individual creativity on the basis of understanding the intention of the movement and its content is the goal each time a Graham work is re-created.

Appalachian Spring became the signature piece of the Graham company and is one of Martha's masterworks. It will be interesting for me to see how these adult, professional dancers, who have never seen the original company perform, will interpret her work. And how it will develop as they continue to perform it. They were given the freedom to create the role, a rare thing for a performer. And they saw Martha's process.

The last thing I said to them was, "I gave you everything that I know and have taught you and guided you. Now I can't wait to sit out there and enjoy what you're doing!"

Bertram Ross

Partnering Martha

Bertram Ross, because of his strong technique and dramatic power, was Graham's partner from 1949 to 1973, and an active participant in contributing to the male roles in her works.

Martha often said that she could not make roles for men because men were too different from women, and she could not portray them accurately. She saw "the other creature" as physically strong, a power symbol, tyrant, messenger, or seer. That gave more leeway to the men in her company to make contributions than it gave her women dancers.

Martha's characters paralleled her relationships with men in her real life: after loving a man in *Appalachian Spring;* uniting with him in *Dark Meadow,* and finding him loathsome in *Cave of the Heart,* she mothered him in *Night Journey.* But typical of Martha and her life-affirming philosophy, she followed that period of angst by portraying loving couples in *Diversion of Angels.*

I saw Martha dance in the late 1940s in *Letter to the World.* I had never seen anything like it. I can still see it in my memory. It was enchanting and heartbreaking at the same time. The music was by a live quintet of musicians, the same as when we went on tour and before tape was used. Clarinet, oboe, piccolo, drums, piano—that was it. Martha was the easiest person to partner I ever knew because she was so strong and we were so attuned to each other's phrasing. Our partnering was as much intuitive as mutually knowing the choreography. Martha was not above improvising on occasion and I had to be there, ready for whatever may come. That gave our work a spontaneity that implied risk, not physical risk, but the excitement of emotional renewal that was fresh each time we performed the same roles.

I remember that she had a torn cartilage in her knee before we went on tour to Europe in 1950. It was the only injury that I believe she ever had, and it was exacerbated on tour. I doubt that the rumor that Erick [Hawkins] dropped her on purpose during a performance was true. She "marked" [indicated the movements] at every rehearsal, which was very unlike her.

After opening night in Paris, Martha's knee swelled and she was unable to dance. She refused surgery. The audience wanted to see Martha perform, and a London engagement had to be canceled. After the tour, Martha went home to Santa Fe and used weights to rehabilitate herself physically and to heal emotionally. Erick had left; Horst had gone back to San Francisco, in disagreement over Hawkins's management of the company, so Martha was alone and injured.

When Erick left Martha, she asked José Limón if he would be interested in dancing with her company. She was afraid to do anything embarrassing, such as having a man who was much too young to partner her. She also offered the same opportunity to John Butler. Neither one was willing to accept such a responsibility.

Martha made an appointment with me and we met at Harlow's Drugstore, on Fifth Avenue between 12th and 13th Streets. [Martha's studio in those days was located at 66 Fifth Avenue.] We had her favorite energy drink—orange juice, raw egg, and ice cream whipped together. She took me into her confidence and discussed her problem in finding a satisfactory partner to assume Erick's roles. She was in a quandary: she didn't want to do anything that was tasteless. And if she had a partner who seemed too young, the results could be disastrous. She told me she felt that I was the most theatrical of the young male dancers in the company and believed I could handle the intricacies of the role of Oedipus. As we sat there, I realized that she wanted a sympathetic ear. "I don't want to do anything embarrassing," she said, referring to being an older woman herself and being an older woman in the role. "But that's the subject of the work," I told her. "We can make it work."

Then she asked me if I would be willing to work with her secretly, learn the Love Duet between Jocasta and Oedipus [her son], and then show it to a trusted member of the company.

One day John Butler began discussing with me Martha's offer to him, which he had turned down: "She's too powerful. She'll destroy any male who plays opposite her." I gulped and replied timorously, "I don't have to worry about that." John didn't know that I'd been rehearsing with Martha.

Came the day of our tryout, Martha and I asked Yuriko Kikuchi to watch us in the Love Duet from *Night Journey* (1947). When Martha and I finished, Yuriko burst into tears. She said she just couldn't believe it: the transformation of her student Bertram Ross into the artist! With enthusiasm she said, "Oh, Martha, now the doors have reopened. You can do all the roles you've wanted to do: *Cave of the Heart, Errand into the Maze,* and Bert would be wonderful in *Every Soul Is a Circus.*

Later I realized that the story, based upon the Oedipus legend of a sexual relationship between a mother and her son, was a reflection of her personal pain in her relationship with Erick, who was young enough to be her son.

At rehearsals of *Night Journey,* she did not like demonstrating for a man because she did not have a man's body—she gave me directions verbally. She said, "Let's talk a bit and see what we have." We experimented with a long scarf that I threw between my legs and over my shoulder. It became a cape, then a symbol of power and a drape of mourning. The lifts turned out to be dead-weight lifts, precarious and an indication of her trust in me. One lift began with a high kick from Martha and a support only from the cup of my hand as she did a back fall. She had enough energy to supplant the usual jumps into a lift and raise her own body to a great extent. It was all in our timing.

David Wood

Creating Movements for Men

David Wood was a member of the Martha Graham company from 1953 to 1967 and acted as rehearsal director as well. He began his career as a performer in Broadway musicals, and the New York City Opera and Metropolitan Opera companies. He also performed with Hanya Holm, Doris Humphrey, José Limón, Charles Weidman, and Alwin Nikolais.

Wood taught for Holm and Weidman at the American Dance Festival at Connecticut College, the High School for the Performing Arts in New York City, as well as in Sweden, in Vera Cruz, Mexico, at Maurice Béjart's Mudra in Brussels, and in Jerusalem, Japan, and Norway. As a choreographer, Wood created works for summer stock, musicals, his own company, and a PBS program. He has been the recipient of NEA fellowships in 1973 and 1979. Wood received a distinguished-teacher award from the University of California at Berkeley.

The technique, the performance, and the choreography of Martha Graham are closely interwoven. The only time I ever heard Martha speak of choreographing for men was at a press conference when she said, "I'm not a man, I've never been a man, and I have no intention of ever being a man. I first suggest, and then I alter, change, and shape the movement that occurs in order to arrive at male choreography." An example of how this happened is when Martha choreographed the Messenger of Death on me in *Clytemnestra* (1958). She spent a month developing the concept and then gave me a pole and a musician and sent me upstairs to work on the movement by myself. After two days, I presented her with what I thought was a marvelous finished product. She looked at it, sighed and began to cut, change, suggest, add, and demand what she wanted. My movement was merely a catalyst that set off her imagination. What she created was totally her own product.

When I first learned the technique, it was said that it was not really good for men. The reason given was that a woman had created it. This made as much sense to me as a statement that ballet should only be done by males because Louis XIV was one of the first performers and protagonists of this art form.

The fact that Graham's work was at first done by women was a factor in this statement. But it did not take into account that the floor work, in particular, challenged the male dancer and was extremely beneficial in expanding the range of motion in the pelvic area while, at the same time, teaching many different qualities of movement.

With the advent of males as members of the company, the technique broadened in scope, but did not basically change. Erick Hawkins's appearance in *American Document* (1938) added weight and strength to the movement it had not had before. Then Merce Cunningham in *Every Soul Is a Circus* (1939), *Letter to the World* (1940), and *El Penitente* (1940) added another dimension in elevation and utilized a certain square approach to movement for men that Martha developed at that time.

Letter to the World used the first male group in a Graham work, but Martha did not greatly alter or make changes to her technique for the sake of male movement. Within some variation, the party scene—the main dance for both males and females—kept the relationship of the sexes, but more by the relationship itself than by the movement.

In *Deaths and Entrances* (1943), the male became more conceptual, with the men's dance and the fight between the Poetic Beloved and the Dark Beloved characters. In *Dark Meadow* (1946), in the sarabande, the men began to support the women, and the very first lifts—simple but beautiful—were done. In the fetish dance, the man became a distinct sexual being.

In *Diversion of Angels* (1948), Martha choreographed two distinct male and female groups. Within one context of lyrical young love, the men and women moved clearly and distinctly in their own works, using their own particular unique strengths. Now and then, the two groups merged their energies to become unified. The sexuality of the White, Red, and Yellow Couples was more clearly discernible against the background of group conformity. I always felt the group movement itself could easily be reversed, because it fit structurally both the male and female bodies. But, here again, the intent was made clear within the sexual relationship rather than the movement.

Phaedra (1962) showed the peak development during this period of male athleticism with the creation of the Bull Dancers. The men's entrance, with the leap and sit to the floor, actually ended with one man diving into the thighs of the other. This sheer physical exuberance opened the door for later acrobatics and athleticism. However, at a later point, when I saw the company on tour, half of the men were replaced by women in this dance, which was a historically accurate thing to do. The women did the movements successfully.

With the arrival of males in the company, there came some new movements: In *Diversion of Angels,* the Bison jumps cut into the air (however, these movements were also performed very fast, dartingly, and brilliantly by Helen McGehee); in *Letter to the World* (1940), the march jumps were introduced by Merce Cunningham (however, in *Night Journey* the women's contraction jumps were basically the same, only more difficult and more powerful); the contraction leaps are brilliantly performed by men (but consider the weighted leaps in *Primitive Mysteries* done by the women—they are powerful and beautiful); in the beginning of *Ardent Song* (1954), the curtain rose with the men on one side and the women on the other side of Yuriko as both groups began the same movement (in the rest of the dance, male and female groups developed separately, but in the beginning, the two sections were one and split apart only later).

The main change brought about by the introduction of male athleticism was the expansion of the movement vocabulary. The inner landscape expanded as the cyclical action began to include the outer landscape. There were never any absolute limits as to which movements were male and which were female, except in class. There, a difference was made for the movement, because a slower pace was given hopefully for the achievement of higher elevation by the men. In class there was always some interchange of quality rather than a development of sexual stereotypes. Robert Powell's extensions were the envy of many a woman; Dudley Williams's fast lightness and Bob Cohan's beautiful lyricism were in evidence.

On the other hand, who could fail to remember the marvelous female power of Pearl Lang as the Seductress Death in *Canticle for Innocent Comedians* (1952) or even more so, all the power of Martha in so many roles, but especially as she did the knee crawls along the red cloth, enticing Agamemnon to his death in *Clytemnestra* (1958).

Male athleticism did affect the expansion and the explosive strength of the technique. But the marvel was that there were no limits placed upon an individual because of his or her sex, but rather the focal point was on the unique projection of the individual as a human being. This development then proceeded to the ultimate, powerful use of the individual by Martha as male or female in its dimension to create her later choreographic complexities.

8 ⟲ EMBATTLED GRAHAM, 2001

In the aftermath of the sale of the East 63rd Street site to a developer to pay Graham's debts, lack of funds to pay the company dancers for the summer of 2000, engagements at the American Dance Festival in North Carolina and the Kennedy Center in Washington, D.C., and the closing of the school led the teachers and dancers to despair and anger. The possibility that the end of the Martha Graham Dance Company and the Martha Graham School of Contemporary Dance might be at hand disturbed the entire dance profession.

Yuriko, who taught the technique at the Peridance studio, when she was between engagements restaging works, and daughter Susan Kikuchi, expanded the classes to include Graham teachers in order not to disappoint foreign summer students and to maintain continuity of the Graham methodology, then called "Graham-based" because of trademark restrictions.

Temporary rented space for classes was also found by the Martha Graham Center, the umbrella organization that consists of a board for Graham activities, at a studio on West 26th Street. Meanwhile, a $75,000 renovation (financed by a State of New York grant negotiated by the trustees of the center) progressed at the East 63rd Street site. The future school will be housed in the basement of the high-rise building that now occupies that site.

The seventy-five-year-old Martha Graham School of Contemporary Dance moved to the 26th Street temporary studio in January 2000 and opened under the direction of Stuart Hodes. A faculty was formed of former Graham stars to teach and once again offer auditions for the Professional Trainee/Certificate Program.

But after the school reopened in January, a bitter legal struggle between the Martha Graham Trust and the Martha Graham Contemporary Dance Center erupted over which owned the rights to Martha's dances and the use of the trademarked words *Graham technique*.

Ron Protas, a long-time "friend" (as designated in Graham's 1989 will), former photographer, and her companion for twenty years, filed suit in Federal Court for the Southern District of New York, claiming that the school did not have the right to use the Graham name without obtaining a license from the Martha Graham Trust, which he directs. Protas, who never danced, became artistic director of the company after Martha's death. It was a turbulent time of firings and painful defections and increasing debts. He had arrived on the scene about 1969, when Martha was seventy-four, and saw her through a bout of alcoholism. He prevented her from going into a fatal coma by walking her all night up and down hospital corridors. She went back to work.

At the reopening of the school, in January 2000, Protas announced the establishment of a Martha Graham School and Dance Foundation, whose plans, he said, included licensing Graham ballets to schools for $1 per year. Protas claims his right to Graham's works stems from her will, which made him executor and principal beneficiary of her estate. Protas gained the right to her personal effects, 180 dance works, musical scores, scenery sets, personal papers, and the use of her name, with the will's request that he consult with other of her friends over the use of those rights and interests.

He proposed that the school and dance company split into separate legal entities and that he control the school and attempt to affiliate it with an academic institution in the city. The center would not be allowed to use Graham's name and would have the same licensing agreement that required payment of a fee for the rights to her dances for a set period and for the services of a restager chosen by Protas, as any other dance company would have. The assumption that Protas was sole owner and dispenser of the rights to Graham's estate, and could stop the center and school from using the name Martha Graham or Graham Technique, set off a bitter legal battle.

For the next few weeks, the testimony from both sides, before Federal Judge Miriam Goldman Cedarbaum, played like a television drama, with members of the Graham company and students listening and watching. Then an expected witness appeared for the center, one of the many professionals who provide free or discounted services to the support of the arts—accountant Rubin Gorewitz, who had assisted Graham in a tax burden forty-five years ago and convinced her to sell her school to a new not-for-profit Martha Graham School, giving it exclusive educational rights to her name. Graham, therefore, became an employed choreographer and teacher, as found in evidence of the 1956 application for tax-exempt status. Although the application was unsigned, Graham was still owed the purchase price, in the 1960s, for her sale of the school, and her agreement that no other school or company use her name also granted theatrical properties, including original Noguchi sets and costumes, to the exempt organization. Choreographers such as Graham and Balanchine were hired by exempt organizations to compose works for them. Such works may or may not be owned by those organizations. (Copyright issues of all choreography rights will be influenced by the decision of the court in this case.)

Where does this leave Protas? Perhaps guilty of fraud in selling Noguchi's sets, trademarking Martha's name, and licensing dances that did not belong to him based on the will, because he withheld answers to questions by his counsel, which led to material misrepresentations to the patent office on their ownership. At this point, the judge has ruled that the words *Graham technique* are no longer under trademark and Martha's works can be reconstructed by the Martha Graham Contemporary Dance Company.

Most Graham dancers and teachers feel that Martha would have delighted in these conflicts and would be laughing over the turmoil.

1. Martha Graham, 1920s, showing her use of cupped hands. Photo by Soichi Sunami. New York Public Library.

2. Martha Graham, East Indian dance, 1920s, showing her strong and flexible feet. Photo by Soichi Sunami. New York Public Library.

3. Michio Ito, famous Japanese dancer who was an influence on Graham's work, 1925. Private collection.

4. Graham in long white dress teaching the first classes at the Neighborhood
Playhouse, 1928. Courtesy of Neighborhood Playhouse.

5. Louis Horst composition class with three students, at the Neighborhood Playhouse, 1930. Left: Anna Sokolow. Courtesy of Neighborhood Playhouse.

6. Anna Sokolow and Anita Alvarez, informally posed, 1931. Sokolow collection.

7. *Primitive Mysteries*, 1931. Back row, Gertrude Shurr, Marie Marchowsky, unidentified third dancer; center, Martha Graham, in white; front row, Anna Sokolow, Anita Alvarez, unidentified third dancer. Photo by Soichi Sunami. Courtesy of Gertrude Shurr.

8. Sophie Maslow and Martha Graham in *Primitive Mysteries*, 1931.
Courtesy of Sophie Maslow.

9. Elizabeth Bloomer (Betty Ford), right, dancing with three other women, 1938. Courtesy of Gerald R. Ford Library.

10. Elizabeth Bloomer (Betty Ford), second from right, in performance, 1938. Courtesy of Gerald R. Ford Library.

11. Tony Randall (center), Eli Wallach (second from left), students at the
Neighborhood Playhouse, 1938. Courtesy of Neighborhood Playhouse.

12. May O'Donnell, standing, with Martha Graham, in *Cave of the Heart*, 1940s. Courtesy of May O'Donnell.

13. May O'Donnell with Erick Hawkins in *Dark Meadow*, 1940s. Courtesy of
May O'Donnell.

14. Martha Graham, Jane Dudley, and Sophie Maslow in *Letter to the World*, 1940s. Courtesy of Sophie Maslow.

15. Martha Graham and John Butler at Connecticut College American Dance Festival, 1940s. Butler collection.

16. Erick Hawkins, Graham, and John Butler in *Deaths and Entrances,* 1943.
Photo by Chris Alexander. Butler collection.

17. *Appalachian Spring*, original cast, 1944. Above, Merce Cunningham; May
O'Donnell, Erick Hawkins, Martha Graham. Photo by Chris Alexander.
O'Donnell collection.

18. Pearl Lang in *Diversion of Angels*, original costume, 1948. Photo by Chris Alexander. Lang collection.

19. Bertram Ross as Oedipus in *Night Journey*, 1940s. Photo by Zachary Freyman.

20. Yuriko with Bertram Ross, Moon section, *Canticle for Innocent Comedians*, 1950s. Photo by Lipnitski, Paris. Ross collection.

21. Yuriko with Glen Tetley (above), Matt Turney, and Bertram Ross in *Embattled Garden*, 1958. Ross collection.

22. Yuriko in *Seraphic Dialogue*, 1950s. Courtesy of Yuriko.

23. Yuriko in *Embattled Garden* (revival), 1950s. Courtesy of Yuriko.

24. Martha Graham company on tour, posed before the Taj Mahal, 1955. Left to right, Stuart Hodes (third from left); Linda Hodes, David Wood, Bethsabee de Rothschild, Robert Cohan, William Marlott (company manager), Martha Graham, Bertram Ross, Donald McKayle, Charles Hyman (stage manager), Matt Turney, Paul Taylor, Ellen van de Hoeven, Alfonso Imana (assistant stage manager), Jessica Golfer (secretary), musician, and two transportation persons. Seated, third from left, Helen McGehee, Ethel Winter. Courtesy of Ethel Winter, personal collection.

25. Marnie Thomas in informal pose, 2000. Marnie Thomas, personal collection.

26. Helen McGehee in revival of *Clytemnestra*, 1966. Courtesy of Helen McGehee.

27. Linda Hodes, studio rehearsal in Israel, 1960s. Photo by Oleaga.

28. Linda Hodes in *Hérodiade*, 1960s. Personal collection.

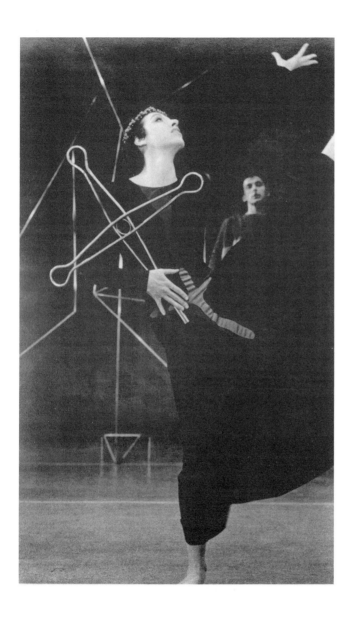

29. Linda Hodes in *Seraphic Dialogue*, 1960s. Personal collection.

30. Linda Hodes with Robert Cohan in *Phaedra*, 1964. Personal collection.

31. Dudley Williams, 1960s. Photo by Kenn Duncan. Courtesy of Alvin Ailey American Dance Theater.

32. Tim Wengert in *Night Journey*, 1960. Photo by Max Waldman. Courtesy of Hannie Gillman.

33. Tim Wengert and Mario Delamo in *Phaedra,* 1960s. Photo by Max
Waldman. Courtesy of Hannie Gillman.

34. Janet Eilber as Cassandra in *Clytemnestra*, 1962. Photo by Max Waldman. Courtesy of Hannie Gillman.

35. Tim Wengard and Peggy Lyman in *Phaedra*, 1960s. Photo by Max Waldman. Courtesy of Hannie Gillman.

36. Joyce Herring in *Night Journey,* 1970s. Herring collection.

37. Peter Sparling in an unidentified dance, 1970s. Photo by Frank Richards. Courtesy of Peter Sparling.

38. Informal photo of Mikhail Baryshnikov, Martha Graham, Rudolf Nureyev, and Maya Plitsetskaya, 1970s. Photo by Vladimir Sladon.

39. Jacqulyn Buglisi and Donlin Foreman in *Tangled Night*, 1986. Foreman collection.

40. Donlin Foreman and Peggy Lyman in *Judith*, 1970s. Foreman collection.

41. Susan Kikuchi (second from left), with Sharon Tylers, Jeanne Ruddy, and Christine Dakin in *Appalachian Spring,* 1978 Metropolitan Opera season. Photo by J. Heffman.

42. Terese Capucilli, with Graham and Larry White, taking a bow after *Rite of Spring*, Tivoli Gardens, Denmark, 1980s.

43. Terese Capucilli in studio rehearsal, 1980s. Photo by Kristin Lodoen.

44. Christine Dakin in *Night Journey,* 1980s. Photo by Michele Ballantini.

45. Christine Dakin, informal pose in unknown work, 1980s. Photo by Chuck Kimball.

46. Peggy Lyman, solo in her own company, 1980s. Photo by David Fullard.

47. Peggy Lyman, informal pose in her own work, 1980s. Photo by John Russell.

48. Martha Graham and Yuriko (as restager), with *Primitive Mysteries* cast, 1982.

49. *Diversion of Angels,* staged by Takako Asakawa for American Ballet Theatre, 1999, with Ashley Tuttle and Keith Roberts. Photo by Rosalie O'Connor.

50. *Appalachian Spring,* the Joffrey Ballet of Chicago, 2000. Photo by Herb Migdoll.

SYLLABUS OF
GRAHAM MOVEMENTS

This syllabus is a basic list from the 1960s of exercises with their variations that indicates advancing levels of accomplishment. The syllabus may or may not be taught in its entirety; the decision is up to the school or the teacher. The number of executions of each exercise is also the choice of the individual teacher. But the sequence of movements is always taught in the same order—floor work, breathings, knees, standing center work, barre work, and traveling across the floor.

The quotations are from Graham; she frequently described movement using ballet terms. The contraction and release principle is used throughout the class work and in almost all exercises. As with all physical activity, none of the movements should be attempted without proper instruction.

Floor Work

1. Bounces executed in a sitting position

   a. In contraction and release, with feet arched, heels off the ground, toes together, knees and thighs lifted

   b. With legs opened into Second Position

   c. With legs together, straight in front, feet flexed

   The back ("tree of life") is kept straight, from the bottom of the spine to the top of the head, as the student sits on the floor. After each set of bounces, the body is centered. It should feel lifted or suspended, "as though you were jumping in the air." The arms are to the side on the floor.

2. Breathings

   a. From contraction to release

   b. Lifting the head

   The throat is felt to be "open" and is centered exactly over the body. The chin is raised when the head is lifted, which permits the head to roll backwards without compressing the neck.

c. Into a spiral with the head

A spiral is a twist from the waist. It should feel as if "an arrow were going through the body from underneath the shoulders to the hip bones." At all times, the dancer should feel "poised, as if in flight," when seated.

d. With an extension to Second Position and quarter turn on the floor

Variation: with centered contraction to back and a quarter turn onto one hip.

3. Soles of the feet together (heels up)

a. Contract and release

b. Contract and release with the body forward

c. Repeat with the legs open in Second Position

Exercises 1–3 finish with a high lift of the back, chest, and head. Arms open from overhead into Second Position. The alignment of the body in Second Position when it bounces forward is described as "parallel to the ceiling and to the floor." The arms are "like wings" when they open to Second Position. The Second Position on the floor "is not a position of rest, but a position of activity." The muscles of the inside of the leg must be firmly held in order not to deform the outside of the leg from overuse.

4. Stretches on four counts forward

a. With arms in Second Position

b. With fingers touching overhead, arms in a diamond shape

c. With arms diagonally up

d. With soles of the feet together (as in exercise 1a, feet arched and heels up) and hands on ankles.

5. Feet coming forward (straightening front, toward the mirror or front of the room)

a. With flex and point in the last position (4d)

b. Flex and point with legs straight

c. Contract and release with feet pointing and flexing in a drawn-up (knees slightly bent) First Position of the feet

Variation: with extension of one leg extended off the floor front and to the side. The leg is lifted about 45 degrees off the floor and placed back into position, not dropped.

6. Legs in Second Position

   a. With one knee slightly bent, flex the foot; straighten the knee, extend the leg, and point the foot

   b. With arms together in front (waist high), or one forward, the other to the side

   c. With spiral in the body. "The body turns only as far as it can with both hips on the floor."

   d. With arms lifted to center overhead (diamond shape)

   Variation: with contraction and release. The variation finds the release in a spiral position with one arm raised, the other to the side. "In the contraction to the side, the shoulder crosses the knee."

7. Sitting in Fourth Position

   The Fourth Position on the floor begins with the front leg, knee up and the foot on the floor. The back leg's inner thigh is on the floor as the starting position. The front knee is dropped to the floor, outer thigh muscles flat when the exercise begins. The body leans slightly backwards and forwards during this exercise. "This series is only possible when the elemental has been mastered."

   a. Spirals with slight lean backwards

   b. Using one arm

   c. Using both arms

   d. Spiral onto the elbow with contraction and release to the front

   Variation: with rise to the knee. "This movement depends not only upon the balance of the body, but on the demonic—fierce—use of the muscles. There is no strain on the knee." The movement of the spiral impels the body onto the back knee in a kneeling position. "There are no exercises for the knees. Only for the muscles surrounding the knees."

   Variation: with quarter turns on the contraction. In these quarter turns, the body slides along the floor in the contraction.

8. Back extensions in Fourth Position

The back leg lifts off the floor to its natural capacity. "The hip, thigh, knee, and foot are lifted as the body turns in the spiral variation in the opposite direction from the lifted leg. The heel of the front leg is kept directly in front of the body in relationship to the navel."

    a. Plain, or extended along the floor, hands on floor

    b. With arm extended front

    c. With quarter turn (a pivot on the front hip that turns the body) along the floor

    d. With double contraction

9. Front and back extensions

    The front extension finds the forward knee extended along the floor at first, and then raised slightly off the floor.

    a. Plain (along the floor, not lifted)

    b. With contraction along the floor

    c. With a high release and rise onto the front knee in a quarter turn

    d. Same as 9c, with a half turn

10. Contraction prone ("This exercise is sometimes called pleading.")

    "As in all the exercises, the timing must be correct" to provide the proper shape and execution of the movement.

    a. Head back on the rise and release

    b. With head rolled forward

    c. With a half turn and release (pivot on the floor)

    d. With one leg extended as the body comes up

    e. With a turn as the leg is extended

11. Sitting in Fourth Position

    a. Extension of front foot to Second Position off the floor

    b. With a quarter turn (pivot on floor as leg opens)

    c. Extension of the back leg off the floor with rise onto the front knee and continuing to bring the back leg to the Second Position and front as in rond de jambe; the foot is placed over the front knee at the end and the sitting position is resumed.

12. Contractions around the leg (a difficult and quickly paced series)

   a. Contraction around the raised knee (as in 11c)

   b. With head dropping to place the ear to the ankle. "The head must drop as close to the floor as possible."

   c. With arms around the raised knee

   d. With arms (side, overhead, diagonal)

   e. With back fall in contraction (leaning slightly to the side opposite the raised knee, arms reaching forward)

   Variation: with arms and fall (arms overhead).

13. Variations on the above with a spiral; various arm positions; extending front leg on the release

   "The strength of one's back, not an arbitrary level, determines the height of the leg in an extension during this exercise."

14. Back falls

   "These falls must never be done unless you are prepared for them and have done them a great, great many times."

   a. Preparation: both feet on the floor, sitting, deep contraction and release

   b. Fall to the floor

   "All falls are into the body—into yourself. The force of the movement returns the body to its original position from the fall."

   c. With half turn on contraction

15. Sitting square front, heels off the floor

   a. Contraction to the back on hip, release to front

   b. With raised arms

   c. With a spiral

   d. With extension of the back leg on the rise

   e. With strike (battement) of the leg to wide Second Position

   f. Adding quarter and half turns

16. Sitting Fourth Position and rising to front

   a. On four counts

   b. On three counts

c. On two counts, lifting head

d. Into a spiral turn

Variation: with leg extension on contraction and release placing leg on floor.

"All these falls (exercises 14–16) are performed with the pelvis up and under. The movement starts in the pelvis in the fall and in the return. The speed with which the falls are performed depends upon how early and carefully you were prepared for them."

17. Back contraction with crossed ankles (spine to the floor up to the shoulders)

"In dance, each time, it may be a mystical or religious connotation that you feel, but principally it is the body exalting in its strength and its own power."

a. With elbows pressed together, hands toward the ceiling

b. With both legs extended front on the rise

c. With arms wrapped around the back of the waist

d. With arms opening to Second Position

e. Rising onto both knees at the end

18. Variation with one foot across the knee, on the floor, over the leg in front in Fourth Position

a. With arms extended

b. With the front foot extended

c. With a quarter turn onto the hip lying on the floor

d. Contraction over to elbows

e. Into Fourth Position

f. With turn on knees to sitting position

19. Sitting in Fourth Position

a. Contract and release with feet off the floor

b. With a quarter turn

c. With a leg extension front, then back

20. Leg extensions to the side (from back falls, as in the preceding exercises)

    a. Leg extension to the back

    "There is no substitute for muscular strength in the body."

    b. With a rise onto one knee and a turn as the leg extends to the side

    c. With a complete back fall and rise onto one knee as the leg extends to
       the side

21. Rise onto one hand in contraction

    a. Release to sit on hip

    b. End in leg extension to the side

    "No matter what the desire, there is nothing but training that will accomplish these movements. The safety in doing these exercises is within the movement itself."

22. Sitting in Second Position

    a. Release to lifted knees, heels on the floor

    "The waist stays still."

    b. Release with extension of the feet, the back in spiral

23. High contraction to front and side

    a. With leg extension side

    b. With release to back bend

    c. With pitch to floor

Variation: with rise to knees, contraction, and rise to knees in back bend.

24. Knee across front

    a. Back fall

    b. With rise to standing position, contraction to floor

    "Always return to center. So be it."

Knees

Graham had a great deal to say about work on the knees. She constantly emphasized that the leg muscles surrounding the knee must be strong enough to take the weight off the bones of the knee: "The muscles of the legs must be strong, and these exercises have nothing to do with the knees themselves."

To safely perform exercises on the knees, attention must be paid to their execution: "In all exercises on the knees, whether a dancer does just one or 150, the execution must be exactly the same each time."

"The body has a lovely animal logic. It is the duty, the joy, and the desire of each generation of dancers to discover more deeply all of its meanings."

1. On one knee in Fourth Position (kneeling on one knee)

"All these exercises must be done slowly and with great concentration. The weight is held in the center of the body during all these movements," or returned to the center after a lunge, tilt, or pitch.

a. Quarter turn to back extension

b. Plié to Second (leg opposite the kneeling side is placed in Second Position, foot on the floor, then the plié is executed)

c. Change to other side (both knees together, then change)

d. To Second Position with body tilt (as in 1b, with tilt)

e. Change (both knees together to change sides)

f. With body tilt

g. Change with tilt of the body

h. With turn into contraction, sit

i. With lunge out

j. Change on knees

k. With lunge onto front leg

l. With pitch fall to elbows

m. With contraction, release on lunge

n. Pitch to elbows, Fourth Position turn

o. Contraction to sit

2. On one knee

    a. Contract to back fall, release to front and up to one knee

    b. Same, changing knees on release

    c. Travel back on the fall

3. On both knees

    a. Spiral contraction into sit, spiral release to right

    "Everything grows on a spiral." In other words, there is a lift in the twist of the body as if to lift the body as it turns, not separately—lift then twist.

    Variation: into back, "hips remain firm."

4. Strikes (battements) in contraction

    a. Foot is placed on the floor to the side on the heel

    b. With spiral contraction and release into roll on the back, into strikes

    c. Ending with a sit on the hip, both legs extended to the side

5. Traveling crawls on the knee in contraction

    a. With deep sit, roll onto knee as the other foot is placed on the floor to support the weight; then roll is repeated onto second knee as first leg supports the weight. The crawl is always supported by one foot on the floor.

    b. Change on knees, using the same knee, crawling on one side

    c. Crawls in a circle, one foot crossing over the knee

6. On one knee

    a. Rise up from one knee onto the front foot in a tilt

    b. Rise up onto one foot from one-knee position with a spiral in the body on the rise

    c. Rise up with the back leg off the floor in attitude

7. Exercise on six counts (begin kneeling on both knees); sometimes called a hinge, as the body swings back and forth on the knees, torso straight

    a. On six (body arches back as hands are placed on ankles)

    b. With roll, straight back falling side, on back, and up the other side

    c. With back fall, falling straight back

Variation: with back fall and roll, falling backwards rolling on side to original hinge position

(It will be noted by students of the Pilates method—a series of rehabilitating and strengthening exercises created by Joseph Pilates in the early 1920s—that some of Graham's exercises on the floor and knees are similar to Pilates's. Although no imitation of the Pilates exercises was intended by Graham, they are comparable—although in a transformed manner—and have been incorporated into the syllabus for creating a harmoniously strong and lean body, with emphasis on the use of the pelvis and breathing.)

Standing Center Work

1. Standing with heels in lengthening and strengthening value. Both rely on together, slightly turned-out feet

   a. Two demi-pliés with contraction and breathing throughout

2. Demi-pliés in First, Second, Fourth, and Fifth Positions (arms slightly away from the body; head turned to the side of the front foot in Fourth Position; body has a slight twist)

   The exercise sometimes includes a rise to demi-pointe as the knees straighten; or the demi-plié may be executed on demi-pointe from the start. As in all exercises, the teacher decides on the needs of the class. Graham describes demi-pointe as "a position of waiting to move."

3. Brushes (battements, on the floor, to 45 degrees; to 90 degrees)

   These battement exercises (3–10) are given at the discretion of the teacher as to sequence. "The dancer's time is spent not only in training the body, but in getting to know what it is capable of doing. The laws of the use of the body are as strict as the laws of architecture."

   a. From First Position, one in four counts; two in two counts; eight ending in demi-plié; repeat to other side; to the side

   "The torso is held and the hips do not move; point from the sole of the foot."

   b. In a faster tempo, sixteen ending in demi-plié; repeat to the other side

4. Parallel brushes, four on each leg to 45 degrees; four to 90 degrees

5. Contraction preparation and shift to brush side at 90 degrees, alternating

6. In parallel position, brush front and side, to 45 degrees and 90 degrees with contraction, two times each direction and height, ending with demi-plié between changes to other side

7. Quick brushes—front, side, back, side—on the floor, and then off the floor, ending in demi-plié in four counts; other side

8. Brushes to side using given arm positions (front or back)

   a. Ending in demi-plié and executed in demi-plié

   b. With tilt of body toward leg, then away from leg

   c. Repeat both sides in contraction

9. Brushes with turns (on the floor, rotating on the side of the supporting leg)

   "The inner thigh muscles work to make this movement smooth."

10. Brushes with arms (First to Second) with a spiral toward the working leg; then away from the working leg; in eight counts, then four times in two counts

11. Turns with the working foot in coupé position (on the ankle) closing in Fifth Position front, then closing in Fifth Position back. To complete one turn, the first coupé closes front without a turn; then a quarter turn is executed with the next coupé closing back. (The turn is performed on the metatarsal of the supporting leg, while the other foot is in coupé position.) By alternating closing front and back, the turn is completed in five coupés. Turns may be en dedans or en dehors.

    a. Turns with the working leg in passé (at the front of the knee of the supporting leg) five times closing front and back (behind the knee), as in the preceding exercise

    b. With a plié at the end of each quarter turn

12. High contraction in grand plié, ending in élevé to demi-pointe

    a. In First Position; in Second Position; in Fourth Position; in Fifth Position

    Variation: with spiral and full circle of arms, ending in relevé (to demi-pointe). "This variation should never be taught unless the classic version has been mastered."

Barre Work

Barre work contains extensive stretching, ending in élevés—a rise to the demi-pointe—the movement, as it is executed in a controlled and smooth tempo, is closer to an élevé than a spring, or relevé. The tempo throughout is a slow 4/4.

1. Demi-plié facing the barre in First Position (approximate) with a spiral (lean) directly side, opposite arm up; end in élevé with both arms up; reverse spiral on next demi-plié; then execute the same exercise with grands pliés in eight counts

   "The spiral is performed without changing the placement of the hips; the knees are free. The exercise is primarily for the inside muscles of the legs, not only for the outside muscles."

2. Stretches at the barre

   a. The working leg performs a développé from a passé position and opens above the barre and is lowered gently onto the barre; then lifted off the barre in sixteen counts

   Variation 1 (with plié): perform the same exercise with a plié as the leg remains on the barre; opposite arm up.

   Variation 2: with a slide toward the same side as the leg on the barre; ending in demi-plié, then élevé upon return to the right-angle position.

   "This all must be done gradually."

   Variation 3 with knee vibration (turned in, then out): the working leg performs a développé to the side from passé position turned in; then is turned out and extended to the side (knee vibration); then the supporting leg rises to demi-pointe and the body turns (in fouetté) away from the raised leg, thus becoming an arabesque

3. As in variation 3, with balances in the side extension and arabesque

   a. As in variation 3, with contraction on knee vibration, release on turning out

   Variation 3 is given at the discretion of the teacher, taking into account the physical limitations of the students.

4. Brushes (grand battements) in a series to the side

   "The leg must be held for one second at the highest point."

a. On the floor; to 45 degrees; to 90 degrees; as high as possible; two each in sixteen counts

5. Brushes with one hand on the barre, from First Position

   a. Three grand battements (brushes) front; passé to extension front in plié; passé to tendu on the floor and battement from tendu (toe is on the floor in tendu)

   b. Same exercise to the side extension

   c. Same to the back

   d. Reverse series beginning with brushes back

6. Extensions (grand battements) to percussive music, with the accent at the height of the position
   "Extensions are an endless part of the dancer's vocabulary."

   This series of exercises is similar to a grand adagio at the barre and, as given by the teacher, may include attitude positions and turning toward and away from the barre in the big poses—attitude or arabesque.

   a. Facing the barre, extend to the side on demi-pointe

   b. With same-side arm raised

   c. With opposite arm raised

7. With one hand on the barre and turning quickly toward the barre to execute the exercise on the other side

   a. With grand rond de jambe (half circle of the leg at waist level) from 90 degrees front to arabesque; in reverse; and en cloche—with bell-like swing from high front to high back

8. Off-center battements with prances: tilts opposite the raised leg; some from développé—as given—and in relevé

9. Knee vibrations as grand rond de jambe

   a. Waist-high extensions front to side; side to arabesque; full half circle; with relevés as given

10. Preparation for hinges (slightly bent knees with the body on a straight line from knees to head)

    a. In a parallel position, demi-plié, lean backwards while holding onto the barre; push through the body to the upright position. This exercise sometimes ends with bounces.

"Push though the body, but never through the knees."

11. Hinge to the ground with one hand on the barre pushing up through the body, "never through the knees"

   a. With a quick drop (heels are off the floor in all hinges)

12. Full fall to floor using one hand on the barre as preparation for falls in the center. Fall is through the contraction preceding the fall; bounce is incorporated into the rise.

13. "Bird" pliés

   "The weight is carried high in the body." Arms are to the side, like a bird's wings.

   a. With the feet parallel, a deep plié is performed, then a swivel is executed after a contraction and the rise is to demi-pointe as the body completes a half turn

   b. The same exercise in Fourth Position (similar to temps lié, but with a deep plié)

   c. Variation: a rise with a straight back leg, in Fourth Position, with the body parallel to the floor

14. Variations on the positions of the rise

   a. In Fourth Position, as in exercise 13, ending with a lift of the back leg, body parallel to the floor

   b. Lifting the leg and adding a rond de jambe as the supporting leg does a demi-plié (heel down); extension ends side

   c. Same as 14b, with a tilt opposite the raised leg

   d. Same as 14b, with no tilt and rond de jambe ending front in plié, close Fifth Position, turn, and execute on the opposite side

15. Preparation for turns (turns are in passé with the supporting foot slightly off the floor but not in demi-pointe

   a. Turn (pivot) from Second Position plié to right or left leg in passé

   b. Same in Fourth Position

   c. Combination: two preparation (no turn); two with a quarter turn; one in half turn; two in a full turn; change sides

16. Preparation for turns from Second to Fourth Position in a lunge

   a. Plié in Second with passé preparation, no turn

   b. Same with quarter turn (supporting foot does not rise to demi-pointe)

   c. Turn half circle

   d. Full turn (passé) and quarter turn, heel on floor as in 16b

Center

This series may be done as two preparations; two quarter turns; one half turn; two full turns. Change to other side.

1. Circular walk with spiral turns (walking on a diagonal, upstage left to downstage right)

   a. As a preparation using temps lié (shifting from one position to another in Second or Fourth through plié). In a series: two preparations for a turn in low arabesque; two in quarter turn; one in half turn; two in full turns ending in a held balance.

"The turn is done in a spiral" (a slight lean toward the direction of the turn).

   b. Variation with a pitch into attitude—two in preparation; two with full turns, hold ending in balance (a pitch finds the body parallel to the ground)

   c. Variation: with a pitch into arabesque ending in pencheé (full lowering of the body—nose to knee) on a straight supporting leg

   d. With a step onto demi-plié in attitude and pitch; two steps back and repeat to the other side (no turn)

   e. Same as 1d, with two half turns

   f. Same as 1d, with two full turns

   g. Same as 1d, in a triplet walk (six counts) with a turn

   h. Same as 1d, in four-count walk, turning in three counts

2. This section may be likened to adagio combinations, because of the control required in the transfer of weight

   a. Preparations: demi-plié "pull" (tilt slightly) to side in First Position; lunge to Fourth Position and transfer leg in tendu to Second Position and balance with leg at 90 degrees in Second Position. No arms are used in this preparation.

   b. Plié in Second Position; raise leg to 90 degrees; return to First Position (execute twice, then change sides)

   c. Repeat arms side, from Fourth Position front and back

   "The shifting of weight forces the body to take the relative position."

   d. Plié in Second; shift weight to one side with foot in passé position (toes to knee of supporting leg); change sides, completing this series twice on each side

   e. Same as 2d, in passé from Fourth Position back; twice change sides

   f. Plié in Second Position, passé, plié in Fourth Position back; full turn with foot in passé (supporting leg is on quarter-pointe during the turn); once each side

   "The weight of the body is exactly over the big ankle bone when the foot is in passé." Hip on supported side is directly over the ankle.

   g. Plié in Second Position, shift weight to 90 degrees in arabesque, rond de jambe to Second Position, rond de jambe again to arabesque (rond de jambe on straight supporting leg; change on sixth count

   Variation: exercise may be done as grand battement to Second Position and into arabesque beginning in Second Position plié.

   h. Turn with feet in First Position, no arms; complete twice on each side (demi-plié in First Position gives impetus for the turn)

   i. Same turn in First Position as in 2h, but performed in Second Position plié with arms at right angles (elbows toward the ceiling); perform twice

   j. Same turn as 2h, with arms held slightly to the side from the Fourth Position back; complete twice

   k. From Second Position preparation into First Position with chassé (triplet) to Fourth back; perform twice; change

   l. Add turn to First Position; perform twice; change

m. Add turn from Fourth Position; perform twice; change

n. A combination of 2k–m; complete twice to each side

A general word must be said here in order to understand the direction of the turns. When the right foot is in passé and the turn is to the right, the turn is en dehors – away from the body. When the same position is assumed, but the turn is to the left, the turn is en dedans—toward the body. The position of the foot does not determine the direction of the turn. "Away from" or "toward" the body are the directions for the turn. Another way to determine these two directions is to observe the heel of the supporting leg: if the heel moves backwards in the turn, the direction is en dehors; if the heel moves forward, the direction is en dedans.

3. From Second Position plié, the leg lifts to Second Position at 90 degrees, with the arms in "declaration," or open slightly to the front (called "presenting the movement" in ballet terminology)

    a. Add a contraction in the Second Position at 90 degrees

    b. Add a slow turn (promenade) in Second Position at 90 degrees; one each side, finish in relevé

4. Contraction in First Position, opening to Second at 90 degrees

    a. With a quarter turn in First opening to Second; twice in quarter turn; once in half turn; twice in full turns with feet parallel, heel of the turning foot slightly raised

    "You don't copy these movements, you feel them."

5. Contraction in Second plié; release into turn in Second Position, quarter turn twice; then half turn once, one full turn twice

6. With brushes (small battements on the floor) twice in Second Position, change to Fourth Position back and turn in First toward the body (en dedans); use the contraction on the turn

    a. Add a release and tilt in the body

7. Same as exercise 6, with foot in passé with contraction from Second and Fourth Positions

    "The Fourth Position is a classic position in Asia as well as in the West."

    a. Add a tilt of the body

8. With preparation on Second in plié, shift to a side tilt and turn in Second

Position in relevé; do the same from Fourth Position, holding a balance at the end of each turn

 a. With contraction on turn

 b. End in a fall to the floor, instead of a balance

9. Split falls

 a. Tendu side, split to the floor, body leans to the floor, leg comes around to Fourth Position front, rise, temps lié (transfer weight) to become Fourth Position, half turn

 b. "Stagger" (Fourth Position to Second Position as if staggering), tendu to split side; same recovery as in 9a

 c. With developpé to the side and a sit to the floor, contraction as feet come together in parallel position and the body does a rise

10. Knee vibrations

"These are called knee vibrations. In reality, they are like ronds de jambe." Various arm patterns may be given for these movements and the contraction-release principle is also added.

 a. From passé, turn the knee in (across the supporting leg), out, into developpé side, and ronde de jambe to attitude

Variation: turn the knee in, out, to attitude

"This movement represents joy or anger, frustration: 'Shall I walk, or shall I not walk?'"

 b. Starting low to the floor with the foot of the working leg no longer on the knee of the supporting leg, but separated by several inches; turn in and out with the supporting leg in plié several times as the body rises; the working leg ends in attitude; twelve counts

 c. Knee in quasi-passé to the side, as in 10a, remains in this position as the foot is thrown front-side-back; the movement ends in Second Position at 90 degrees; twelve counts

 d. Combination of movements as in 10a–10c, with back movement ending on the outer thigh on the floor, followed by a roll on the back and rising on one leg in attitude

 e. Same as 10d, rising in Second Position to the side

11. From a parallel position, grand battement with a flexed foot front, four times, increasing in height; opposite arm pushes forward, ends on shoulder; finish with a half turn

   a. With battements front and Second; four times reaching Second on the count of three (3/4 tempo)

   b. In a handstand, beat and recover to upright position once forward, once side, eight times on three, in 3/4 tempo

   The handstand is supported on one hand, elbow straight; the body is straight, with legs overhead in parallel position. One leg beats or bounces off the other. The recovery is accomplished by placing one leg in Fourth Position front with bent knee onto the floor and returning to upright position. This movement is not a "walkover."

   c. The handstand movement may be given in combinations to the front or to the side

12. Rond de jambe front to back while bending supporting leg until the movement is on the floor, eight times on the "and-one" count (similar to a movement in *Night Journey*)

   Combinations from Graham dances are sometimes given in the class, such as: *American Document* step: glissades and small emboîtés (coupés in a small jump with the raised foot a small distance away from the ankle), all to the front. The counts are: six, seven, six, seven, two for the combination.

13. Preparation for sitting from various positions

   "The weight in all sits to the floor moves down through the center of the body."

   a. From Fourth Position, a grand plié is executed to a sit on the floor as the back foot rotates so that the weight is on the outer thigh; rise on the supporting leg—front foot

   b. Same as 13a, with a contraction on the sit

14. In wide Second Position and straight legs, fall to the front using the hands for support; the body is rotated (right or left) to permit a roll on the back; rise on either foot

15. Beginning with two grands battements front and a rond de jambe to Second, the body lunges toward the leg in Second; as the other leg is thrown back the body rotates on the back leg; rise

a. Same as 15, with a rond de jambe going directly to Fourth Position back and rise ending in a side extension

b. Add a contraction to 15

c. Add a contraction to 13a

d. Add a contraction to the sit and rise in a side extension (15a)

16. Grands battements to the side; rond de jambe front to attitude position; sit; rise in same attitude position

17. Pitch turns (pencheé in positions in attitude or arabesque)

"... with a deep contraction as preparation and a high release on the rise."

a. Preparation with two steps and arabesque, pitch, no turn

b. Preparation and full turn in eight counts on a straight leg

c. Full turn on four counts; two full turns in three counts (the sole of the foot remains on the floor as it pivots, the heel raises slightly to accommodate the turn)

18. Pitch turns on one knee. Walk into contraction in Fourth Position (or Second); raise a leg into a small attitude or arabesque position and turn on the front knee (it is placed gently on the floor); recover by swinging the back raised leg front to Fourth Position and rise

"The knees are not in danger because of the preparation in earlier exercises. The weight is up into the body itself, never down into the knees."

a. Add a side extension

b. Standing in side extension, pitch turn with the head almost touching the knee of the supporting leg

19. Prances (marchlike steps with knees lifted high or low, as given) through a roll from flat to demi-pointe and a small push off the floor—catlike

"These prances and turns are done on both sides," and are usually performed on the diagonal across the studio

a. Preparation: hold each prance for four counts, four times; two counts, four times; and alternating feet for sixteen counts

b. Two prances with sharp passé and a tilt toward the lifted foot

c. Two prances with a half turn in passé

d. Two prances with a full turn

e. Two prances with a side extension on demi-pointe into a full turn

20. Jumps from two feet to two feet, and to one foot (sissonnes)

    a. Big jump from parallel position to Second, ending with one leg in Second Position; close to parallel; jump in First

    b. Big jumps in First with bent knees, soles touching

    c. Continuous big jumps in Second Position

    d. Jumps with parallel feet

    e. Two jumps to the side, ending on two feet (sissonne fermé)

    f. Two jumps with movement backwards, and with forward movement

21. Jumps from parallel First Position to a turned-out position in the air, knees side, soles together at the crest of the jump and landing in First Position

    a. From parallel First Position, jump with one foot in passé position, the other straight out in a lowered Second Position; repeat to the other side. Jump continuously.

22. *Aegisthus* jump: from parallel position, jump continuously with both legs in attitude derrière (to the back)

Traveling across the Floor

1. Walks

    a. Simple walk across the floor on diagonal: "These are brushes." The foot passes along a straight line, the body and head turn slightly.

    b. The arms swing on the fourth count

    Variation: walk with knee bent, foot raised in back

    c. Walk two steps and step on heel into a low arabesque; roll down to the flat foot

    d. Step on each count in arabesque

    e. Two arabesque steps, changing direction with a half turn on the second arabesque; do two in the opposite direction from the first two steps in the same pattern

f. Two arabesque steps with contraction to floor, head back
"You are held by the upper back and the thighs."

g. Four walks and hold balance, bent knee, working foot in passé position

h. Four walks and quick développé side

Variation: grand battement front and swing through First Position as the body does a half turn (fouetté); and the same leg does a grand battement to the front. (When a leg is extended and stays still while the body rotates, the movement is described as a fouetté, of which there are several kinds.) The movement is bell-like in the legs.

Variation: same exercise, with grands battements back

2. Low walks with back leg dragging, knees slightly bent, arms swinging, and with increasing speed. At full speed, this movement is known as the *Diversion of Angels* run.

3. Triplets

"The weight is held as in flight."

a. Three steps: first count, step in demi-plié; second step is higher; third, same as second step. (The plié and rise are slight, giving the impression of a slight accent similar to the one count, as in a waltz).

b. A turn on every second step (without, then with arms). The working leg is 45 degrees in front.

c. A turn on each step (without, then with arms)

d. Turn as in 3c, and hold on fourth count

e. Same as 3c, holding a balance (rise to demi-pointe on fourth count)

f. Two walks and an arabesque on the heel on the third count

4. Diagonal Walks

a. Walks in Second Position to Fourth—step right in Second, step left in Fourth (right foot held at the ankle in back)

b. Same as 4a, with foot held in passé back

c. Same as 4a, with arm swing opposite raised foot

d. Same as 4a, with a slight jump, without arm

e. Same as 4a, with slight jump adding opposite-arm movement

5. Skips

a. Alternating legs

b. Skip on same leg, with step on opposite leg between skips

6. Skips in large poses

   a. Step, step, sauté (jump) in attitude front, then in attitude back

   b. Same as 6a, with grand jeté (large jump) on third count

   c. Same as 6a, with grand jeté on the same leg on second count

7. Hops while executing a low rond de jambe, back to front

   a. While turning

8. Step-draws (glissade-like steps)

   a. Slow glissade right and left ending in a coupé (foot at ankle front or back)

   b. With small 45-degree battement followed by a glissade or "draw"

   c. Same as 8a, with relevé on supporting leg, passé on working leg, ending in glissade

   d. Arabesque, swing front, fouetté (the leg remains placed and the body turns; as opposed to a rond de jambe, for instance, where the leg moves, but the body remains placed); and draw or glissade (same leg movement)

9. *Seraphic Dialogue* strikes

   a. Battement to Second, "draw" working leg to passé and turn, movement alternates

   b. Battement side with half turn each step

10. Pitch (pencheé) attitude on right, half turn, step on left, with right in Second Position completing second half of turn

11. Contraction and release turns in Second with pitch "It's something you learn and something you develop."

    a. In Second Position, contract and release facing diagonal corner and traveling

    b. With a turn in Second facing upstage, changing sides to Second Position facing downstage

    c. Contraction on half turn; release on next half turn

    d. Same as 11c, ending in Fourth Position lunge

e. Same as 11c, with slight pitch forward in Fourth

12. Contraction drops performed traveling in the diagonal

   a. Turns in attitude in contraction

   b. Same as 12a, ending in sit to floor

   c. Same as 12a, ending in sit and turn on floor

13. Turns with hips parallel in attitude

14. Arabesque turns contracting into attitude, without, then with, a turn

15. Walking backwards in contraction-release "profile"

16. Traveling in diagonal with grand battement front in contraction

   a. *Gospel of Eve* contraction: grand battement front, jump into attitude turn (pitch)

17. *Cave of the Heart* turn: in arabesque, pitched, with variation opening to Second. Turn on the one count, step, step

   "This turn can be done in a joyous manner or may indicate jealousy or anger."

18. *Electra* turns: a series of arabesque turns ending in Second, left leg bent when turn is on right side

19. *Diversion of Angels* turn: Traveling attitude turn with strike into attitude

20. *Clytemnestra* turn: Arabesque turn on heel finishing with forward contraction; palm of hand on forehead of supporting side in "anguish"

21. Circular walks

   a. Back leg lifts to Second Position, falls front, repeat other side

   b. Same as 21a, with relevé in Second Position and pitch attitude in tombée (fall) front

   c. Same as 21a, with two steps between

22. Développés in Second Position, arabesque, and front tombée, plié

Across the Floor in Diagonal

1. Traveling prances (march in parallel position using the knee to raise each foot off the floor in the image of a prancing horse)

   a. Prancing across the floor in a diagonal

b. With a strike (battement) to the floor on the eighth count

c. With a small jump on the eighth count

d. With changes of direction and a turn on the eighth count toward various directions: half, quarter, and full turns

e. With a bend to the side on the seventh count in passé, to attitude back on the eighth count

f. Prances to Fourth Position—jump on the tenth count

2. Jumps in Second Position with a tilt to the side on a given count

a. Jumps with a tilt side, straight, other side

b. Jumps in Second Position with a contraction to make the torso almost parallel with the floor

3. Bell jumps (grand jeté—shape should reach a crest as if going over a hurdle)

a. Straight forward on the same leg

b. With two steps between and alternating sides for jump

4. Jumps with an arabesque at a given count from prances

a. Jumps into Second Position in contraction with hands touching feet (Cossack jump)

5. *Seraphic Dialogue* jump: jump with one leg in Second Position at 90 degrees side; step on raised leg; repeat in side pattern; arms between legs in jump, hands clasped

6. "Sparkle" jumps: Arabesque sauté jumps with two steps between— arabesque alternates, repeats in a series with arms shooting up on the arabesque

a. Continuous arabesque sautés alternating sides, arms up on each sauté (jump)

7. Traveling sits: step, step, sit (a crouch, both knees bent, buttocks not on the floor)

a. With a small jump before the sit, rise with leg side, body in contraction

8. Traveling split/fall: 90 degree side jump with fall straight forward, hands breaking the fall

a. Big jump ending in a sit (crouch) instead of a fall forward

9. Split to side, fall forward, roll on side to back, and come up in Fourth Position; may be repeated as a traveling step

    Variations: front split, one leg bent, rise in plié, other leg in Second Position; same but rising in arabesque

10. *Diversion of Angels* jumps: prancelike emboîtés with leg raised higher in front—a series of small jumps alternating feet, body in contraction forward, arms to the side

    Variation: with feet raised in emboîtés back, body pitched forward or legs in arabesque jumps

11. "Butterflies": emboîtés back with step, step between. They may be imaged as temps de flèche derrière (back) with two steps between

12. March jumps: continuous jumps into attitude back alternating legs and in contraction (from a parallel position)

13. *Diversion of Angels* step: jump in Second Position at 90 degrees with a tilt to the side, step, step. (All traveling steps may be executed separately, or continuously without two steps between.)

14. Straight leg jumps: grand battement front with a jump, step, step

    a. With a contraction and tilt forward, parallel to floor

15. "Stranger" jump: a crouch with two knees up to the chest, body in contraction

16. "Stranger" with chasing run: traveling "Stranger" jump from parallel position

17. *Cortège of Eagles* jump: sauté in Second Position, land in attitude back

18. "Barrel" jumps: two knees up, arms back, "as in jumping over something"

19. Assemblé front with parallel feet; land in attitude side—knee bent and parallel to hip

    a. With contraction on the landing in attitude

    b. "Bison" jump: front and back leg in attitude in the air—approached from a run, or step, step; land in attitude back

20. Pas de chat (without turning out) from four emboîtés, pas de chat on the fifth count

    a. Jeté (brush side, land in modified coupé) four times, then pas de chat

    b. Pas de chat with jeté, jumping onto front foot in combinations

c. "Stag" leap: big jump with front leg in passé, knee forward, back leg in arabesque: step, jump; step, jump. Exit step: two arms up or in Fourth Position.

Variation: a series of emboîtés and pas de chats with a turn.

21. *Primitive Mysteries* jumps: arms behind, body in crouch, series of jeté jumps front, leg in attitude back at landing

22. "Furies" jump: series of grand jetés across the floor with the left arm thrust forward; jump on the same leg—fast exit

23. *Diversion of Angels* jump: from-the-floor jump in Second Position, fall to floor and hop into attitude from floor (with or without a turn)

24. Triplet combination: step, step, turn à la seconde, sauté on third count— traveling step

25. "Lake Placid" combination: a series of three jetés, with a fall front onto the chest, a rise à la seconde

26. Combination: contraction with leg à la seconde, swing raised leg behind supporting leg now in plié, roll on back, rise on same supporting leg in Second Position at 90 degrees, with or without plié. During roll on back, legs may be straight or bent, knees to the chest

27. Knee walks ("keep the upper body held high"): step, step, kneel on back leg, rise on next step; alternates in traveling series

   a. Continuously step, kneel

28. Knee boureés: boureés (small steps, one foot closely following the other) on knees sideways

   a. Bourée front

29. Free series of falls: passé in contraction, développé side, rond de jambe to attitude back, fall on thigh of attitude leg, rise in given position

   a. From kneeling position, body falls backward, roll on side. Knees come up to chest during roll on back, come up in given position.

   b. From relevé on supporting leg, other leg in à la seconde, fall and roll on back with rise in side attitude, hand on ankle

   c. "The simplest fall": from parallel position, bend knees and contract forward, roll onto shoulders and come up on knees. During roll on back, legs may be straight or bent close to the chest.

THE DANCES OF MARTHA GRAHAM
AND HER COMPOSERS

Martha Graham choreographed over two hundred dances for the company she founded in 1926. In addition to this list of company dances, Graham choreographed an unknown number of dances when she was a member of the Denishawn company in the 1920s, short dances for demonstrations at Bennington College in Vermont from 1934 to 1942 (she was artist-in-residence from 1942 to 1944), and dances for plays performed at the Neighborhood Playhouse in New York City in the 1930s and 1940s. This list is a revised and enlarged version of lists compiled by Louis Horst, Alice Helpern, and Don McDonagh.

1926
April 18, 48th Street Theatre, NYC

Chorale, César Franck (from Prelude, Chorale, Fugue)

Novelette, Robert Schumann (from *Bunte Blätter,* Op. 99)

Tänze, Franz Schubert

Intermezzo, Johannes Brahms (*Intermezzo no. 18 in C Major for Piano,* Op. 119, no. 3)

Maid with the Flaxen Hair, Claude Debussy (*Preludes for Piano,* book 1, no. 8)

Arabesque no. 1, Claude Debussy (*Arabesque no. 1 for Piano*)

Clair de lune, Claude Debussy (from *Suite bergamasque: Clair de lune*)

Danse languide, Alexander Scriabin (*Danse languide for Piano,* Op. 51, no. 4)

Désir, Alexander Scriabin (*Désir for Piano,* Op. 57, no. 1)

Deux valses sentimentales, Maurice Ravel (from *Valses nobles et sentimentales,* nos. 2 and 3 for piano)

Masques, Louis Horst (*Masques for Piano*)

Trois gnoissiennes: Gnoissienne/Frieze/Tanagra, Erik Satie (from *Trois Gnoissiennes for Piano*)

From a Twelfth-Century Tapestry (retitled a *Florentine Madonna*), Sergei Rachmaninoff

A Study in Lacquer, Marcel Bernheim

Danse rococo, Maurice Ravel

The Three Gopi Maidens (excerpt from *The Flute of Krishna*), Cyril Scott
The Marionette Show, Eugene Goossens
Portrait—After Beltram Masses (retitled *Gypsy Portrait*), Manuel de Falla

May 27, Kilbourne Hall, Rochester, N.Y.
The Flute of Krishna, Cyril Scott
Suite from *Alceste,* Christopher Willibald von Gluck
Scène javanaise, Louis Horst
Danza degli angeli, Ermanno Wolf-Ferrari
Bas Relief, Cyril Scott

August 20, Mariarden, Peterboro, N.H.
Ribands, Frédéric Chopin

November 28, Klaw Theatre, NYC
Scherzo, Felix Mendelssohn (Op. 16, no. 2)
Baal Shem, Ernest Bloch (*Baal shem*)
La soirée dans Grenade (retitled *The Moth*), Claude Debussy (*Soirée dans Grenade* from *Estampes*)
Alt-Wien, Leopold Godowsky, arranged by Louis Horst
Three Poems of the East, Louis Horst

1927
February 27, Guild Theatre, NYC
Peasant Sketches: Dance/Berceuse/In the Church, Vladimir Rebikov, Alexander Tansman, Peter Tchaikovsky
Tunisia (Sunlight in a Courtyard), Eduard Poldini
Lucrezia, Claude Debussy
La canción, René Defossez

August 2, Anderson-Milton School, NYC
Arabesque no. 1 (revised), Claude Debussy (*Arabesque no. 1 for Piano*)
Valse caprice, Cyril Scott (Op. 74, no. 7)

October 16, the Little Theatre, NYC
Spires, J. S. Bach (*Chorale: Schwing dich auf zu deinem Gott*)
Adagio (retitled *Madonna*), George Frideric Handel (*Adagio* from *Second Suite*)

Fragilité, Alexander Scriabin (Op. 51, no. 1)

Lugubre, Alexander Scriabin (Op. 51, no. 2)

Poème ailé, Alexander Scriabin (Op. 51, no. 3)

Tanzstück, Paul Hindemith (from *Reihe kleiner Stücke*, Op. 37)

Revolt (originally *Danse*), Arthur Honegger (from Danse section of *Trois pièces*)

Esquisse antique, Désiré Emile Inghelbrecht (from *Esquisse antique*, no. 2 Driades)

Ronde, Rhené-Baton (from *Au pardon de Rumengol*)

December 10, Cornell University, Ithaca, N.Y.

Scherza, Robert Schumann

1928

February 12, Civic Repertory Theatre, NYC

Chinese Poem, Louis Horst

April 22, The Little Theatre, NYC

Trouvères (*The Return of Spring, Complaint, A Song, Frank and Gay*), Charles Koechlin

Immigrant (*Steerage Strike*), Joseph Slavenski (from *Suite aus dem Balkan*)

Poems of 1917, Leo Ornstein (from *Poems of 1917*)

Fragments (*Tragedy, Comedy*), Louis Horst

Resonances (*Matins, Gamelan, Tocsin*), Gian Francesco Malipiero

Tanagra, Erik Satie

1929

January 20, Booth Theatre, NYC

Dance, Arthur Honegger

Three Florentine Vases, Domenico Zipoli

Four Insincerities (Petulance, Remorse, Politeness, Vivacity), Serge Prokofiev (from *Visions fugitive*, Op. 22, nos. 14, 12, 6, 11)

Chants Magic (Farewell, Greetings), Fedérico Mompou (from *Chants magics*)

Two Variations (Country Lane, City Street), Alexander Gretchaninoff (from *Sonatina in G*, Op. 110, no. 1, movements 1, 3)

January 24, Bennett School, Millbrook, N.Y.

Figure of a Saint, George Frideric Handel

March 3, Booth Theatre, NYC

Resurrection, Tibor Harsányi

Adolescence, Paul Hindemith (from *Prelude and Song* from *Reihe kleiner Stücke*, Op. 37)

Danza, Darius Milhaud

April 14, Booth Theatre, NYC

Visions of the Apocalypse (Theme and Variations), Herman Reutter (from variations on Bach's chorale, *Komm' süsser Tod*)

Moment rustica, Francis Poulenc (from *Sonata for piano*, four hands, second movement "Rustique")

Sketches from the People, Julien Krein (from *Eight Preludes*, Op. 5, nos. 4, 2, 7)

Heretic, anonymous ("Breton Tetus" in collection *Chansons de la fleur de lys*, arr. De Sivry)

date and place of premiere unknown

Sarabande and Courante, J. S. Bach

Prelude in Black (Song in White), Paul Hindemith

1930

January 8, Maxine Elliott's Theatre, NYC

Prelude to a Dance (retitled *Salutation*), Arthur Honegger (from *Counterpoint no. 1 for Piano*)

Two Chants (Futility, Ecstatic Song), Ernst Krenek (*Piano Sonata*, Op. 59, no. 2)

Lamentation, Zoltán Kodály (from *Piano Piece*, Op. 3, no. 2)

Project in Movement for a Divine Comedy, no musical accompaniment

Harlequinade, Ernst Toch (from *Klavierstücke*, Op. 32)

1931

February 2, Craig Theatre, NYC

Two Primitive Canticles, Heitor Villa-Lobos

Primitive Mysteries (Hymn to the Virgin, Crucifixus, Hosanna), Louis Horst

Rhapsodics (Song, Interlude, Dance), Béla Bartók

Bacchanale, Wallingford Riegger

Dolorosa, Heitor Villa-Lobos

December 6, Martin Beck Theatre, NYC

Dithyrambic, Aaron Copeland (*Piano Variations*)
Serenade, Arnold Schoenberg
Incantation, Heitor Villa-Lobos

1932
February 28, Guild Theatre, NYC
Ceremonials, Lehman Engel

June 2, Mendelssohn Theatre, Ann Arbor, Mich.
Offering, Heitor Villa-Lobos
Ecstatic Dance, Tibor Harsányi
Bacchanale no. 2, Wallingford Riegger (from *Bacchanale*)

November 20, Guild Theatre, NYC
Prelude, Carlos Chavez
Dance Songs (Ceremonial, Morning Song, Satyric Festival Song, Song of Rapture), Imre Weisshaus
Chorus of Youth—Companions, Louis Horst

1933
February 20, Fuld Hall, Newark, N.J.
Tragic Patterns (Chorus for Supplicants, Chorus for Maenads, Chorus for Furies), Louis Horst

May 4, Guild Theatre, NYC
Elegiac, Paul Hindemith (from *Music for Unaccompanied Clarinet*)
Ekstasis, Lehman Engel (*Ekstasis*)

November 19, Guild Theatre, NYC
Dance Prelude, Nikolas Lopatnikoff (from *Fünf Kontraste,* last movement)
Frenetic Rhythms (Three Dances of Possession), Wallingford Riegger

1934
February 18, Guild Theatre, NYC
Transitions (Prologue, Sarabande, Pantomime, Epilogue), Lehman Engel
Phantasy (Prelude, Musette, Gavotte), Arnold Schoenberg

February 25, Guild Theatre, NYC

Celebration, Louis Horst
Four Casual Developments, Henry Cowell

April 22, Alvin Theatre, NYC
Intégrales (Shapes of Ancestral Wonder), Edgard Varèse (from *Intégrales*)

November 11, Guild Theatre, NYC
Dance in Four Parts (Quest, Derision, Dream, Sportive Tragedy), George Antheil
American Provincials (Act of Piety, Act of Judgment), Louis Horst

    1935
February 10, Guild Theatre, NYC
Praeludium (no. 1), Paul Nordoff
Course, George Antheil

April 28, Guild Theatre, NYC
Perspectives (Frontier, Marching Song), Louis Horst (*Frontier*), Lehman Engel (*Marching Song*)

August 14, Vermont State Armory, Bennington
Panorama (Theme of Dedication, Imperial Theme, Popular Theme), Norman Lloyd

November 10, Guild Theatre, NYC
Formal Dance (retitled *Praeludium no. 2*), David Diamond

April 7, Philharmonic Auditorium, Los Angeles
Imperial Gesture, Lehman Engel
Panic (choral movement)

    1936
February 23, Guild Theatre, NYC
Horizons, Louis Horst
Salutation, Lehman Engel

December 20, Guild Theatre, NYC
Chronicle, Wallingford Riegger

1937

July 30, Vermont State Armory, Bennington
Opening Dance, Norman Lloyd
Immediate Tragedy, Henry Cowell

December 19, Guild Theatre, NYC
Deep Song, Henry Cowell

December 26, Guild Theatre, NYC
American Lyric, Alex North

1938

August 6, Vermont State Armory, Bennington
American Document, Ray Green

1939

December 27, St. James Theatre, NYC
Columbiad, Louis Horst
Every Soul Is a Circus, Paul Nordoff

1940

August 11, College Theatre, Bennington, Vt.
El Penitente, Louis Horst
Letter to the World, Hunter Johnson

1941

August 10, College Theatre, Bennington, Vt.
Punch and Judy, Robert McBride

1942

March 14, Chicago Civic Opera House, Chicago
Land Be Bright, Arthur Krentz

1943

December 26, 46th Street Theatre, NYC
Salem Shore, Paul Nordoff
Deaths and Entrances, Hunter Johnson

1944
December 30, Library of Congress, Washington, D.C.
Imagined Wing, Darius Milhaud (from *Jeux du printemps*)
Hérodiade, Paul Hindemith
Appalachian Spring, Aaron Copeland

1946
January 23, Plymouth Theatre, NYC
Dark Meadow, Carlos Chavez (from *Hija de Colquide*)

May 10, McMillin Theatre, Columbia University, NYC
Cave of the Heart, Samuel Barber

1947
February 28, Ziegfeld Theatre, NYC
Errand into the Maze, Gian Carlo Menotti

May 3, Cambridge High School, Cambridge, Mass.
Night Journey, William Schuman

1948
August 13, Palmer Auditorium, New London, Conn.
Diversion of Angels, Norman Dello Joio

1950
January 4, Columbia Auditorium, Louisville, Ky.
Judith, William Schuman

January 22, 46th Street Theater, NYC
Eye of Anguish, Vincent Persichetti
Gospel of Eve, Paul Nordoff

1951
December 5, Columbia Auditorium, Louisville, Ky.
The Triumph of St. Joan, Norman Dello Joio

1952
April 22, Juilliard School, NYC
Canticle for Innocent Comedians, Robert Ribbink

1953
May 27, Alvin Theater, NYC
Voyage, William Schuman

1954
March 18, Saville Theatre, London
Ardent Song, Alan Hovhaness

1955
May 8, ANTA Theater, NYC
Seraphic Dialogue, Norman Dello Joio

1958
April 1, Adelphi Theater, NYC
Clytemnestra, Halim El-Dabh

April 3, Adelphi Theater, NYC
Embattled Garden, Carlos Surinach

1959
May 14, City Center, NYC
Episodes: Part I, Anton Webern (from *Passacaglia,* Op. 1, *Six Pieces for Orchestra,* Op. 6)

1960
April 27, 54th Street Theater, NYC
Acrobats of God, Carlos Surinach

April 29, 54th Street Theater, NYC
Alcestis, Vivian Fine

1961
April 16, 54th Street Theater, NYC
Visionary Recital, Robert Starer

April 20, 54th Street Theater, NYC
One More Gaudy Night, Halim El-Dabh

1962

March 4, Broadway Theater, NYC
Phaedra, Robert Starer

March 5, Broadway Theater, NYC
A Look at Lightning, Halim El-Dabh

August 17, Palmer Auditorium, New London, Conn.
Secular Games, Robert Starer (*Concerto a tre*)

October 25, Habima Theatre, Tel Aviv, Israel
Legend of Judith, Mordecai Seter

1963

September 6, Prince of Wales Theatre, London
Circe, Alan Hovhaness

1965

November 2, 54th Street Theater, NYC
Witch of Endor, William Schuman

November 3, 54th Street Theater, NYC
Part Real—Part Dream, Mordecai Seter

1967

February 21, Mark Hellinger Theatre, NYC
Cortege of Eagles, Eugene Lester

February 24, Mark Hellinger Theatre, NYC
Dancing Ground, Ned Rorem (from *Eleven Studies for Eleven Players*)

1968

May 25, George Abbott Theater, NYC
A Time of Snow, Norman Dello Joio

May 29, George Abbott Theater, NYC
The Plain of Prayer, Eugene Lester

May 30, George Abbott Theater, NYC
The Lady of the House of Sleep, Robert Starer

1969
April 11, City Center, NYC
The Archaic Hours, Eugene Lester

1973
May 2, Alvin Theater, NYC
Mendicants of Evening, David Walker

May 3, Alvin Theater, NYC
Myth of a Voyage, Alan Hovhaness

1974
April 30, Mark Hellinger Theater, NYC
Chronique, Carlos Surinach
Holy Jungle, Robert Starer

July, Jerusalem, Israel
Jacob's Dream (retitled *Point of Crossing*), Mordecai Seter

1975
July 19, Uris Theatre, NYC
Lucifer, Halim El-Dabh

December 8, Mark Hellinger Theater, NYC
Adorations, classical guitar
Point of Crossing, Mordecai Seter

December 22, Mark Hellinger Theater, NYC
The Scarlet Letter, Hunter Johnson

1977
May 17, Lunt-Fonnance Theater, NYC
O Thou Desire Who Are About to Sing, Meyer Kupferman (from *Fantasy for Violin and Piano*)

May 24, Lunt-Fontanne Theater, NYC
Shadows, Gian Carlo Menotti (*Cantilena e scherzo*)

1978

June 26, Metropolitan Opera House, NYC
The Owl and the Pussycat, Carlos Surinach

June 27, Metropolitan Opera House, NYC
Ecuatorial, Edgard Varèse (*Ecuatorial*)

June 28, Metropolitan Opera House, NYC
Flute of Pan, traditional

1979

December 9, Metropolitan Museum of Art, NYC
Frescos, Samuel Barber (two arias from *Antony and Cleopatra*)

1980

April 29, Metropolitan Opera House, NYC
Judith, Edgard Varèse

1981

February 26, Kennedy Center, Washington, D.C.
Acts of Light, Carl Nielsen

1982

June 9, City Center, NYC
Dances of the Golden Hall, Andrzej Panufnik

June 23, City Center, NYC
Andromache's Lament, Samuel Barber

1983

July 1, Herod Atticus Theatre, Athens, Greece
Phaedra's Dream, George Crum

1984

February 28, New York State Theater, NYC
Rite of Spring, Igor Stravinsky

1985
April 2, New York State Theater, NYC
Song, traditional

1986
May 27, City Center, NYC
Temptations of the Moon, Béla Bartók (from *Dance Suite*)

June 4, City Center, NYC
Tangled Night, Klaus Egge

1987
October 3, City Center, NYC
Persephone, Igor Stravinsky (from *Symphony in C*)

1988
October 13, City Center, NYC
Night Chant, R. Carlos Nakai

1989
October 3, City Center, NYC
American Document (revised), John Corigliano

1990
October 3, City Center, NYC
Maple Leaf Rag, Scott Joplin

1991
October 8, City Center, NYC
The Eyes of the Goddess, Carlos Surinach

BIBLIOGRAPHY

Armitage, Merle, ed. *Martha Graham*. 1937; reprint, New York: Dance Horizons, 1966. Collection of articles.

de Mille, Agnes. *Martha: The Life and Work of Martha Graham*. New York: Random House, 1991. Anecdotes and opinionated gossip.

Garfunkle, Trudy. *Letter to the World: The Life and Dances of Martha Graham*. Boston: Little, Brown, 1995. Concise account for young people.

Graham, Martha. *Blood Memory*. New York: Doubleday, 1991. Graham's selective account of her life and career published the year she died, probably with input from other persons.

———. *The Notebooks of Martha Graham*. Edited by Nancy Wilson Ross. New York: Harcourt Brace Jovanovich, 1973. An array of thoughts, observations, scenarios, steps, diagrams, and drawings, with quotations from literary and philosophical sources. Incomprehensible sometimes, but offers insights into Graham's mind at work.

Helpern, Alice. *The Technique of Martha Graham*. Dobbs Ferry, N.Y.: Morgan and Morgan, 1994. Nonspecific account of Graham's technique, with vintage photos by Barbara Morgan.

Leatherman, LeRoy. *Martha Graham: Portrait of the Lady as an Artist*. New York: Knopf, 1966. Text by her personal manager, with 200 photographs of performances in the fifties and sixties.

McDonagh, Don. *Martha Graham: A Biography*. New York: Praeger, 1973. First full-length account of her life and work, from public and private records and personal interviews.

Morgan, Barbara. *Martha Graham: Sixteen Dances in Photographs*. 1941; reprint, Dobbs Ferry, N.Y.: Morgan and Morgan, 1980. A classic by her famous photographer, revised to include dramatic action photographs of Graham in performance.

Pratt, Pamela Bryant. *Martha Graham*. San Diego: Lucent Books, 1995. A biography for young people.

Stodelle, Ernestine. *Deep Song: The Dance Story of Martha Graham*. New York: Schirmer Books, 1984. A biographical study of Graham's performing and choreographic achievements, including detailed descriptions of all major works.

Terry, Walter. *Frontiers of Dance: The Life of Martha Graham.* New York: Crowell, 1975. A biography for young people by a dance critic and personal friend of Graham.

Marian Horosko attended the Cleveland Institute of Music, the Juilliard School as a piano major, the Russian Imperial Ballet School in Cleveland, and the School of American Ballet in New York City, and she studied with Anatole Vilzak and Mme. Anderson-Ivantsova. She performed in several Broadway musicals, including *Oklahoma!* and in three Hollywood films, including *Royal Wedding* with Fred Astaire and *An American in Paris;* she was soloist with the Metropolitan Opera Ballet and a member of the New York City Ballet.

She has produced radio and television (WNET and WCBS) programs on dance, created five film seminars on dance for the Harkness Foundation for Dance ("One Hundred Years of American Dance"), and taught at the High School for the Performing Arts and at Fordham University at Lincoln Center.

She was a longtime education editor at *Dance Magazine* and has authored four books on dance technique, two in reprint for the University Press of Florida, Gainesville. She is listed in *Who's Who in America* and the *Oxford Dictionary of Dance* as a performer, educator, and author.